.50

COMPUTERS AND THEIR
SOCIETAL IMPACT

COMPUTERS AND THEIR SOCIETAL IMPACT

MARTIN O. HOLOIEN
MOORHEAD STATE UNIVERSITY
MOORHEAD, MINNESOTA

JOHN WILEY & SONS
New York
Chichester
Brisbane
Toronto

Library of Congress Cataloging in Publication Data:

Holoien, Martin O   1928-
    Computers and their societal impact.

    Includes bibliographies and index.
      1.   Computers and civilization.   I.   Title.
QA76.9.C66H64   001.6′4   77-5520
ISBN 0-471-02197-0

Printed in the United States of America

10 9 8 7 6 5 4

Lovingly dedicated to:
Edie
Lee
Cindy and David
Dan and Merry
Renee and Bill

PREFACE

Almost everyone in the world is directly or indirectly affected by computers. Those few people who remain untouched will soon feel their influence. Because of the ever-increasing role that the computer plays in our world, it is extremely important that every adult know something about these machines. *Computers and Their Societal Impact* was written with that end in mind.

Not only should people be aware of ways in which others use computers, but each person should find out about potential personal benefits derived from knowing how to use a computer. That is a secondary goal of this book.

Perhaps not everyone needs to know how to write a computer program, but by acquiring that skill one will surely learn about computers. Practicing that skill and learning about computer applications that affect all of us are pedagogically sound means for becoming knowledgable about societal impacts of computers. Furthermore, this method of teaching seems to appeal to mathematics and computer science educators, one large group of people who are assuming the task of making people aware of the influence of computers on our society.

The first two chapters present a historical survey of computers that will help students gain an appreciation of the centuries of effort that led to the development of the computer and the many people who played significant roles in its creation. As the accomplishments of these contributors are reviewed, their humanness is also depicted.

Computer programming is introduced in Chapter 3 with special emphasis on the BASIC language. By the time students complete the first three chapters, they will have some knowledge of digital computers and will be able to write simple programs for them.

In Chapters 4 through 8, the use of computers in six areas that affect a great many people is discussed. Not only are students made aware of computer applications by others but they are urged to apply their new-found programming skill to developing simplified versions of the applications presented. It is felt that such active participation by students will help them to more clearly comprehend the numerous ways in which computers can and already do affect their lives.

Chapter 9 examines possible future applications of computers.

The book was developed for a one-quarter freshman-level college course meeting four times a week, or for a one-semester eleventh or twelfth grade high school course meeting five times a week. Although mathematics is not stressed in this book, the student who has had at least one high school algebra course will find the discussion of computer programming easier to understand.

MARTIN O. HOLOIEN

CONTENTS

1
A HISTORY OF COMPUTATIONAL DEVICES

2
TWENTIETH CENTURY INFORMATION PROCESSING MACHINES

3
COMMUNICATING WITH A COMPUTER

4
COMPUTERS IN THE EDUCATIONAL ENVIRONMENT

5
COMPUTERS IN
BUSINESS AND INDUSTRY 115

6
COMPUTERS, POLITICS,
AND GOVERNMENT 146

7
COMPUTERS
AND CRIME 175

8
COMPUTERS
AND YOUR HEALTH 191

9
COMPUTERS
AND YOUR FUTURE 211

APPENDIX A
FLOWCHARTING:
A PROBLEM-SOLVING
TECHNIQUE 233

APPENDIX B
USING A
TERMINAL 254

Index 261

1 A HISTORY OF COMPUTATIONAL DEVICES

Since the beginning of recorded time, a significant amount of human activities has been given to organizing and processing information so that it could be more easily understood, and so that learning could more effectively take place. History verifies that those people who improved methods for handling information and communicating it to others have had a disproportionately large impact on the rest of the world's population. When we use the term information in this book, we are referring to all kinds of knowledge: numerical, linguistic, pictorial, and any other kind. The modern electronic digital computer is essentially a machine for organizing and processing information. It is appropriate then that, in a book concerned with investigating the influence of the computer on society, we consider some of the computer's forbears and the effects they had on the people of their times. Such an investigation will lead to a better understanding of today's computer.

ANCIENT COUNTING METHODS

From the very beginning of human existence quantitative or numerical information has been vital. The question of "how much" or "how many" has always concerned people. The earliest records show that people quickly developed methods of one-to-one correspondence to help them communicate about numbers of objects. The very form of human appendages, our fingers, toes, and hands, has provided us with a ready set of objects with which to keep track of objects being counted. From body parts it is not a big step to using a correspondence between other readily available objects and objects being bought, sold, or stored. It is believed, for example, that early shepherds used piles of small pebbles to keep track of their sheep and other animals. As each sheep passed out of the pen in the morning, a pebble was placed in a special pile (the sheep-out pile), and in the

1

evening as each sheep returned to the enclosure a pebble was taken from the sheep-out pile and placed in another special pile (the sheep-in pile). If, after all the sheep were in, pebbles remained in the sheep-out pile, the shepherd knew some sheep were lost. It seems reasonable that the sheep owners who first "counted" their flocks in this way reduced the percentage of loss in their operations and very likely became the wealthiest sheep owners around. It is probable, then, that even this early innovation in the handling of information had its societal effects, beneficial to some people, harmful to others.

For thousands of years people counted by correspondence without having any number-words in the language, and even today the method is used by some primitive societies. In his book *Number Words and Number Symbols,* Karl Menninger tells about a tribe living on the island of Ceylon who do their counting by sticks. If a merchant wishes to count coconuts, for example, he will collect a pile of sticks, then for each coconut counted he will place a stick in a special pile. He can tell whether anyone has stolen any coconuts by matching sticks with coconuts.

Early Romans also used the counting by correspondence method. The Roman historian Pliny described an ancient law that required that the senior praetor (magistrate) drive a nail into the right wall of the Temple of Jupiter at a specified time of the year. The collection of nails on the wall was a sign for the number of that year. Apparently, the number of nails in the wall of the temple was associated with the time during which important events occurred. The praetor or other officials who knew the system, and could thus relate past incidents with the present, surely must have had a significant influence on the people of that era.

THE COUNTING BOARD AND THE ABACUS

Clearly, once the concept of correspondence between physical objects and things being counted was accepted, it was logical that marks on a board would be used to represent things being counted. Some archaeologists believe that ancient Arabs developed a device used primarily for counting that consisted of a slab of material (perhaps wood) on which sand was strewn to provide a writing surface. In fact, some scholars suggest that the word "abacus" is derived from the Phoenician word "abak." Other scholars, however, believe that "abacus" is derived from the Latin or from the Greek word "ábax."

Whatever the case, evidence indicates that Babylonians living hundreds of years before Christ traced symbols with their fingers on such sand-strewn boards. As time went on, such boards came to be used only for counting and computing. Perhaps the temporary nature of markings in sand made them more useful as scratch pads for computing than for anything more permanent. Later, wax-covered boards were introduced, then counting boards on which loose pieces of bone were the counters, and still later pieces of glass or metal were used. By 450 B.C. the abacus consisted of beads strung on rods, and the *position* of a counter on the board came to determine the value associated with it. Writings of the Athenian lawgiver Solon, who lived in the seventh century B.C., compare a ruling tyrant's favorite person to a counter on a counting board. The present worth depends on the position it is given by the person who pushes it around the board. Archaeologists tell us that lines were carved into the boards to indicate positions of different values, and certain positions represented units, tens, hundreds, and so on.

The reckoning boards discussed to this point were probably all very large, about the size of a table (see Figure 1.1). In "opera historica et philogica" (1682),

FIGURE 1.1   Counting table [Bildarchiv Preussischer Kulturbesitz, Berlin].

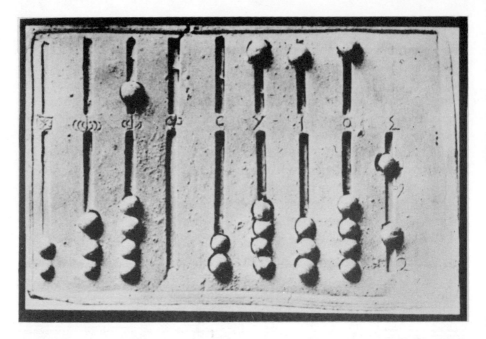

FIGURE 1.2   Roman hand abacus. Almost full size [Courtesy Cabinet des Médailles, Paris].

FIGURE 1.3   A Roman reckoner with hand abacus [Courtesy Museo Capitolino, Rome].

4

FIGURE 1.4   **Chinese suan pan. Size: 6 × 45 cm [The Bettman Archive].**

the Augsburg scholar Marcus Welser describes a hand-sized abacus in which grooves were cut and objects similar to cut-off nails were inserted in the grooves and used as counters (see Figure 1.2). Such abacuses were usually made of bronze and were probably used for only the simplest computations, such as the addition of two numbers. A gravestone carved in the first century A.D. shows us that such devices were popular in the Roman Empire. The gravestone depicts a nobleman dictating to a reckoner standing with his counting board held in one hand moving the counters with the other (see Figure 1.3).

Although historical evidence indicates that *small* counting instruments did not take hold as they might have among the Romans, they had considerable influence in the Far East. By the sixth century B.C., the Chinese had developed abacuses that used bamboo rods as counters. Later, about the twelfth century A.D., a hand-held abacus called a "suan pan" (literally "reckoning board") came into use (see Figure 1.4). From China the hand-held abacus was transported to Japan, probably during the sixteenth century A.D., where it was called a "soroban." Figure 1.5 shows a modern soroban.

The abacus was last used as a general computing device in Spain and Italy in the 1500s, and in France during the 1600s. England and Germany stopped

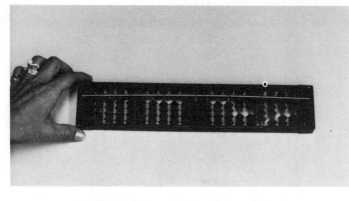

FIGURE 1.5   **Japanese soroban.**

using the abacus in a general way during the 1700s. To this day, however, the abacus is used in certain parts of Russia, Iran, China, and Japan.

We cannot attribute the greatness of the Phoenician, Greek, Roman, and Chinese societies to their adoption of the abacus. However, their use of this early number processor is one indicator of their inventiveness and their willingness to embrace changes that furthered the influence their cultures had on other peoples. In addition, we can deduce that the more advanced numerical processing techniques developed in response to needs within these societies and helped ensure their predominance.

STONEHENGE: THE STONE AGE COMPUTER

A curious arrangement of large stones stands on the Salisbury Plains of southern England. The largest stone weighs 55 tons or more, and some stones form huge arches while others stand as sentinel pillars. Archaeologists believe that Stonehenge (literally "hanging stones") was constructed sometime between 1900 and 1200 B.C., probably around 1500 B.C., a thousand years after the building of the Egyptian pyramids. The stones at Stonehenge are so large that no one knows how they could possibly have been placed into position (see Figure 1.6). Geologists have determined that a number of the stones, the bluestones, must have come from the Prescelly Mountains. The primitive builders of Stonehenge had to transport 80 or more stones, weighing as much as 5 tons, some 240 miles to their present location. But why was this tremendous effort made, and what is the significance of the peculiar arrangement of the stones?

Professor Gerald S. Hawkins in his interesting book *Stonehenge Decoded* deduces that Stonehenge was closely associated with the religion of those people.

Hawkins begins with the theory proposed by several archaeologists and anthropologists that the people of that day were sun and moon worshippers and, after analyzing large amounts of information, he concludes that Stonehenge was used to view extreme positions (rises and settings) of the sun and moon in what must have been some kind of temple. He believes further that it was used to predict special events involving the sun and moon, in particular, to forecast eclipses.

Besides the carefully positioned stones there are 56 holes dug into the ground to form a huge circle. These holes have come to be called Aubrey holes in honor of John Aubrey, an Englishman who lived and wrote during the 1600s. Aubrey was digging around the remains of Stonehenge and recording some things about it in his writings, *Brief Lives*. The Aubrey holes vary from 2½ to nearly 6 feet in diameter and in depth from 2 to 4 feet. Their spacing at 16-foot intervals around a circle of circumference 904 feet with no more than a 21-inch deviation along the circumference and no more than a 19-inch deviation along the radius must be considered a remarkable engineering feat. Figure 1.7 provides a visual means of bringing into perspective the amazing project known as Stonehenge.

Professor Hawkins, after poring over page after page of printed output from a modern digital computer, has proposed the only serious explanation of the Aubrey holes. He believes that they were used by the priests who likely presided over activities at Stonehenge to predict eclipses of the sun and moon. If the people of Salisbury Plain were worshippers of the sun and moon as many believe they were, then the unusual disappearance of their gods (as in eclipses) would arouse intense feelings of stress and fear. If these danger periods could be predicted and

FIGURE 1.6   Stonehenge as it appeared July 1963.

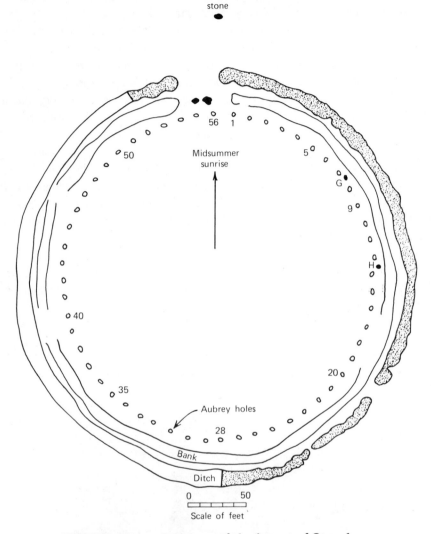

Heel
stone

56   1

Midsummer
sunrise

50

5

G

9

H

40

20

35

Aubrey holes

28

Bank

Ditch

0   50

Scale of feet

FIGURE 1.7   Diagram of the layout of Stonehenge.

explained by the priests as a natural temporary departure by the gods, the people would surely be less fearful. Clearly, the prophets who could predict such periods would be highly regarded.

If we accept Hawkins' hypotheses we see another example of how people created a device that helped them process information, in this case astronomical information. The end result of better information handling was almost surely a strong and direct effect on the people of Salisbury Plains and maybe of a much larger region.

It is interesting to note that the theory that Stonehenge was a stone-age computer (a special purpose computer for astronomical data) could not have been developed without the aid of a modern electronic digital computer. Hawkins and his associates used an IBM 7090 computer to perform hundreds of thousands of computations and comparisons in order to arrive at the plausible conclusions which they did. Had no such machine been available there is every reason to believe that there would be no explanation of the mystery of the Aubrey holes.

NAPIER'S LOGARITHMS

Long after Stonehenge was built and sometime during the period when the abacus was gaining popularity in China and Japan, John Napier of Merchiston, Scotland, was born. Napier was born on July 7, 1550, and lived a productive life for almost 67 years. His father was a titled and wealthy citizen of Scotland, and John had the benefits of education and comfortable home that such positions afforded.

The Napiers were devout Protestants, and in John Napier's youth Presbyterianism became the state religion of Scotland and John Knox, the Protestant theologian, was very influential there. However, in the rest of Europe at this time the Roman Catholic Church was dominant. That the Scottish Parliament adopted Presbyterianism can be seen as a kind of rebellion by the Scots.

The mighty Spanish Armada set sail in 1588 when Napier was 38. One of the major objectives of the Armada was to bring the rebel Scottish and English governments back under the control of the Pope.

Like his father, John Napier was active in politics. He believed he must do all in his power to protect the church, and to him this meant participation in government. His natural abilities led him to spend much of his time studying mathematics. Using the things he learned, Napier developed many instruments of war that he believed should be used to defend his country and his church. He was also a serious student of scripture and wrote a lengthy paper on the last book in the Bible, the "Revelation of St. John."

One of his major contributions to the world was his invention of logarithms. By the time Napier was born, science and mathematics had progressed to the point that mathematical computations, especially divisions and multiplications, were numerous and lengthy. Napier's logarithms made it possible to do division and multiplication by performing subtraction and addition. His first paper on logarithms was published in 1614, and in that paper, entitled *The Construction of the Wonderful Canon of Logarithms,* examples of computations using logarithms were presented as were detailed rules for computations of various kinds. During this time Napier also devised some mechanical aids to computation, small rods with appropriate markings on them (see Figure 1.8). These rods came to be called "Napier's bones" and their use was described in another of Napier's papers, *Rabdologia*, published in 1617, the year in which Napier died. The last of Napier's publications *Mirifici Logarithmorum Canonis Constructio* is his most complete and lucid presentation of the method of computation using logarithms. It was published two years after his death by his son, Robert.

Napier's contribution must surely be considered a major milestone in humanity's struggle to improve methods of processing information. By Napier's time the numerous scientific computations were done by tedious paper-and-pencil methods. Napier showed mathematicians how the more cumbersome operations of division and multiplication could be done by subtraction and addition. His ideas, both in the theory of logarithms and in the use of computation rods, led directly to the invention of the slide rule some years after his death.

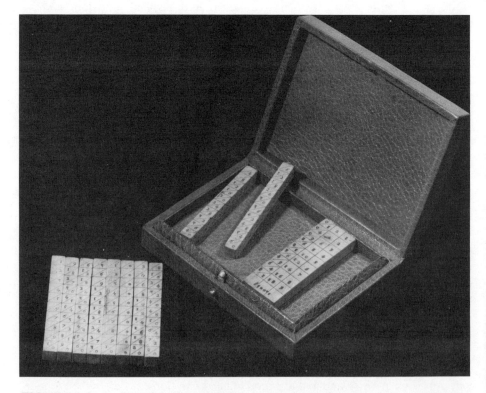

FIGURE 1.8   Napier's bones (Smithsonian Institution Photo No. 58996D).

It is difficult to assess the impact Napier's improvements in computing had on the world. But recognizing the emergence at that time of England as a world power on the seas, and the calculations needed to provide accurate navigational data, we can believe that Napier's logarithms and his calculating rods, and Edmund Gunter's later invention of the closely related slide rule, produced far-reaching effects. Until recently, in fact, the slide rule has been the standby of all engineers as their computational device.

PASCAL'S MECHANICAL CALCULATOR

About the time that the first slide rule came into existence, Blaise Pascal was born, on June 19, 1623, to Étienne and Antoinette Pascal. Blaise grew up in a family of three children, an older sister, Gilberte and a younger one, Jacqueline.

Blaise's great-grandfather, Jean, left his native village of Cournon in the Auvergne region of southwestern France to seek his fortune in the nearest large city, Clermont. Jean did quite well as a merchant, but his eldest son, Martin, Blaise's grandfather, did better than Jean ever hoped to do. Not only did Martin do well financially but he married into nobility so that his social standing was assured. The wealth and social position led to political power, and Martin eventually rose to the office of representative to the French Treasury serving a large region of France.

Étienne was thus born into a wealthy and influential family and attended a school in Paris for the education of magistrates. Upon returning to Clermont, Étienne used family wealth and influence to acquire a government post in financial administration. Later he was appointed to the important governmental position as Second President of the Cour des Aides, a post similar to our tax commissioner. This was an esteemed position in seventeenth-century France and made Étienne both widely known and highly honored.

As Étienne Pascal's children grew, it became increasingly clear to him that his children were unusually intelligent, and more and more he found himself absorbed in the interesting job of educating them. So great was this interest that four years after the death of his wife (Antoinette Pascal died when Blaise was three years old) Étienne sold his job to a brother, disposed of his property, and moved with his three children to Paris to dedicate himself to studying science and educating his children.

Étienne had unorthodox ideas about education; he did not follow the education curriculum customary in that age. For example, at that time drill and practice in Latin was the starting point of all education (beginning at age eight), but Étienne told his children nothing about formal aspects of language until they were twelve. He believed curiosity was the point from which learning should start, and to encourage curiosity he used games to teach many aspects of geography, history, and mathematics. Traditional subjects such as grammar, philosophy, and religious education were not omitted from the Pascal curriculum, but their manner of presentation and their time of introduction were not traditional. Science was Étienne's greatest delight, an interest just as intensely shared by his son. His concern for science and his experimental approach to learning would probably have earned for Étienne Pascal a prominent place in educational history had he written down his ideas. We know of them today only because his daughter Gilberte mentions them in her writings.

Because Étienne Pascal assumed responsibility for his children's education, there is no record that Blaise ever attended school nor even that he ever had any dealings with boys his own age. His whole life evolved around associations with his father and his sisters and those scholars that came to talk science with his father. Physical education was completely ignored as were those aspects of human development that come from interacting with people of one's own age. As a result, Blaise Pascal seemed to live in a constant sense of separation from the world. Perhaps the only feeling of group membership which he experienced was the result of participating in a society much like today's Academy of Sciences. When he was only thirteen, his father allowed him to begin attending weekly meetings of this organization of scientists and, in spite of his youth, the boy was among the most vocal and knowledgeable people there. The freedom of expression and climate of love in the Pascal home certainly fostered the development of a genius like Blaise Pascal.

When Blaise was seventeen the family moved to Rouen, where Étienne accepted a position as tax commissioner. The unending computations resulting from his work with tax assessments forced Étienne to call on his son to use his considerable computational ability to help. Blaise, who had by this time encountered some of the frontiers of theoretical mathematics, detested the tedium of summing, multiplying, subtracting, and dividing the unending lists of numbers which his father's work demanded. So, at the age of 19, Blaise Pascal began designing a machine that would do this hateful arithmetic for him. His plans called for wheels with pins placed around their perimeters; each wheel affected the rotation of the wheel immediately to its left. It took three years to obtain a working model of the machine. Perhaps the most amazing thing about Pascal's calculator is that it was constructed before anything resembling gears with accurately meshing teeth had been conceived. Furthermore, the principle of having one complete rotation of one wheel move the adjoining wheel only one-tenth of a rotation had apparently never occurred to anyone before Pascal. We who have grown up seeing the odometers (mileage meters) on our cars display the distance traveled, observing that the "tenths" wheel rotates a complete revolution in order to produce a move-

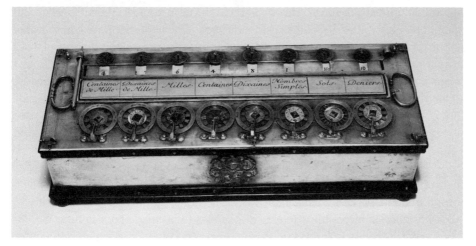

FIGURE 1.9   Pascal's calculating machine (courtesy IBM).

ment of one mile on the "mile" wheel, find it hard to imagine the seriousness of the
obstacle faced by Pascal. Those who have examined Pascal's calculator first hand
agree that the way he accomplished this communication of movement from wheel
to wheel is perhaps the most ingenious part of the entire device. In any case, the
principle originated with Pascal and has been the foundation for all mechanical
calculators developed in the 300 years since (see Figure 1.9).

Although a Rouen watchmaker attempted to copy Blaise's device, Étienne
Pascal acquired for Blaise an exclusive license to build and market the machines.

Blaise continued to perfect his invention, and in 1645 he was ready to
make it public. He sent one machine to Chancellor Seguier, the official who had
granted him exclusive license to make the machines, and one to his scientist friend
Roberval. Gilberte Pascal records that Blaise dreamed his machine would bring him
wealth and fame. It did bring fame; even the renowned mathematician Descartes
wrote to inquire about the calculator. But the calculator did not bring wealth.
Although his father was not poor, Blaise's experimentation in the development of
his calculator had cost dearly. He wanted badly to recover some of these costs for
his father and to acquire some wealth in his own right. As a promotional effort,
Blaise sent a model of the machine to Queen Christina of Sweden and to other
influential potential customers. His machine was used in his father's tax offices in
Rouen, and he probably gave many demonstrations of its capabilities in the un-
likely role of a salesman.

Blaise Pascal's machine was remarkable. When operated by Pascal or one
of his associates it was capable of performing all four arithmetic operations with

previously unheard of speed. But wealth was never to come to Pascal through this invention or any other. Potential customers were afraid of its cost (the equivalent of about $250), the lack of people skilled in its operation, and the fact that only Pascal or one of his workmen could make repairs. These fears together with the knowledge that even if the machine could do the work of six or more men it was cheaper to hire the men, kept sales to a very small number. The same three reasons, cost, lack of people to operate them, and lack of people to service them, have been used as arguments against the acceptance of almost all machines of any significance ever invented.

Although Pascal's calculator was a truly amazing device and well ahead of its time, it did not become the potent force it might have been. Here, indeed, was an information processing machine whose computational capabilities might well have hastened some of the scientific discoveries to be made later in history.

We do know that this was the only machine of any consequence invented by Pascal. He has long been famous for numerous discoveries in mathematics and science, but only since the coming of the modern computer has it become widely known that Pascal also possessed this inventive genius.

The next nine years of Pascal's life were spent in pursuing the study of mathematics and science. Then, on November 23, 1654, Pascal had an unforgettable experience in which he says he talked with God for two hours. After that experience Pascal was a devout believer in Jesus Christ as his own personal savior from sin. From that time on, Pascal seemed to feel that mathematics and science were less important than his new-found desire to express some of the deep feelings about his developing relationship with God. Some of the most beautiful religious poetry ever written came from the mind of Pascal during this last period of his life.

Pascal, never a healthy person, died at the age of 39 on August 19, 1662 from a hemorrhage of the brain. Thus, one of the greatest of all human minds came to the end of its existence, leaving for all mankind to follow many of the greatest of scientific discoveries not the least of which was his wonderful calculating machine.

The reader interested in the life of Pascal should consult any of the books on the topic listed at the end of this chapter. Morris Bishop has written a particularly complete and readable book.

JACQUARD'S ATTACHMENT TO THE LOOM

About 100 years after the death of Pascal, France produced another man who would affect the course of information processing. On July 7, 1752, Joseph Marie Jacquard was born in Lyons, a city known for its production of fine cloth. Little is known about Jacquard's family but it is quite probable that his father worked in one of the many factories in Lyons that produced woven cloth. It is likely that Joseph Jacquard also began working in a cloth mill, and used the knowledge he gained there to develop the device for which he is famous. This device is known as the Jacquard attachment to the loom, although Jacquard himself was not the original inventor of the loom.

The identity of the first person or group of people to use a loom in weaving cloth is lost in history. Records exist in many civilizations indicating the use of some version of a loom. Even though it may not have originated there, the city of Lyons produced more than its expected share of improvements to the loom. In the 1720s a Lyonnaise inventor named Vaucanson introduced the use of needles and hooks to control the formation of designs in the cloth. Vaucanson's needles and hooks were controlled by cords pulled by assistants to the weaver called drawboys. The various designs were determined by the order in which the cords were pulled. The master weaver was responsible for ensuring that the right cords were pulled at specified times so as to produce cloth of a predetermined design.

Another citizen of Lyons named Bouchon introduced the concept of using a perforated roll of paper wrapped around a cylinder to specify which cord to pull. The selected design was built into the pattern of holes punched in the paper. As the cylinder around which the paper was wrapped turned, specially positioned needles dropped into the holes in the paper, indicating which cords to pull in order to produce a given design. The result was that the master weaver could plan the cloth design in advance and when the actual weaving process was taking place, the perforated roll of paper kept track of which cords to pull so that the end product contained the intended design.

Shortly before Jacquard's birth, another artisan of Lyons, Falcon, invented a device that significantly increased the number of needles controlling the sequence of pulling cords, thus making it possible to weave more complex designs into the cloth. Falcon also recorded the design on rectangular cards rather than a roll of paper. Each card, punched in a certain manner, produced a specific portion of the entire design. Then any number of cards were fastened together in a chain-like fashion producing the entire design.

These devices were part of many of the looms in France in 1804 when Jacquard was commissioned by the Conservatory of Arts and Crafts in Paris to overhaul one of Vaucanson's looms. This was apparently one of Vaucanson's last looms because it incorporated many of the improvements invented by Bouchon and Falcon. While rebuilding the loom, Jacquard was able to make workable an idea unsuccessfully attempted by Vaucanson. Jacquard mounted the shedding device (automatic selection of cords to be pulled to create the design) on top of the loom and, as the needles dropped into the holes in punched cards, the weaver was able to use the treadle to control the actual pulling of cords. With this new invention the weaver not only planned the designs of the cloths, but could also produce the cloth without the assistance of drawboys. A look at Figure 1.10 might make it easier to visualize the function of Jacquard's invention.

The Jacquard attachment, as it was called, was vehemently opposed by the

FIGURE 1.10   Drawing of a loom. [The Bettman Archive].

silk weavers of Lyons, who felt it would cause widespread unemployment of the drawboys. But the machine's advantages outweighed its disadvantages, and Jacquard's attachment soon became generally used. Jacquard made his invention public in 1805. The next year, Napoleon, then dictator of France, granted Jacquard a lifetime annual pension of 1000 francs for his invention. And despite violent protests against the first use of the machine, by 1812 11,000 looms with a Jacquard attachment were operating in France.

Clearly, the social impact of Jacquard's invention was significant. Although drawboys were put out of work, the cost of producing a yard of cloth decreased so that more people than before could buy the products of fabric mills. Those drawboys who had learned enough about weaving and could finance a loom of their own became independent producers. France became more famous than ever for its textiles.

How does the Jacquard attachment fit into our study of information processing machines? Clearly, Jacquard's device made it possible for the master weaver to effectively handle the flow of information needed to produce a beautiful piece of cloth. This information control consisted first of storing a coded equivalent of some portion of the design in a punched card. (By the way, Jacquard was the first to use rectangular holes rather than round ones.) Then, by fastening various cards together into endless loops, the weaver was able to create many different designs, again a means of controlling information. But it is equally significant that, more than 200 years ago, Jacquard and his immediate predecessors provide the first examples of storing information on a punched card.

CHARLES BABBAGE AND HIS CALCULATING MACHINES

Many people have called Charles Babbage the "father of the computer." For that reason and because of his genius, we will devote considerable time to his life and his inventions.

Charles Babbage was born to Benjamin and Betty Babbage on December 26, 1792 in the coastal town of Totnes in southwestern England. Benjamin was a banker of considerable wealth. Several children were born to the Babbages but only Charles and a sister survived infancy. In 1805, when Charles was 13, his father retired from banking and moved the family to London, some 150 miles away, and retained a seacoast house as a summer home.

Because Charles Babbage was not a healthy child, he was sent to a church school for two years and received the personal attention of a minister/teacher. Unfortunately, the teacher was more concerned about Charles's health than his education; however, the year before the family moved to London, Charles was well enough to attend a neighborhood school. In London, Babbage was sent to Forty Hill School where he studied for three years. In addition to this formal study, Charles had the benefit of private tutors from Cambridge University hired by his father.

When he was 19, Charles began his university study at Cambridge. His greatest love was mathematics but he soon discovered that he was more proficient in that subject than his Cambridge teachers. Understandably, this experience somewhat soured him on Cambridge. In June 1814, Charles Babbage married Georgiana Whitmore, and, while Charles was studying at Cambridge, they became parents of a boy whom they named Herschel, in honor of Babbage's friend John Herschel. Charles was finally awarded a master's degree and left the university in 1817.

By 1819, Babbage had learned much about mathematics and especially about calculus. He was most interested in functions that could be represented as sums of infinite series, and this interest probably led to his work on calculating machines. He had a well-equipped laboratory and shop and was beginning to spend time designing his first machine, which he called the Difference Engine. Babbage knew that if he could compute differences rapidly and accurately he could simplify certain tables of numerical values. He had found so many errors in navigation tables used by the British Navy that he was certain that ships had been lost simply because the navigational charts were wrong. He was determined to correct such errors and he was convinced his Difference Engine was the key. By 1822 he had built two experimental models of the Difference Engine and hoped to use these to convince others of the usefulness of this invention.

On July 3, 1822, Babbage wrote to Sir Humphrey Davy, President of the Royal Society (the highly respected and influential scientific organization of that day) describing his Difference Engine and asking the support of the Society in his bid for money from the British government. Davy agreed and Babbage was subsequently awarded funding in the amount of about 7000 English pounds (approximately $16,300 in today's U.S. dollars). The initial payment was to be 1500 pounds, with supplemental amounts to be paid over a three-year period.

Babbage was delighted at the government financing, which reduced his dependence on his father for support. Although he had completed the drawings for the Difference Engine and had even built experimental versions of it, Babbage was unable to acquire the equipment needed to complete his newly funded project, since the technology of his time could not provide him with the tools he needed. Within the next three years he developed a new system of notation for his mechanical drawings and proposed methods never before used in the making of tools and equipment, so that definite progress was made in the construction of the Difference Engine.

In 1824, a group of London businessmen interested in forming an insurance company asked Babbage to become a partner and prepare insurance tables and other data related to life insurance. Babbage responded by providing even more than he was asked for in a book entitled *A Comparative View of the Different Institutions for the Assurance of Life*. His book contained the most reliable tables published to that date. Although the insurance company was never formed, Babbage's book was shortly thereafter used by German insurance agents, and remained the standard English insurance tables for the next 45 years. The venture produced no income for Babbage, however.

By 1827, government representatives began to ask when the Difference Engine would be delivered. After all, government funds had been committed to it. Unfortunately the machine was nowhere near completion, largely because of Babbage's own inventive mind. As construction proceeded Babbage made endless improvements that made it necessary to discard what had been done and start over. Many times the machinists he employed would come with parts and assemblies made according to Babbage's drawings only to be told they were obsolete. Of course, a major difficulty with which Babbage struggled was the low level of technology as compared to the grandeur of his ideas. Had the technological development been on par with his creativity, Babbage may well have seen his Difference Engine completed and his genius would have been recognized in his own time.

Because there was little apparent progress toward the actual construction of a working Difference Engine, the government refused to provide any more money after 1827. As it was, government funds were only sufficient to cover the salary of the supervising engineer. Babbage donated all of his time to the project and his father provided the cost of materials as well as salaries for the machinists and other workers they employed.

In that same year, 1827, illness claimed the lives of two of Babbage's children and his father, and Georgiana Babbage died in childbirth. Babbage was left to care for his two sons Herschel and Henry. He was crushed and bitter at his personal tragedies, especially at the death of his beloved Georgiana. He tried to forget she had ever existed; Babbage never spoke of his wife for 54 years, until he himself was dying.

At this point in his life Babbage, who had never been very healthy, seemed to lose what health he had. His doctor advised him to leave England for a complete rest. With the sizable inheritance left by his father, Babbage was able to finance a trip through much of Europe, spending most of his time in Italy. All along the way his curious mind would constantly watch for any new ideas which he might use in some way. He had occasions, especially in Italy, to discuss his Difference Engine with other scientists, and he discovered that some of them were intensely interested in the project, an attitude he rarely encountered in his homeland.

In January 1829, Babbage returned to England. He contacted influential friends, seeking their help in once more obtaining government funding to complete the Difference Engine. Through the efforts of John Herschel, he finally succeeded in getting another grant of 1500 pounds (about $3500.00). As happened with his other grants, this one was soon spent and progress toward having an actual machine was hardly apparent. Two more government grants, each in the amount of 3000 pounds, were awarded within that year, so by 1830, the British government had donated 9000 pounds to Babbage's Difference Engine. Resistance began developing against providing any more government funds.

Sensing this developing feeling, Babbage ordered his remaining workmen to assemble enough of his machine to prove that the project was really worth the government's continued support. The result of this feverish activity was a small portion of the calculating mechanism of his machine (see Figure 1.11). It performed beautifully, but, alas, was not enough to convince the authorities that it was a worthwhile project.

Charles Babbage could not stop his work on the Engine because of this new setback. He had discovered that by adding a few more gears he could feed information back into other parts of the machine. This made him think that his machine could perform tasks that required information not available when the problem was first posed. Thus the machine might be given instructions as to how to proceed once certain computed information was available. This concept caused him to begin thinking about a whole new computing machine which he began calling his Analytical Engine.

Babbage had been greatly influenced by the writings of Leibnitz, the German mathematician, and of Jacquard, the French weaver discussed previously in this chapter. As he planned his Analytical Engine he thought more and more about Jacquard's attachment to the loom. Here is what Babbage wrote about this time in his life in his book *Passages from the Life of a Philosopher,* published in 1864:

> The Analytical Engine is therefore a machine of the most general nature. Whatever formula it is required to develop, the law of its development must be communicated to it by two sets of cards. When these have been placed, the engine is special for that particular formula. The numerical value of its constants must then be put on the columns of wheels below them, and on setting the Engine in motion it will calculate and print the numerical results of that formula.
>
> Every set of cards made for any formula will at any future time recalculate that formula with whatever constants may be required.
>
> Thus the Analytical Engine will possess a library of its own. Every set of cards once made will at any future time reproduce the calculations for which it was first arranged. The numerical value of its constants may then be inserted.

FIGURE 1.11   Small portion of the Difference Engine (British Crown Copyright. Science Museum, London).

This excerpt clearly expresses two of the fundamental ideas of today's digital computers: (1) the use of a previously prepared set of instructions for the machine (which is today called the "program"), and (2) a place that stores intermediate as well as final results (which is today called the computer memory). Beyond that, the last paragraph of the excerpt shows that Babbage envisioned libraries of instruction sets for solving many common problems. Here is the germ of the idea which computer people today call system software, collections of prepared instructions for accomplishing certain tasks. Remember, Babbage was thinking like this around 1853, 100 years before any kind of computer had ever been constructed.

Interesting, also, is Babbage's estimate of how quickly his machine could perform arithmetic and to what degree of accuracy the results would be given.

> *The Analytical Engine I propose will have the power of expressing every number it uses to fifty places of figures. It will multiply any two such numbers together, and then, if required, will divide the product of one hundred figures by a number of fifty places of figures.*
>
> *Supposing the velocity of the moving parts of the Engine to be not greater than forty feet per minute, I have no doubt that*
>
> *Sixty additions or subtractions may be completed and printed in one minute.*
> *One multiplication of two numbers, each of fifty figures, in one minute.*
> *One division of a number having 100 places of figures by another of 50 in one minute.*

Although English scientists had expressed only a limited interest in the Analytical Engine, an Italian mathematician and engineer named L. F. Menebrea was very enthusiastic. Menebrea fully understood the workings of the machine and his 1842 paper, written in French, won wide acclaim.

CONTRIBUTIONS OF LADY LOVELACE TO THE ANALYTICAL ENGINE

A 26-year-old Englishwoman named Ada Augusta Lovelace was fascinated by Menebrea's paper. Lady Lovelace (the wife of the first Earl of Lovelace) was the only legitimate daughter of the famous poet, Lord Byron. Lady Lovelace was well educated and showed an unusual ability in mathematics; at eighteen she regularly attended public lectures at the Mechanics Institute in London. It was there that she was first introduced to the Difference Engine. When she read Menebrea's paper, she set about translating it because she knew that no such description of the Analytical Engine existed in English. As she translated, she would insert long descriptive notes about aspects she apparently felt needed elaboration. She published her translation, with notes, under the initials A. A. L. (It was not dignified at that time for noblewomen to spend time writing scientific papers!) Most of her friends in the scientific community knew, however, that A. A. L. was Ada Augusta Lovelace. The translation and explanatory notes were so well done that Babbage's image gained considerable stature. In fact, Babbage began to make new inquiries into the possibility of more government support but with no success.

An indication of how well Lady Lovelace understood the machine is that she knew it could operate on *any* elements for which logical relations existed, not just on numbers. Read this excerpt from her published notes:

> *The operating mechanism can even be thrown into action independently of any object to operate upon (although of course no result could then be developed). Again, it might act upon other things besides number, were objects found whose mutual fundamental relations could be expressed by those of the abstract science of operations, and which should be also susceptible of adaptations to the action of the operating notation and mechanism of the engine. Supposing, for instance, that the fundamental relations of pitched sounds in the science of harmony and of musical composition were susceptible of such expression and adaptations, the engine might compose elaborate and scientific pieces of music of any degree of complexity or extent.*

It is quite likely that Lady Lovelace understood Babbage's concept of a computing machine better than anyone else would for a hundred years.

Scholars cannot agree about what fostered a rather tragic collaboration between Charles Babbage and Lady Lovelace. Perhaps Babbage was desperately searching for ways to finance his Analytical Engine or Lady Lovelace may have needed an outlet for her love for gambling. In any case, Babbage and Ada began secretly devising a scheme for picking winning horses using the Difference Engine to perform the calculations. When they were ready to try it out, they confided in Ada's husband, the Earl of Lovelace, and all three placed bets according to the scheme. The first few times, they won handsomely. Then the losses began to come, one after the other, until both Babbage and the Earl pulled out. But Lady Lovelace was hooked on both gambling and the scheme for winning; she secretly placed bets, sometimes pawning valuable family jewels to do so. Twice her mother, Lady Byron, redeemed the jewels. Lady Lovelace's passion for gambling outweighed her interest in mathematics and science. This extremely talented woman would make no further contributions to science. She died of cancer in 1852, just 10 short years after reading Menebrea's paper; she was only 36 years old.

When Ada Augusta Lovelace died, Charles Babbage lost his one friend who fully understood and believed in his computer. He was saddened and embittered by Ada's death and by his lack of recognition for his design of the calculating engines, but Babbage remained active in writing scientific articles as well as inventing. Among other interests were his inventions of the coronagraph (for studying the sun's corona), an ingenious lighthouse signalling device, a hand-lantern for signalling, an unpickable lock, and the cowcatcher on a locomotive.

One of the happiest times in Babbage's life must have been in 1855 when a working model of his Difference Engine was brought to England for display by George Scheutz, a Swedish printer. This machine was based on Babbage's ideas, which Scheutz had read 20 years earlier. Babbage was pleased to have a part in promoting the machine and used the occasion to scold England for not having believed in him. He also called attention to the fact that he now had designed an even more powerful computer. Figure 1.12 shows the Scheutz machine.

At last, when the inventor was 70 years old, the British government invited Babbage to display his Difference Engine. But even this invitation was not an unmixed blessing for Babbage. His proposal that the Scheutz engine be displayed beside his own, both machines working slowly so people could see what they were for, was refused. Babbage was told that the Scheutz machine was "far too busy computing life insurance information" to be put on display. Furthermore, the management of the London Exhibition claimed it could not afford to hire a person to be at the display to explain the machines workings. So the proud Charles Babbage spent every day at the Exhibition explaining his machine to all who would listen.

In 1864, Babbage published his autobiography, *Passages from the Life of a Philosopher*. From the preface of that book we gain some insight into his deep disappointment at not being recognized for his genius in conceiving his calculating machines.

FIGURE 1.12   Scheutz's version of the Difference Engine (British Crown Copyright. Science Museum, London).

FIGURE 1.13   **The Mill and printing parts of the Analytical Engine (British Crown Copyright. Science Museum, London).**

I have frequently had applications to write my life, both from my countrymen and from foreigners. Some caterers for the public offered to pay me for it. Others required that I should pay them for its insertion; others offered to insert it without charge. One proposed to give me a quarter of a column gratis, and as many additional lines of elege as I chose to write and pay for at ten-pence per line. To many of these I sent a list of my works, with the remark that they formed the best life of an author; but nobody cared to insert them.

I have no desire to write my own biography, as long as I have strength and means to do better work.

The remarkable circumstances attending those Calculating Machines on which I have spent so large a portion of my life, make me wish to place on record some account of their past history. As, however, such a work would be utterly uninteresting to the greater part of my countrymen, I thought it might be rendered less unpalatable by relating some of my experience amongst various classes of society, widely differing from each other, in which I have occasionally mixed.

Charles Babbage died on October 18, 1871, almost 79 years old. Newspapers took little notice of his death, and, aside from his family and the undertakers, only one friend was present at the funeral.

Seventeen years later, in 1889, Babbage's son Henry succeeded in demonstrating a working model of the "mill" portion (today called the arithmetic unit) of Babbage's Analytical Engine (see Figure 1.13). The machine worked perfectly and Henry Babbage used it to calculate and print a table of certain multiples of the number pi correct to 29 significant digits (see Figure 1.14). At last, Charles Babbage was vindicated.

The impact of Babbage's computing machines on the society of his day is difficult to assess. Some of his ideas certainly affected people outside of England; for example, the use of his insurance tables by the Germans and the application of the Scheutz machine to astronomy in the United States. His work with navigational

00001	03141592653589783238462643383
00002	06283185307179566476925286768
00003	09424777960769349715387930149
00004	12566370614359132953850573532
00005	15707963267948916192313216915
00006	18849555921538699430775860298
00007	21991148575128482669238503681
00008	25133741228718265907701147064
00009	28275333882308049146163790447
00010	31415926535897832384626433830

FIGURE 1.14   **Multiples of pi as printed by the Analytical Engine.**

tables must have helped the British Navy retain its dominant position. But probably the most important impact of Babbage's inventions on people is the rich collection of ideas contained in his drawings and the papers written about them. Babbage was the source of numerous ideas about computing machines in the years after his death. In 1944, all of the facets of Babbage's Analytical Engine were encompassed in the first information processing machine.

EXERCISES

1.1 Order the following information processing devices chronologically: counting board, Stonehenge, counting pebbles, Pascal's calculator, Napier's logarithms, Babbage's Analytical Engine, Jacquard's attachment.

1.2 What external forces gave impetus to the development of the following devices:
>   (a) hand-held abacus
>   (b) Napier's bones (logarithms)
>   (c) Pascal's calculating machine
>   (d) Jacquard's attachment

1.3 What personality weakness did Babbage have that prevented him from completing his Analytical Engine?

1.4 Why is Charles Babbage often called the "Father of the Computer"?

1.5 What features in Babbage's Analytical Engine were ahead of their time?

1.6 Write a paper or give a talk about how to use the abacus.

1.7 The Inca people of South America had an elaborate record-keeping system based on knots tied in cords (quipu). Prepare a paper on the topic.

1.8 Although we sometimes see Roman numerals today, the Roman counting system is no longer in use. Research the topic and discuss why Roman numerals are no longer popular as a counting system.

1.9 Write a paper or give a talk describing Professor Hawkins' theory of how the Aubrey holes of Stonehenge were used.

1.10 Gottfried Wilhelm Leibnitz of Germany designed and constructed a mechanical calculator that was an improvement over Pascal's machine. Write a paper on Leibnitz's calculator.

1.11 Prepare a proposal to be presented to the British Parliament urging the granting of 10,000 pounds to support the development of Babbage's Analytical Engine.

1.12 Prepare a justification for not granting Babbage money to construct the Analytical Engine.

1.13 Suppose Babbage's Analytical Engine had been completed during the inventor's lifetime and that it worked as Babbage had envisioned. Use your imagination to describe some of the likely effects on the people of England, in particular, and on the people of Europe and the rest of the world.

SELECTED REFERENCES

BOOKS

Bernstein, Jeremy, *The Analytical Engine,* Random House, New York, 1964.

Bishop, Morris, *Pascal: The Life of Genius,* Greenwood Press, New York, 1968.

Diebold, John, editor, *The World of the Computer,* Random House, New York, 1973.

Dorf, Richard C., *Computers and Man,* Boyd & Fraser, San Francisco, 1974.

Halacy, Dan, *Charles Babbage Father of The Computer,* The Macmillan Company, New York, 1970.

Harmon, Margaret, *Stretching Man's Mind: A History of Data Processing,* Mason/Charter Publ., New York, 1975.

Hawkins, Gerald S., *Stonehenge Decoded,* Doubleday, New York, 1965.

Menninger, Karl, *Number Words and Number Symbols,* M.I.T. Press, Cambridge, 1969.

Moseley, Maboth, *Irascible Genius: A Life of Charles Babbage,* Regnery, Chicago, 1964.

Morrison, Philip and Emily Morrison, eds., *Charles Babbage and His Calculating Engines,* Dover Publications, New York, 1961.

Napier, John, *The Construction of the Wonderful Canon of Logarithms,* Dawsons of Pall Mall, London, 1966.

Rosenberg, Jerry M., *The Computer Prophets,* Collier-Macmillan Ltd., London, 1969.

PERIODICALS

Gleiser, Molly, "Lady Lovelace and the Difference Engine," *Computer Decisions,* May 1975, pp. 39—41.

Kean, David W., "The Computer and the Countess," *Datamation,* May 1973, pp. 60—63.

2 TWENTIETH CENTURY INFORMATION PROCESSING MACHINES

Although Charles Babbage never lived to see the grand ideas in his plan for the Analytical Engine become reality, he did greatly influence the development of information processing machines.

HOLLERITH AND THE PUNCHED CARD

Eleven years before the death of Charles Babbage, Herman Hollerith was born to George and Franciska Hollerith at Buffalo, New York. The date was February 29, 1860. Although it is undeniable that the card processing machine Hollerith was to develop was an important precursor to the modern computer, neither Hollerith nor his invention was mentioned in a book entitled *Great Inventions* published in 1932 by the Smithsonian Institution Series.

Hollerith grew up in Buffalo and apparently enjoyed a normal childhood. He was an extremely bright boy, but like many schoolchildren, he detested spelling. He spent some years in public schools but, perhaps because his parents recognized his unusual ability, he was withdrawn and given private tutoring by a Lutheran minister of Buffalo. The private instruction must have been good for Hollerith because he was able to enroll at Columbia University's School of Mines at a relatively young age, and, in 1879 at the age of 19, he was awarded his bachelor's degree from that school.

It is quite possible that Hollerith read a report published in 1878 by the Committee of the British Association summarizing Babbage's work. It is also likely that Hollerith researched Jacquard's attachment to the loom. In any case, he began to be more and more interested in the storing and processing of information via punched cards.

One of Hollerith's professors at Columbia was also a consultant for the

United States Census Bureau for the 1880 census, and he asked Hollerith to work with him on a census-related research project. So in October 1879, Herman Hollerith began working at the Census Bureau. At dinner with one of his colleagues at the Census Bureau, Dr. John Billings, Director of Vital Statistics at the Bureau, the concept of processing census information by machine was proposed. Apparently that idea and the friendship with Billings' daughter, Lucia, both developed from that day on, because Lucia and Herman were married on September 15, 1890, and the first patent for a data processing machine was issued to Herman Hollerith on March 31, 1884.

In Hollerith's machine, a strip of perforated paper passed between pins and a tray of cups filled with mercury. Whenever a hole was encountered by a pin, the pin would make contact with the mercury below, thus allowing a flow of electricity through a specific circuit which included a meter for recording that fact. Hollerith credits many of the ideas he incorporated to Babbage, Jacquard, and a railroad conductor punching tickets. Hollerith recognized that the punches placed in a ticket by the conductor recorded certain information about the passenger. He reasoned that strips of punched paper could be similarly used to record essential census information about every person in the United States.

His first tabulating machine utilized a roll of perforated paper, but as he began preparing for the 1890 census, he decided to switch to individual cards. The first such set of cards was prepared for the city of Baltimore, and were 3¼ by 8⅝ inches in size. Information was recorded, using a conductor's punch, by punches in any of 192 positions. There were three rows of 32 positions at the upper part of the card and three rows of 32 at the bottom. The system ultimately used for the 1890 census consisted of cards 3¼ inches wide and 6⅝ inches long, divided into quarter-inch squares positioned in 12 horizontal rows and 24 vertical columns. The four leftmost columns were used for geographical data and the other 20 for personal data. Hollerith's machine is illustrated in Figure 2.1.

Hollerith began working independently on his machines in March of 1884, when he resigned from his position with the Census Bureau. The Bureau was under no obligation to use the machines he developed. In 1889, the Superintendent of the Census, Robert P. Porter, appointed a committee to evaluate methods of tabulating the 1890 census. Three systems, among them Hollerith's, were recommended for testing. The data to be tabulated were those collected in four census districts of the city of St. Louis, Missouri. The results of the test indicated that Hollerith's system required only one-tenth the time of his nearest competitor. The committee estimated that by using the Hollerith system, the Census Bureau would save $650,000 on the 1890 census and complete the tabulating process in much less time than it had ever been done before. Of course, the committee recom-

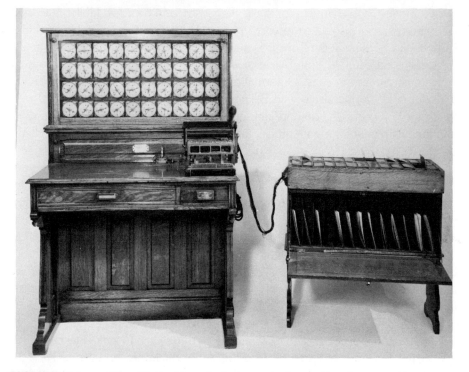

FIGURE 2.1   The Hollerith tabulating machine (Smithsonian Institution Photo No. 64563).

mended that the Bureau contract with Hollerith to use his equipment for the census. As it later turned out, the tabulation took even less time than anticipated. The first count of the United States population, released June 1, 1890, took six weeks, but the accurate, official count of 62,622,250 people was announced on December 12, 1890. The census a decade earlier had taken several years to complete, and then the results were not reliable. Hollerith and his machines had made the grade.

The contract awarded Hollerith for the 1890 census kept him financially solvent. He became convinced of the commercial value of his machines and in 1896 formed the Tabulating Machine Company. All the equipment used for the 1900 census was leased from that firm. And in 1900 Hollerith completed his "automatic tabulating machine." Previously cards had to be inserted into the machine one by one. Now he had devised a machine that would accept batches of cards and automatically examine single cards. It was also about this time that he made the first electric sorting machine, one that could sort cards according to information on them.

Meanwhile, the Chief of Agriculture for the United States government began criticizing the Census Bureau for spending so much money on the use of Hollerith's machines. The criticism made Hollerith look more diligently for customers outside of the government. He was successful in many places, both in the United States and abroad. The Tabulating Machine Company became known throughout the world. The Census Bureau, largely because of the criticism from Agriculture, set up its own machine laboratory, and the new Director of the Census was determined to improve on Hollerith's machines. He hired a statistical engineer (the same title previously given Hollerith) named James Powers. Powers had the foresight to make the government agree to let him keep any patent rights to machines he might develop. In time for the 1910 census, Powers had developed a card punch, a sorter, and a tabulating machine. The director was so pleased with the machines that he purchased 300 of them to be used for the 1910 census. In that year Hollerith brough suit against the Census Bureau, claiming some of his patent rights had been infringed upon by the Bureau in the design of Powers' machines. No significant settlement ever came of the suit and Hollerith never again had any dealings of consequence with the Census Bureau.

Powers, naturally enough, formed his own company, the Powers Accounting Machine Company, and left the Census Bureau in 1911. Powers' company continued to produce card-processing equipment and, in 1927, became the Tabulating Machines Division of the Remington-Rand Corporation. Still later, in 1955, the Remington-Rand Corporation became the Sperry-Rand Corporation and the Tabulating Machines Division became the Univac Division. (Univac was the name of the first computer made for commercial purposes, and it was made for the Sperry-Rand Corporation in 1951.)

Hollerith continued to be active in his company, increasing the efficiency of his machines. In 1911 his company merged with three others to form the Computing, Tabulating, Recording Company (CTR). That firm was renamed the International Business Machines Corporation (IBM) in 1924, then under the management of Thomas J. Watson. It is interesting to note that the competition that began between Herman Hollerith and James Powers over the 1910 census continues to this day in the corporations spawned by the companies those two men began.

Hollerith wrote his last plans to develop a tabulating machine in 1923 but, because of illness, was unable to carry them through to completion. He died on November 17, 1929 at the age of 69 from a heart attack.

Through the efforts and abilities of Hollerith, the ideas of Pascal, Jacquard, and Babbage were put to even more sophisticated uses in the processing of information. Pascal had thought only of numbers, and Jacquard of beautifully complex cloth designs, but Hollerith had worked with information of various kinds. The effects on business and commerce of having accurate, current information about the country's population can only be guessed. The ability of large companies to keep track of their inventories, to compile cost data, and analyze payroll information fast enough that management decisions could change the profit outcome has affected many people. Slowly, but surely, people were gaining the ability to organize and utilize large amounts of information. An increase in that ability by one segment of society has always produced effects (good for some and bad for others) on society as a whole. Information processing would never again be the same as it was before Hollerith.

AIKEN AND THE FIRST COMPUTER

Although Hollerith conceived of remarkable applications for the punched-card concepts of Jacquard and Babbage, his machines had none of the analytical aspects proposed in Babbage's design. Not until 1944 was anything built that had most of the capabilities of the Analytical Engine. In that year, a machine called the Mark I was completed under the direction of Howard H. Aiken.

Howard Aiken was born on March 9, 1900 at Hoboken, New Jersey, to Daniel and Margaret Aiken. He attended the Hoboken schools and earned a bachelor's degree from the University of Wisconsin in 1923. He worked in Wisconsin and Illinois for the next eight years, and in 1931 began graduate study in physics at Harvard University. While he was researching his doctoral thesis, Aiken became concerned about a calculating machine. The mathematics used in the research was such that solutions to certain equations could not be obtained explicitly. The only known methods of solution were numerical approximation methods requiring extremely long calculations. Aiken began to consider mechanical methods of doing the calculations and, in the process, invented a machine for evaluating simple polynomials. Over the next few years, he developed other machines capable of solving more complex problems. Reflecting on the various machines he had designed, Aiken realized that their logical organization was identical. The major differences lay in the kinds of information each machine could handle. This realization set him to thinking about the possibility of a general-purpose machine, one that could handle any of the problems for which his various machines were designed. He completed his doctoral research, using the separate calculating machines, and in 1939 was awarded a Ph.D. from Harvard.

That same year he approached IBM about providing financial support for the new machine he envisioned. IBM accepted his proposal and he began work immediately at one of that company's locations, working closely with four IBM engineers. Strange as it may seem, Aiken had worked three years in the development of a computer before he discovered the writings of Babbage. He was amazed to read that 100 years earlier Babbage had struggled with some of the same machine design problems that had bothered him. The machine on which Aiken and his collaborators were working was initially called the Automatic Sequence Controlled Calculator but that was soon changed to Mark I. Aiken was instructor of physics at Harvard at that time, and on January 7, 1943 was married to Agnes Montgomery.

The Mark I was an electromechanical machine; that is, the functioning parts were mechanical but were driven by electricity. Electromechanical devices use a relay switch, an electromagnet, a device that is magnetic as long as electric current is flowing but loses its magnetic capabilities when the current is shut off. At the instant the device is magnetized, the magnetic effect causes physical movement that closes a switch, activating a circuit in which a counter or similar device is moved ahead. When the electric current is cut off, the magnetic effect is lost and the switch is opened again by the force of a spring attached to it. About 3000 such relay switches were used in the Mark I, and each could be opened or closed in about a hundredth of a second. The computer had about 760,000 electrical components, including switches, wheels, and vacuum tubes. It required about 500 miles of wire to form all the various circuits. The machine was 8 feet high, 51 feet long, and about 3 feet deep. Figure 2.2 shows a picture of the Mark I. It was housed in a separate red brick building just behind the physics building on the Harvard campus.

The Mark I handled numbers in decimal form (as opposed to binary numbers most later computers used), and did its arithmetic to 23 digits of accuracy. The time required to perform an addition operation was 0.3 second. Multiplication and division were done by using a multiplication table built into the machine's circuitry. Numbers were stored in strings of relay switches, on punched paper tape, and on a series of hand-manipulated switches set up for each computation. The sequence of instructions (the program) was prepunched in numerical form into a ribbon of paper tape, which was moved forward automatically by the machine, instruction by instruction. When first built, the Mark I was used to compute tables of ballistic data for the Armed Services during World War II. After the war it was running almost continuously, producing mathematical tables of various kinds. It was retired from operation after 10 years of service and is exhibited today in the Smithsonian Institution.

Aiken continued improving the Mark I, and introduced a new version, the Mark II, in 1947. Although significantly faster as a calculator, the Mark II was still an electromechanical machine. Aiken designed and directed the construction of two later computers while at Harvard, called the Mark III and Mark IV.

Howard Aiken accepted a faculty position as Professor of Information Technology at the University of Miami, Florida in 1947. He was still living in Florida

FIGURE 2.2   The Mark I computer (Smithsonian Institution Photo No. X4724).

when he died in March 1973. A tribute to him appeared in the May 1973, issue of *Communications of the ACM.* Here is the first paragraph of it:

> *It was the olden days, when computers were still laboratory projects. Howard Aiken was one of the first of our era to envision large self-sequenced machines which would relieve scientists of the burden of computation, and his initial efforts in the late thirties had produced the Harvard Mark I Calculator. He held in respect the lesson of Babbage, that too high a level of untested technology could do you in, and seldom bit off more than he could chew. Yet he was always on the lookout for new and better ways to do things. Under his direction had been constructed four machines, of progressive sophistication, while other groups were still attempting to get one into operation.*

About the same time that Aiken was developing his machine, a mathematician working at Bell Telephone Laboratories named George Stibitz was also constructing a computer. Stibitz designed his machine entirely around existing tele-phone parts, using the relay as the key device. His computer was completed in 1946 and was quite similar to the Mark I. It got its instructions from loops of punched paper tape, each instruction requiring from one to two seconds to exe-cute. Stibitz included one innovation not found in Aiken's machine; his machine could store data. Stibitz's computer was the first to have storage facilities, although it could store only 20 seven-digit numbers.

Aiken began planning his computer because he needed to complete some research for graduate study. The computer was completed while the United States was at war, and it was quickly put into use serving the war effort. Stibitz's machine was being developed by Bell Laboratories for war use. Both computers played significant roles in direct military applications and in military-related scientific re-search. Military operations entered the age of the computer, and undoubtedly the war effort was strengthened by the use of these machines. Clearly, these sophisti-cated information-processing machines played a significant role in shaping the structure of both domestic and foreign affairs of most of the world's nations. Not only that. The Mark I revolutionized scientific and statistical research. Those first computers made it realistic for researchers to apply mathematical and statistical techniques not previously used because of the tremendous amount of calculations they required.

ATANASOFF, MAUCHLY, ECKERT, AND THE FIRST ELECTRONIC COMPUTER

While Aiken was developing his computer, three men, John V. Atanasoff, John W. Mauchly, and J. Presper Eckert, were working on calculating machines destined to be even more powerful than the Mark I. All three men are living today (January 1977).

John Vincent Atanasoff was born in 1904 to an Iowa couple of Bulgarian descent. He earned his bachelor's degree from Iowa State University and his Ph.D. from the University of Wisconsin, the latter degree being awarded in 1930. He, like Aiken, had been frustrated many times during his doctoral research by the lack of a satisfactory calculating machine. Atanasoff returned to Iowa in 1930 as an assistant professor of mathematics at Iowa State University in Ames. His deep concern for the need for an adequate calculator was reinforced as he guided graduate students in mathematics research. After thinking about such a machine for more than eight years, during the winter of 1937—38 some of the basic concepts came to him which later became the bases for the electronic computer which he built. He wrote the ideas down, expanded on them, and began to design the machine.

In the fall of 1939, the same fall that war was declared in Europe, Atanasoff

FIGURE 2.3   The ABC computer (courtesy John V. Atanasoff).

hired a promising graduate student, Clifford Berry, and started building the computing machine. In December 1940, Atanasoff attended a meeting of the American
Association for the Advancement of Science in Philadelphia. There he met Dr.
John Mauchly, who showed intense interest in Atanasoff's computer. Atanasoff
invited Mauchly to Ames to study the devices already constructed and to discuss
the ideas he and Berry had about the design of their computer. One of Atanasoff's
and Berry's innovations was the representation of numbers internally as binary
numbers (numbers whose base is the decimal number two) rather than as decimal
numbers (numbers whose base is ten). The Atanasoff-Berry Computer (ABC), as
they called it, was completed in 1942. This machine incorporated the vacuum tube
as the basic counting device (rather than the relay used by Aiken and Stibitz) and
was capable of solving large systems of algebraic equations (see Figure 2.3).

      Because the ABC project was not directly related to the war effort, Berry
was eligible for the draft. Consequently both men sought jobs more directly helpful
to their country's defense effort. Atanasoff accepted a position with the Naval
Ordnance Laboratory (NOL) in Washington, D.C., and Berry went to an engineering firm in Pasadena, California.

      Since the work of Atanasoff, Mauchly, and Eckert bear on each other, let us
consider some facts now about Mauchly and Eckert. John W. Mauchly was born in

Cincinnati, Ohio, in 1907. He attended the Washington, D.C. public schools, was admitted to the Johns Hopkins University School of Engineering in 1925, and was awarded the Ph.D. in physics from that university in 1932. He taught at various colleges, becoming more and more aware of the need for a fast computing machine if the physics problems then being discussed were ever to be solved. In 1941 he accepted a position at the Moore School of Engineering at the University of Pennsylvania in Philadelphia.

J. Presper Eckert was born in Philadelphia in 1919 and attended the William Penn Charter School in Germantown, Pennsylvania. In 1941 he was awarded his bachelor's degree from the Moore School of Engineering and was asked to remain there as a teacher. By June 1943 he had earned his master's degree from the Moore School and had accepted an invitation to work with Dr. John Mauchly on a secret defense contract. As a graduate student, Eckert had studied under Mauchly and had worked with him on some research. During 1942 both men were working on separate projects for the Ballistic Research Laboratory of the U.S. Army Ordnance Department.

The work that Mauchly and Eckert embarked on in 1943 was to be done under a contract between the University of Pennsylvania and the Ballistic Research

FIGURE 2.4   The ENIAC (courtesy Sperry-Univac).

Laboratory. Essentially, the task was to design and build a large-scale computing machine. The project was given high priority by the government because of its great potential for helping the military effort. Thirty months after the designing was begun in earnest, the machine was completed, in February 1946. At its dedication, the machine was named ENIAC, acronym for Electronic Numerical Integrator and Calculator. It was an enormous thing consisting of 47 panels of electronic parts and wires, each panel being 2 feet wide, 9 feet high, and 1 foot thick. Among its components were 19,000 vacuum tubes, 70,000 resistors, and 10,000 capacitors, it also had 500,000 soldered joints. It used 150,000 watts of electrical power each day when operating, and, when the ENIAC was switched on at night, so much power was drained from the city's electrical system that the lights of north Philadelphia dimmed. It could perform 5000 additions of ten-digit numbers each second. It had a memory of 20 storage locations. It did everything Aiken's Mark I had done but much faster, about 1700 times faster. It also incorporated the memory feature of Stibitz's machine. Figure 2.4 shows the ENIAC and the room in which it was located. The machine weighed 30 tons and occupied 15,000 square feet of floor space. The essential counting device in the ENIAC was the vacuum tube, as it was in the Atanasoff-Berry Computer. Because vacuum tubes create considerable amounts of heat, the problem of keeping the ENIAC's room cool enough was no small matter. Nevertheless, the air-conditioning problem was solved satisfactorily enough to keep the ENIAC running from February 15, 1946 to October 2, 1955. On that day it was retired, and it stands on display now in the Smithsonian Institution.

Although Atanasoff and Berry's computer was really the first electronic digital computer, it is the ENIAC that is generally cited as having that honor. However, all three men, Atanasoff, Mauchly, and Eckert, must be credited with contributing greatly to humanity's persistent efforts to effectively manage information.

Not long after the end of World War II, Atanasoff formed his own company, the Ordnance Engineering Corporation. That firm was sold in 1962 to Aerojet General, the company with which Atanasoff is still associated. After the ABC project, Atanasoff never again worked directly in the development of computers. On the other hand, Mauchly and Eckert formed their own computer company and in 1951 it was purchased by the Remington Rand Corporation with Eckert being made the vice president of the computer division.

VON NEUMANN AND THE FIRST STORED-PROGRAM COMPUTERS

During this same period of time, the 1940s, a mathematician named Dr. John von Neumann was a consultant at the Aberdeen Proving Ground. He became enthusiastic about the secret project going on at the Moore School of Engineering when he realized Mauchly and Eckert were well on their way toward developing a machine that could perform more than a thousand times faster than existing electromechanical ones. He joined the Eckert-Mauchly team in 1946.

John von Neumann was born on December 28, 1903 in Budapest, Hungary, into a wealthy banker's family. Johnny, as he was later called by all who knew him, was recognized as a brilliant child and was given special tutoring throughout his youth. He was especially gifted in mathematics and was recognized as a professional mathematician from the publication of his first paper when he was not yet 18. He earned doctorates in mathematics and chemistry in Budapest and Zurich, respectively, in 1926, and accepted a visiting professorship at Princeton University in 1930. In 1933 he was invited to join the Institute for Advanced Study at Princeton (a most prestigious place for scientific study) as that institution's youngest member of the permanent faculty. While he was a member of that faculty, the U.S. government called upon him to lend his talents in solving some of the scientific problems facing a nation at war. Thus it was that von Neumann became associated with the Aberdeen Proving Ground.

Von Neumann's innovation in computer science was the concept of storing the program (the set of instructions for the machine) in the memory of the machine along with the information (numbers) on which those instructions would operate. The design of such a computer, called the Electronic Discrete Variable Automatic Computer (EDVAC) was begun in the spring of 1946. Before the project could be completed, Eckert and Mauchly left Aberdeen Proving Ground to form their own computer company. Von Neumann returned to his position at the Institute for Advanced Study and continued his work in computer design there. A new team of scientists was brought in to continue the work on EDVAC, but that machine was not completed until 1950.

Meanwhile, at Cambridge University in England, a team headed by Maurice V. Wilkes developed a machine patterned after the EDVAC. The Electronic Delay Storage Automatic Calculator (EDSAC), as Wilkes' group called their computer, performed its first automatic calculation in May 1949. Thus the EDSAC was the world's first stored-program computer. All earlier machines, including the ENIAC, were given their instructions one at a time either by way of punched paper tape or through elaborate circuit plugboards that had to be rewired for every new computational problem (see Figure 2.5).

The EDSAC was a much smaller machine than the ENIAC; it contained only 3000 vacuum tubes compared to the ENIAC's 19,000. It required only 15 kilowatts of power to operate while the ENIAC took 150 kilowatts. It operated with about one-seventh the speed of the ENIAC, being capable of executing about 700 additions per second. But the important advantage inherent to the EDSAC was its ability to store instructions in its working memory. Thus, for the first time, informa-

FIGURE 2.5   ENIAC showing wiring panels (courtesy Sperry-Univac).

FIGURE 2.6   The EDSAC, first stored-program computer (reproduced by permission of Pitman Publishing Limited).

42

tion computed by the machine, not known in advance by the person setting up the problem, could be used by the machine to modify its internally stored instructions according to procedures established by the human being. Here, at last, was Babbage's Analytical Engine with all its capabilities! It could perform its operations faster than Babbage could possibly have imagined. Figure 2.6 shows a picture of this marvelous product of humanity's ingenuity.

Although Eckert, Mauchly, and Atanasoff are still active in their respective positions, John von Neumann is gone. He had been a man of excellent health until 1954 when he began to show evidence of illness. In 1955 he was told he had cancer, and he died on February 8, 1957 at the age of 53, another outstanding mind lost to humanity.

UNIVAC I: THE FIRST COMPUTER BUILT TO SELL

All the machines discussed to this point were research machines or computers intended for special governmental applications. With the purchase of the Eckert-Mauchly Computer Company, the Remington-Rand Corporation planned to produce computers for profit. Eckert was vice president of the firm's Computer Division and once more he and Mauchly found themselves partners in supervising the development of a computing machine. Their product, delivered by Remington-Rand to the U.S. Bureau of the Census in 1951, was dubbed the Univac, for Universal Automatic Computer. This machine was able to perform just under 4000 additions of five-digit numbers in one second. Its instruction set made it possible to process both numeric and alphabetic information (when coded in binary form) (see Figure 2.7).

The Univac I was used by the Census Bureau 24 hours a day, seven days a week until October 1963, when it was retired and placed in the Smithsonian Institution. It had been in operation for more than 73,000 hours. The Univac I cost Remington-Rand Corporation nearly $12 million to produce, although later models of it were undoubtedly less costly. Thus this corporation was the first in the world to market computers.

The IBM Corporation was not long in developing its own version of an electronic computer for the marketplace. Largely because of that firm's emphasis on a good sales program and excellent support from its service department, it is today well ahead of any other computer manufacturer in value of computer equipment installed. Interestingly enough, from one commercial computer in 1951, by September 1962, it is estimated that 16,200 computers had been installed in the United States alone. By 1975, this figure was well over 80,000. According to reliable estimates of the distribution of computers in the world today, IBM has sold

FIGURE 2.7   Univac I, first commercial computer (courtesy Sperry-Univac).

or leased about 70 percent of the machines, the Univac Division of Sperry-Rand about 7 percent, Honeywell Information Systems about 7 percent, with the remaining 16 percent of the market shared by all other manufacturers.

COMPUTER GENERATIONS

The ABC, ENIAC, EDSAC, and Univac I were the first electronic computers, and they used vacuum tubes as the basic counting device. During the 1950s many of these vacuum-tube computers were built and marketed. This group of computers is now referred to as first-generation computers. Their computation speed was in the range of 1000 to 5000 additions per second, a tremendous increase in computational speed over precomputer days.

In 1947 an electronic device called a transistor was invented by physicists at Bell Laboratories in New Jersey. This device could perform most of the functions that a vacuum tube could perform but much faster, consumed only a fraction of the energy required by vacuum tubes, and created only a small amount of heat. It seemed to be the answer for computer designers of the late 1950s and very early 1960s who had been fighting the problem of keeping computer rooms cool enough that these electronic marvels would operate properly. Also, the computing power made available by first-generation computers enabled users to consider more and more complex mathematical problems. As a result, users began to wonder if even faster computers could be made and if larger-capacity memory devices could be included. These forces accelerated the development of computers using transistors as the basic counting device. Thus, from 1958 to 1964 a large number of such computers were built and marketed. Computers utilizing transistors came to be known as second-generation computers. It should be noted that transistors utilize solids as the medium in which the electronic functions occur rather than empty space, as do vacuum tubes. Consequently, transistors were the first so-called solid-state devices. Second-generation computers had calculating speeds ranging from 2000 additions per second for the small machines to 500,000 per second for large machines like the IBM 7090. Memory capacities were large enough in some of the machines to provide 65,000 storage locations in main memory (the working memory of the computer) and several million storage locations in auxiliary memory (the secondary memory from which information could be retrieved at a slower rate).

In 1957 the first integrated circuit was produced; after 1964 it would have a

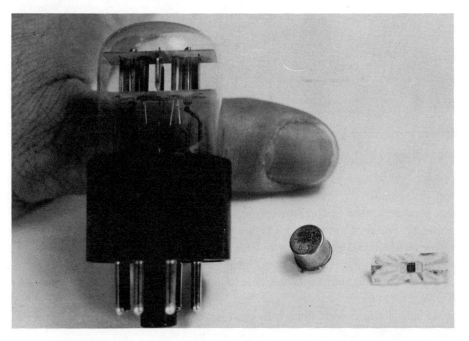

FIGURE 2.8   Vacuum tube, transistor, integrated-circuit.

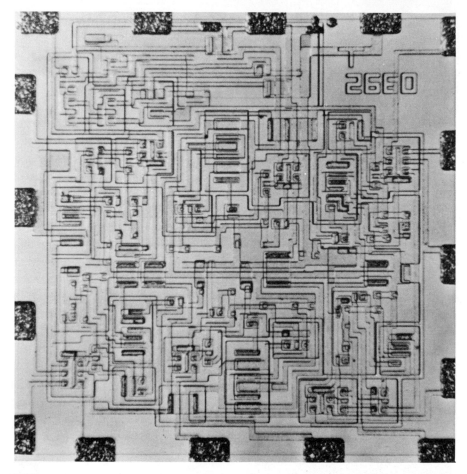

FIGURE 2.9   **Integrated circuit magnified a hundred times (courtesy Bell Laboratories).**

tremendous effect on computer development. An integrated circuit (IC) is a device that combines all of the capabilities of many transistors and other circuit components into one tiny "chip" of solid material about one-sixteenth of an inch square and a few hundredths of an inch thick. (See Figure 2.8 for a comparison of a vacuum tube, a transistor, and an integrated circuit.) This marvelous electronic device is manufactured by a mechanized microphotographic process, hence the cost of production is very low. Therefore, not only does the IC make it possible to construct still faster computers with larger memories than ever, but the *cost* of a given computer capability is less than it was before.

As you look at Figure 2.8, note that the IC is only the center square of the rightmost object in the picture. The IC is mounted on insulating material about ⅝ inch by ¼ inch. The IC itself is only one-sixteenth of an inch square, yet it performs the same functions as several thousand vacuum tubes. Figure 2.9 illustrates the complexity of this marvel of the space age. Clearly, the space program, because of the need to miniaturize on-board equipment, played a major role in the development of integrated circuits, and thus computers. And to the average consumer, the availability of an electronic pocket calculator for $15 or less is an even more direct consequence of the space program.

The integrated circuit, like the transistor before it, is a solid-state device. Computers utilizing IC's as the basic counting device are referred to as third-generation computers, and have been marketed from about 1964 to the present time. Because of certain special features, some manufacturers refer to their current models as fourth-generation machines, but the counting devices remain unchanged. The IC is still the fastest, smallest counting device available (although some refinements have been made in its manufacture) and the latest computers still use it. Third-generation computers perform as many as 10 million additions per second (a speed claimed by the makers of the ILLIAC at the University of Illinois) and may have main memories of more than 100 million storage locations, as well as an auxiliary memory of several hundred million locations. At last researchers need hardly concern themselves with problem limitations imposed by computer capability.

This tremendous facility for handling information has already been applied to a great many functions in society, and the list of applications continues to grow. Today, virtually everyone is affected in some aspect of their lives by computers.

EXERCISES

2.1 Identify the following computers by name:
      (a) the first electronic digital computer made;
      (b) the first stored-program computer;
      (c) the first digital computer;
      (d) the first computer made for commercial purposes.

2.2 List in chronological order of development the following machines: ENIAC, MARK I, ABC, UNIVAC I, EDSAC.

2.3 Describe how the Census Bureau used card-processing machines, and discuss any benefits to the Bureau resulting from their use.

2.4 Prepare a paper on the early business applications of card-processing machines.

2.5 Compare the computation speeds of the MARK I, the ENIAC, the EDSAC, and the Univac I. How do their speeds compare with that of Babbage's proposed Analytical Engine?

2.6 Describe the difference between an electromechanical computer and an electronic computer.

2.7 Which computer company provided financial and technical support for the development of the MARK I?

2.8 How do the first, second, and third generation computers differ?

2.9 Identify the following as being characteristic of a vacuum tube, a transistor, or an integrated circuit:

> (a) uses most energy;
>
> (b) occupies least space for the number of operations it performs;
>
> (c) solves the problem of excessive heat produced by vacuum tubes;
>
> (d) uses least amount of energy;
>
> (e) solid-state device;

2.10 List in chronological order the inventions of the following men: Aiken, Mauchly, Hollerith, von Neumann.

2.11 Prepare a table in which you compare the amount of change having occurred over the past 400 years in certain key aspects of life. A table similar to the following might be used:

	400 yrs ago	300 yrs ago	200 yrs ago	100 yrs ago	50 yrs ago	25 yrs ago
Miles traveled per day						
Years of formal education						
Hours required to communicate a message across 100 miles						
Computation speed (Additions per minute)						

Use the table as the basis for a panel discussion on the societal effects of change and rates of change.

2.12 Prepare a paper on the effect the first computers had on the development of the atomic bomb.

2.13 Write a paper on the impact of computers on the space program.

SELECTED REFERENCES

BOOKS

Bowden, Bertram V., *Faster Than Thought,* Sir Isaac Pitman & Sons, London, 1953.

Proceedings of a Symposium on Large Scale Digital Calculating Machinery, Harvard University Press, Cambridge, 1948.

PERIODICALS

Bulletin of The American Mathematical Society, May 1952, Part II.

McLaughlin, Richard A., "The ENIAC: Feb. 15, 1946—Oct. 2, 1955," *Datamation,* June 1973, p. 122.

Mollenhoff, Georgia B., "John V. Atanasoff, DP Pioneer-Part I," *Computerworld,* March 13, 1974, pp. 1—13.

Mollenhoff, Georgia B., "John V. Atanasoff, DP Pioneer-Part II," *Computerworld,* March 20, 1974, pp. 15—16.

Mollenhoff, Georgia B., "John V. Atanasoff, DP Pioneer-Part III," *Computerworld,* March 27, 1974, pp. 9—10.

"News in Perspective," *Datamation,* January 1974, p. 78.

"News in Perspective," *Datamation, February 1974, p. 82.*

3 COMMUNICATING WITH A COMPUTER

STORING INFORMATION IN A COMPUTER

Now that you know something about the historical development of digital computers, and have been introduced to some of the hardware aspects of these incredible machines, you are ready to consider how to make them accomplish work. To do this, we must first examine the software portion of a computer system. By software we mean the instructions stored in the memory of a computer, some of which are developed by the computer manufacturer and others by the computer user. We look first at how information is stored in a computer. The particular form in which a computer processes information depends on the design of the computer and the coding scheme used. In general, however, computers process any piece of information as if it were a collection of 1's and 0's stored physically next to each other in what is called a computer "word" (see Figure 3.1). That is, a computer word represents information to be handled by a computer, coded into 1's and 0's, and stored in a specific location. Without going into any of the technical aspects of why coding schemes use only 1's and 0's (binary digits or bits), let it be said that the least expensive, most reliable device for storing information is one that can maintain either of two stable conditions, where one condition (like a switch in the ON position) represents a 1 and the other condition (like the OFF position of a switch) represents a 0. In Figure 3.2 12 light bulbs (ON-OFF devices) are used to represent information coded as 100110110011. In today's computers the one-zero devices would not be light bulbs, however, but electronic devices called semiconductors.

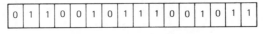

| 0 | 1 | 1 | 0 | 0 | 1 | 0 | 1 | 1 | 1 | 0 | 0 | 1 | 0 | 1 | 1 |

FIGURE 3.1   **Computer word.**

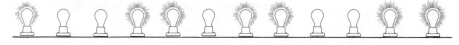

FIGURE 3.2   ON-OFF devices representing information.

There are several one-zero codes (binary codes) used by designers of computer systems. The fact that not all computer manufacturers use the same coding scheme has been the cause of much frustration among computer users. What is interpreted by one computer as the letter A might mean a comma to another computer. Cooperative efforts of computer users, computer manufacturers, and governmental agencies have resulted in the development of some standardized codes although none has yet been adopted by all computer manufacturers. The code most widely used and most generally advocated by U.S. government agencies is the American Standard Code for Information Interchange (ASCII). Users will benefit if all computers are designed to process information in ASCII, because information designed for processing on one computer system can be processed properly on all other computers. Because this is not the case today (1977), much time and effort is wasted in converting instructions and data from one

TABLE   3.1
EIGHT-DIGIT ASCII CODE FOR SELECTED CHARACTERS

CHARACTER	CODE	CHARACTER	CODE	CHARACTER	CODE
0	10110000	F	11000110	U	11010101
1	10110001	G	11000111	V	11010110
2	10110010	H	11001000	W	11010111
3	10110011	I	11001001	X	11011000
4	10110100	J	11001010	Y	11011001
5	10110101	K	11001011	Z	11011010
6	10110110	L	11001100	.	10101110
7	10110111	M	11001101	(	10101000
8	10111000	N	11001110	+	10101011
9	10111001	O	11001111	$	10100100
A	11000001	P	11010000	+	10101010
B	11000010	Q	11010001	)	10101001
C	11000011	R	11010010	%	10101111
D	11000100	S	11010011	,	10101101
E	11000101	T	11010100	=	10111101
				blank	10100000

form to another. Table 3.1 shows the eight-digit ASCII code for 46 of the most commonly used characters.

MACHINE LANGUAGE

Even if the letter A, the decimal digit 7, or any other character were to have the same binary code in all computers, computer designers would still develop a set of instructions unique to each given computer (or family of computers). Individualized instructions enable users to take full advantage of the special features of each computer. Thus each computer has associated with it an instruction set (usually formulated in binary digits) called its *machine language*. Only instructions presented to the computer in its machine language are "understood" by the computer and actually produce any response from it.

To clarify the concept of machine language one might compare it to the native language of a human being. If you speak only one language, anyone wishing to communicate with you must do so in your language. Similarly, each computer has its own native language, its machine language. If it is to carry out your instructions, those instructions must be given in machine language. Since machine language is always numeric and usually expressed in binary digits, learning such a language is not easy for most people. It is quite likely that few people would use a computer if they had to communicate with it in machine language. Therefore, languages have been devised that make it easier for humans to communicate with machines. Such languages, designed to be easily used by people working in a specialized area, are called *problem-oriented languages*.

PROBLEM-ORIENTED LANGUAGES

Problem-oriented languages use words and symbols specific to a given problem area. For example, one widely used problem-oriented language has the name COBOL. (The name comes from *Common Business Oriented Language*.) COBOL was designed for use in a business and financial environment where large files of information are processed, usually to produce some kind of financial report. Consequently the language includes special words such as READ, MOVE, MULTIPLY, AND WRITE that pertain to the handling of collections of information. A portion of a COBOL program follows:

```
PROCEDURE DIVISION.
BEGIN.
        OPEN INPUT INPUT-DATA, OUTPUT OUTPUT-FILE.
        READ INPUT-DATA RECORD AT END GO TO JOB-DONE.
```

```
        WRITE OUT-LINE FROM HEADER AFTER ADVANCING TO TOP.
        MOVE ZERO TO MONTHS-FROM-NOW.
        MOVE NEXT-MONTH TO WHICH-MONTH.
        PERFORM CALCULATION ROUTINE
        NUMBER-OF-MONTHS TIMES.
   JOB-DONE. CLOSE INPUT-DATA, OUTPUT-FILE, STOP RUN.
   CALCULATION-ROUTINE.
        ADD 1 TO MONTHS-FROM-NOW.
        IF WHICH-MONTH IS GREATER THAN 12 SUBTRACT 12
        FROM WHICH-MONTH.
        MULTIPLY MONTHS-FROM-NOW BY PERCENTAGE
        GIVING SALES.
        ADD BASE TO SALES.
        MOVE MONTH(WHICH-MONTH) TO MONTH NAME.
        WRITE OUT-LINE FROM PRINT-RECORD AFTER
        ADVANCING 1 LINES.
        ADD 1 TO WHICH-MONTH.
```

Even without knowledge of COBOL, you can see that this language uses words that make the program at least readable. Some computer users think COBOL requires too many words to define a given job. But if the language is easily learned by those who need to use the computer, the quantity of words is a small price to pay.

Another popular problem-oriented language is FORTRAN. (The name is taken from the two words, *FOR*mula *TRAN*slation.) This language is used to solve problems in mathematics, chemistry, and physics, or any problems that can be represented as formulas or equations. A FORTRAN program that computes the area of a triangle if the lengths of the base and height are given is the following:

```
READ,B,H
A=.5*B*H
PRINT,B,H,A
END
```

Even if you do not know the FORTRAN language it is easy to see that this program calls for input of two numbers referred to as B and H. Then the product of .5, B, and H is found and stored in A. Finally the values of B, H, and A are printed. The fact that certain words and nonnumeric symbols can be used in problem-oriented languages makes programs written in such languages quite readable and under-standable, even when no comments are given with the instructions. This is especially true if the program solves a problem in a subject area with which you are familiar.

Since only machine language instructions actually cause a computer to do work, the instructions written in COBOL or FORTRAN must be translated. Fortunately, this translation can be done by the computer in conjunction with a translating program previously stored in the computer's memory. Figure 3.3 illustrates how problem-oriented instructions become machine-language instructions and are then performed (executed) to complete the specified job. The dashed lines represent instructions entered into the input device of the computer in problem-oriented language form. The processor part of the computer cannot execute the dashed-line instructions so passes them on to computer memory. There the language translator (also called a *compiler*) converts the words and symbols into machine language form (solid lines). Since the machine language instructions *can* be executed by the processor, the processor carries out the tasks specified by those instructions and produces the desired results on the output device.

BASIC: A BEGINNER'S PROBLEM-ORIENTED LANGUAGE

Now that you have an idea about how a computer can be instructed to do useful tasks using words and symbols other than numbers, let us consider a problem-oriented language in more detail. We consider the language called BASIC (from *B*eginner's *A*ll-purpose *S*ymbolic *I*nstruction *C*ode). It was developed in the

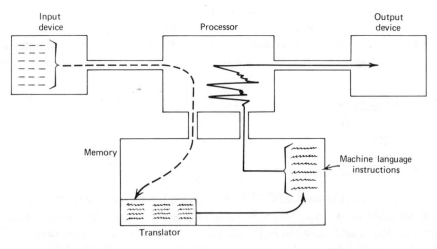

FIGURE 3.3   Translation of problem-oriented language.

mid-1960s by John G. Kemeny and Thomas Kurtz of Dartmouth College and has come to be one of the most widely used programming languages of the many available. Its popularity is probably due to the ease with which the average person can learn enough of its rules to be able to use a computer effectively. One of the major goals of this chapter is to enable the student to do just that, use a computer effectively.

Identifying Storage Locations

We begin our consideration of BASIC by reviewing the means available for identifying computer memory locations. Any information to be processed must, of course, first be properly stored in the computer's memory. This implies that there are ways to specify individual memory locations. Memory locations are specified in BASIC according to the changeability of information stored. If a memory location contains the same information throughout the execution of a given program and whenever that program is run, such a memory location is called a *constant*. On the other hand, if a memory location may contain different information at different times, it is called a *variable*.

BASIC CONSTANTS   There are three forms available to specify numerical constants. The first of these is called integer form. To name an integer constant the number is simply written without a decimal point. Following are some examples of integer constants: 5, 296, 27, 4765, 97483.

The second form we call the standard-decimal form and involves the use of a decimal point. Here are some examples of standard decimal constants: 3.7, 4.016, 1762.5, 49398.2, 45., .064.

The third form is called exponential form and is much like the scientific notation of the sciences and mathematics. This form is usually used for very small or very large numbers. Here are some examples of exponential constants: .647E12, .59324E-8, 14.95E+9. Notice that in exponential form there are three parts to each constant: the digits that identify the number (like .647 in the first example) the letter E (which stands for exponent); and the digits that specify the exponent (like 12 in the first example). The exponential constant .647E12 means $.647 \times 10^{12}$, which is equal to 647,000,000,000. Similarly, the exponential constant .59324E-8 means $.59324 \times 10^{-8}$, which equals .0000000059324. In effect, an exponential constant is evaluated by looking at its fractional part and moving the decimal point to the right (if the number following E is unsigned or positive) or to the left (if the number following E is negative). The number of places the decimal point is moved is indicated by the number following E.

In the case of all three constant forms, the name of the constant is numeri-

Constant name	Memory location and contents
17	17
15.7	15.7
.52E4	5200
.7E−3	.0007

FIGURE 3.4   **Constant names and memory locations.**

cally equal to its contents. Consider Figure 3.4. The constant name is in the left-hand column and the memory location with its contents is shown in the right-hand column.

Sometimes it is desirable to store nonnumeric information in memory locations. Any collection of characters such as letters, letters and numbers, or letters, numbers, and punctuation marks is called a *string*. For example,

I FEEL GREAT, DON'T YOU?

is a string. A string is often a message or information that identifies numbers which have been printed. In the BASIC language, a string constant is indicated by enclosing the string information in quotation marks. In a BASIC program the fact that

I FEEL GREAT, DON'T YOU?

is to be treated as a BASIC constant is indicated by placing quotation marks before and after it as follows:

"I FEEL GREAT, DON'T YOU?"

BASIC VARIABLES.   There are three rules for naming memory locations whose contents are not fixed:

1. The first character must be a letter;

2. The second character (if there is one) must be a digit;

3. A maximum of two characters is permitted.

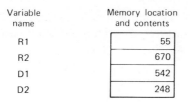

Variable name	Memory location and contents
R1	55
R2	670
D1	542
D2	248

FIGURE 3.5   Variable names and memory locations.

In accordance with these rules four examples of BASIC Variable names follow:

A   X   B2   D7

The name of a BASIC variable has no relationship to its contents except in the mind of the person creating the name. In Figure 3.5, for example, R1 and R2 might refer to the rate of travel via automobile and airplane, respectively. D1 and D2 might refer to two different distances to be considered. The names R1, R2, D1, and D2 are chosen by the person writing the program for their meaningfulness in the given problem situation. Their contents might be as shown in Figure 3.5 at one point in the execution of the program.

If a variable is to contain a string, the rules for naming it are the same as those given for numeric variables except that the second character must be a dollar sign instead of a digit.

Here are four examples of names for BASIC string variables:

A$ X$ B$ D$

Any of the memory locations thus named could be used to store string information such as names, street addresses, or city names.

Getting Information into a Computer

Now that we know how to identify specific memory locations we are ready to find out how to place information in them. In BASIC this is done by using either the READ/DATA pair of instructions or the INPUT instruction. Before these instructions are considered, however, let's examine the form of a BASIC instruction.

LINE NUMBERS   Every line in a BASIC program must begin with a unique number called the line number. This number may be as small as a single digit or as large as 99999. The line number is used by the programmer (the person developing the program) to indicate the order in which the instructions are to be performed by the computer. Following is an example of a very short BASIC program:

```
10   READ P,R,T
20   DATA 1500,.075,36
30   PRINT P*R*(T/12)
40   END
```

You will notice that the line numbers increase from 10 to 40 in steps of 10. Although these numbers were selected arbitrarily, there was a reason for using multiples of 10. Suppose the program as written had been entered into the computer. If an instruction had been left out, say, between lines 20 and 30, a new line could be entered following line 40 and given a line number of, say, 25. It would not be necessary to reenter the entire program. The program would now look like this:

```
10   READ P,R,T
20   DATA 1500,.075,36
30   PRINT P*R*(T/12)
40   END
25   PRINT P,R,T
```

The computer would execute the instructions in the following order:

```
10   READ P,R,T
20   DATA 1500, .075, 36
25   PRINT P,R,T
30   PRINT P*R*(T/12)
40   END
```

If, however, the program had been entered originally as

```
1   READ P,R,T
2   DATA 1500,.075,36
3   PRINT P*R*(T/12)
4   END
```

then the only way to insert a program statement between lines 2 and 3 would be to reenter the entire program including the new line 3 and renumber as follows:

3   **PRINT P,R,T**
4   **PRINT P*R*(T/12)**
5   **END**

It is good practice, then, to use line numbers that are multiples of 10 so that omitted instructions can be inserted easily.

READ AND DATA STATEMENTS   One method provided in BASIC for placing information in memory is the READ statement.

10   **READ A,B,C**

Notice the line number (which must be at the beginning of *every* statement) and the special word READ. The letters A, B, and C are variables. This program line means "store the first number provided to you in a memory location named A, the second number in a location named B, and the third in a location named C." The actual numbers to be stored are made available to the computer in a DATA statement like this:

20   **DATA 4,6,10**

If the lines

10   **READ A,B,C**
20   **DATA 4,6,10**

were entered into a computer as lines in a BASIC program the computer would assign the names A, B, and C to three memory locations and store the number 4 in location A, the number 6 in location B and the number 10 in location C. Notice that the READ and DATA statements work together as a pair. The READ statement names the memory locations and the DATA statement provides the information to be stored in them in the order that corresponds to the variables in the READ statement. To emphasize the importance of order, suppose the statements had been

```
10   READ A,C,B
20   DATA 4,6,10
```

Figure 3.6 shows how memory is affected by executing these statements. Note that since C was the second variable in the READ statement, the second number in the DATA statement was stored in location C. The variables in the READ statement are referred to as the *list* of the READ statement. If there are more variables in the list of the READ statement than there are numbers provided in the DATA statement, most BASIC systems provide for an error message such as "NOT ENOUGH DATA AT LINE 10." Line 10 would refer to the READ statement in which data were being called for but for which none was provided. The following pair of statements would cause such an error message:

```
10   READ A,B,C,X,Y,W
20   DATA 3,6,9,12,15
```

On the other hand, if there are more numbers provided in the DATA statement than there are variables in the associated READ statement, no error message occurs. In other words, as long as there are at least as many numbers in the DATA statement as there are variables in the READ statement, the correct data are stored. There is, of course, no valid reason for having more numbers in the DATA statement than are called for by a READ statement.

INPUT STATEMENT   Another way to place information in memory involves the INPUT statement.

```
10   INPUT A,B,C
```

This statement has the same general appearance as the READ statement except for the word INPUT. It can be interpreted to mean "accept three numbers, storing the first one in location A, the second in location B, and the third in location C." The

Variable name	Memory location and contents
A	4
B	10
C	6

FIGURE 3.6   Memory contents after a READ execution.

INPUT statement differs from the READ in that the numbers to be stored are provided by the user at the time the program is executed. In the case of the READ statement the numbers to be stored are provided when the program is written by using the DATA statement. Thus the INPUT statement does not take an associated DATA statement. Instead, when it is processed by the computer it causes a question-mark to appear on the output device. This cues the user to key the appropriate number or numbers called for by the INPUT statement.

In all three statements, READ, DATA, and INPUT, the comma is used to separate variables or different items of information. There may be as many variables in a READ or INPUT list as space on the line allows. Similarly, in a DATA statement only the length of the line (72 characters) limits the amount of data that may be included.

Getting Information out of a Computer's Memory

Just as important as placing information into memory is the process of displaying to the computer user the contents of given memory locations. In BASIC this is done by the use of the PRINT statement.

PRINT STATEMENT   The PRINT statement has the same characteristics as the READ and INPUT statements. Here is an example:

    20   PRINT A,B,C,X

Notice the presence of a line number, the word PRINT, and the variables A,B,C, and X. Of course, as is true for the READ and INPUT statements, any variables may appear in the list of a PRINT statement. There is a difference between the output statement, PRINT, and the two input statements, however. The locations in a print list must have had numbers stored in them before they appear in the PRINT statement. If not, the computer outputs values of zero. In other words, in the example

    20   PRINT A,B,C,X

it would be foolish to ask for the printing of information from locations A, B, C, and X unless some values had been stored there. However, if the programmer does give such a foolish instruction, the computer functions as if a value of zero had been stored wherever the programmer has not stored any values. For example, if the following program statements were executed,

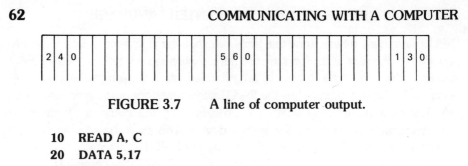

FIGURE 3.7   A line of computer output.

```
10   READ A, C
20   DATA 5,17
30   PRINT A,B,C
```

the resulting output would be the line

5   0   17

Since no number had been stored in location B the computer prints a zero in the output line in the position corresponding to the position of B in the PRINT list.

COMMA AS A SEPARATOR   The comma used to separate the variables in a PRINT statement has a special function. It causes the output to be spaced across the line every 14 spaces. To help you understand this concept consider the following BASIC statements:


```
10   READ X,Y,R
20   DATA 130,240,560
30   PRINT Y,R,X
```

Figure 3.7 shows the line of output that would result. The fact that Y, R, and X are separated by commas in line 30 causes the value of R to begin in space 15 and the value of X to begin in space 29. (The vertical lines in Figure 3.7 designate spaces.) As you can easily verify, if a full line has 72 spaces and if 14 spaces are allocated to each number in the output line, one line can have a maximum of five numbers in it. If a PRINT statement contains more than five variables all separated by commas, the computer will print five numbers on the first line (spaced every fourteen spaces) and print the sixth number on a second line, directly below the first number. Here is an illustration:


```
10   READ A,B,C,D,E,F,G,H,I,J,K,L
20   DATA 2,4,6,8,10,12,14,16,18,20,22,24
30   PRINT A,B,C,D,E,F,G,H,I,J,K,L
```

FIGURE 3.8   Numeric computer output.

Figure 3.8 shows the resulting output. Notice the spacing from left to right and the vertical positioning of the numbers. This pattern of output results from the use of the comma as a separator (also called a delimiter) in a PRINT statement. A set of spaces next to each other (like each group of 14 horizontal spaces in Figure 3.8) is called a *field*. Thus the use of the comma as a delimiter in a PRINT statement produces fields of 14 spaces.

PRINT STATEMENT AND ALPHABETIC OUTPUT   In the preceding section the use of the PRINT statement to produce numeric output was considered. The PRINT statement can also be used to produce nonnumeric output such as headings, sentences, or any kind of printed characters. Consider this example:

10   PRINT "LENGTH", "WIDTH", "HEIGHT"

Figure 3.9 shows the output that would result.

Notice that in the PRINT statement nonnumeric output is achieved by using string constants like "LENGTH", "WIDTH", and "HEIGHT". Again the use of commas as delimiters causes 14-space fields to be generated in the output line. The only limitation on the number of characters permitted in a string constant is the length of the line, that is, 72 characters. These 72 characters must include the line number, the word PRINT, and any punctuation marks or spaces used in the line.

SEMICOLON AS A DELIMITER   Sometimes the 14-column field is not desirable. The BASIC language provides for that possibility and requires the use of the semicolon as the delimiter. Consider this portion of a program.

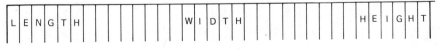

FIGURE 3.9   Alphabetic computer output.

| 8 | 4 | 2 | | | 4 | | | 2 | . | 5 | | 6 | 3 |

FIGURE 3.10   Numeric output using semicolons.

15   READ R,S,T,V
20   DATA 2.5,4,63,842
30   PRINT V;S;R;T

In the output the semicolon causes two spaces to be left between the values of the variables. In particular, the output produced by the preceding example is as shown in Figure 3.10. Notice that output values are separated by two spaces because semicolons were used as delimiters between numeric variables.

In the case of string constants the semicolon produces no spaces following the string information. For example,

10   READ X,Y,Z
20   DATA 15.7,8,749
30   PRINT "X IS";X;"Y IS";Y;"Z IS   ";Z

would produce the output shown in Figure 3.11. In the output no space falls between the "S" of "X IS" and the number 15.7 because a semicolon follows the string "X IS" in the PRINT statement (line 30). Similarly there is no space following the "S" of "Y IS". Although a semi-colon follows the string "Z IS", a space follows the "S" of "Z IS" in the output because a space is included following the "S" in the string "Z IS ". In other words, semi-colons following strings in PRINTstatements produce spaces following those strings in the output unless spaces are included in the strings themselves. Notice in Figure 3.11, however, that two spaces appear after the output of numeric variables as a consequence of using semicolons.

As shown in the preceding example, string constants may be mixed with numeric variables in a PRINT statement. It is, in fact, possible to have any combination of string constants and variables and numeric constants and variables in a single PRINT statement. Figure 3.12 shows another example of a portion of a BASIC program and the output that it would produce. Note especially the mixture

| X | | I | S | 1 | 5 | . | 7 | | Y | | I | S | 8 | | Z | | I | S | | 7 | 4 | 9 |

FIGURE 3.11   Alphabetic and numeric output using semicolons.

```
10 READ A, B, C$
20 DATA 25, 150, "MULTIPLIER"
30 PRINT "ALTITUDE = "; A; C$;" IS "; B
```

| A | L | T | I | T | U | D | E | | = | | 2 | 5 | | | M | U | L | T | I | P | L | I | E | R | | I | S | | 1 | 5 | 0 |

FIGURE 3.12   Mixed information in PRINT and resulting output.

of numeric variables and string constants and variables in the PRINT statement, line 30. Note also the spacing produced in the line of output. In Figure 3.12 the READ statement contains two numeric variables and one string variable. The associated DATA statement has two numbers and one string, with the string enclosed in quotation marks. In this book all strings, whether in PRINT statements or in DATA statements, are enclosed in ordinary double quotation marks. In some BASIC systems single quotation marks (or apostrophes) must be used. The reader should determine which convention applies to the system he/she is using because incorrect use will result in error messages.

Before we conclude this discussion of the PRINT statement, the student should be made aware of the fact that both commas and semicolons may be used in the same PRINT statement. Each delimiter has the effect on the output as previously described. In particular, the use of the comma always causes spacing to the next 14-column field. Consider this portion of a program:

10   READ A,B
20   DATA 2,4
30   PRINT "AXIS IS   ";A,"BASE IS",B

Figure 3.13 shows the corresponding output. The blank in space 8 is the result of including a space after "IS" in the "AXIS IS   " and using a semicolon as the delimiter. The "B" appears in space 15 because in the PRINT statement a comma follows the variable A. The comma signals the computer to space to the next available 14-column field before printing the string "BASE IS". Similarly, the comma after "BASE IS" in the PRINT statement informs the computer to space to the next available 14-column field (which begins in space 29) before printing the value of the variable B.

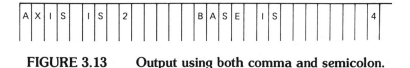

| A | X | I | S | | I | S | | 2 | | | | | | B | A | S | E | | I | S | | | | | | | | 4 |

FIGURE 3.13   Output using both comma and semicolon.

Beginning and Ending a BASIC Program

When you write programs it is usually helpful to include information that makes it easy to identify them. With longer programs it is often worthwhile to include descriptive information about sections of the program. Such identifying or descriptive information is useful for other people who may read the program, but are of no use to the computer in accomplishing the job defined by the program. In BASIC such descriptive information is recorded in the REMARK or REM statement.

REMARK STATEMENT   The REMARK or REM statement enables the programmer to include information useful to people who look at the program; information that will be ignored by the compiler. Here is what a REM statement looks like.

10   REM PAYROLL PROGRAM. COMPLETED 12/1/76

Like every BASIC statement, a REM statement must have a unique line number. The word REMARK or simply REM signals the compiler to omit the translation of this line into machine language. Following REM, any information whatsoever may be entered on the line. Thus in the example just given, the line identifies the program as a payroll program completed on December 1, 1976. Obviously, this information is not useful in actually computing the payroll but is valuable to anyone reviewing the programs on file at the computer installation. Should it be necessary to change payroll procedures, the REM line above would help greatly in locating the program to be modified. Furthermore, if the change deals with the computation of the income tax deduction, one might look for a line in the program similar to this:

150   REM INCOME TAX DEDUCTION COMPUTATION

Such a line in the program would pinpoint the exact portion where the change should be made.

Remember, REM statements are not intended as steps in the accomplishment of the programmed job. Therefore, any information useful to the person writing the program or anyone who might later look at the program may be included in a REM statement. Often, the first lines of a program contain descriptions of the instructions that follow, hence these first lines would be REM statements.

END STATEMENT.   Although the inclusion of a REM statement as the first line in a program is optional, the way a program concludes is clearly specified in BASIC. The line with the largest line number (and hence the last line to be executed) must be the END statement. It takes the following form:

500   END

As you can see, this is probably the simplest statement in the whole program. All you must do is see that the line number is larger than any other line number in the program and spell the word END correctly. What could be easier? Despite its simplicity, the END statement is very important. Every program must have one and there must be only one such statement.

COMPLETE BASIC PROGRAMS.   Now you have enough information about BASIC to write a program that could actually be processed by a computer having a BASIC compiler. To help you toward this goal, look at the following examples of complete programs and see if you can determine what the output for each would be:

Example 1

```
10   REM THIS IS SAMPLE PROGRAM ONE.
20   REM IT REQUIRES A LITTLE INTERACTION
30   REM BETWEEN THE COMPUTER AND THE USER.
40   PRINT "AFTER THE QUESTION-MARK"
42   PRINT "PLEASE TYPE YOUR NAME."
45   PRINT "THEN PRESS THE RETURN KEY."
50   INPUT N$
60   PRINT "HI,"; N$; "HOW ARE YOU?"
70   PRINT "WOULD YOU MIND TELLING ME YOUR AGE?"
75   PRINT "REMEMBER TO PRESS THE RETURN KEY"
78   PRINT "AFTER YOU ANSWER."
80   INPUT Q$
90   PRINT "YOU SAID ";Q$;N$;
100   PRINT "BUT I KNOW HOW SENSITIVE PEOPLE"
110   PRINT "ARE ABOUT THEIR AGES, SO WE WON'T"
120   PRINT "PURSUE THAT TOPIC ANY FURTHER."
130   PRINT "IN FACT, MAYBE WE SHOULD STOP THE"
140   PRINT "ENTIRE CONVERSATION."
150   END
```

Example 2

```
10   REM THIS IS SAMPLE PROGRAM TWO.
20   REM ALL IT DOES IS TO PRINT ANY FOUR
30   REM NUMBERS TYPED IN THE REVERSE ORDER
```

```
40   REM IN WHICH THEY WERE GIVEN.
50   PRINT "FOLLOWING THE QUESTION-MARK, PLEASE"
60    PRINT "TYPE ANY FOUR NUMBERS SEPARATING THEM"
70   PRINT "BY COMMAS. AFTER THE 4TH ONE"
80   PRINT "PRESS THE RETURN KEY."
90   INPUT N1,N2,N3,N4
100   PRINT "THE NUMBERS YOU GAVE ME TYPED"
110   PRINT "IN REVERSE ORDER ARE ";N4;N3;N2;N1
120   END
```

Now, why not try to design some of your own programs? Then you'll be all set to test the computer's ability to respond to your instructions. You will need to find out how to gain access to the computer at your institution. If yours is a timesharing system, the next section will help you understand its operation. Appendix B describes some details of the procedure for connecting to and disconnecting from one specific timesharing system.

Timesharing Computer Systems and How to Use Them

Most computers that have BASIC available as a language are timesharing computers. In the mid-sixties it became apparent to some people working with computers that the devices in a computer system which performed the arithmetic computations and the decision-making functions were not being fully utilized. (This part of a computer system is called the central processor, or central processing unit.) In fact, the central processor was busy only a small portion of the time because the input and output devices operated much more slowly than the central processor; information that took several minutes to input and print out was analyzed in a fraction of a second by the central processor. Some people who observed this situation wondered if it would be possible to attach several input/output devices to the same central processor. The idea eventually became reality and the first timesharing computer system was built. Figure 3.14 will help you understand how a timesharing computer works. The figure shows the central processor, the circular device with a rotating pointer, and the five terminals. ("Terminal" is another name for the input/output device in a timesharing computer system.) The circular device is divided into five equal segments, and each segment is linked to one of the terminals. As the pointer rotates over segment 1, the central processor is in contact with terminal 1 and is controlled by instructions sent to it from that terminal. It is also able to send information back to terminal 1 during this portion of the pointer's rotation. In other words, terminal 1 has the use of the central processor for one-fifth of the total time. A similar arrangement is true for segments 2, 3, 4, and 5 with

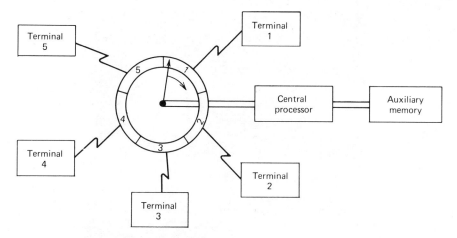

FIGURE 3.14   Diagram of timesharing computer system.

respect to terminals 2, 3, 4, and 5. Information sent on its way to each terminal is stored in a temporary holding place, called a buffer, and transmitted to the terminal as the terminal can accept it. This way the central processor is free to serve the other terminals while the buffers release information to keep their respective terminals busy. The timesharing system makes much more efficient use of the central processor's time than would be possible if only one input/output device were attached to the central processor.

In Figure 3.14, the jagged line connecting each terminal to the circular rotor represents a physical connection in the form of a cable or telephone line. The terminals may be in the same room as the central processor, or they may be several thousand miles away. Electrical signals may be generated by any terminal to produce a response in the central processor and the central processor may in turn send signals to any terminal to cause it to display information.

Another block to note in Figure 3.14 is the one labeled "auxiliary memory." Auxiliary memory is a storage area for information not immediately needed by the central processor. For example, programs that could be useful to any computer user (like finding the square root of a number) are called library functions and are typically stored in auxiliary memory until needed by the user and are then called into the central processor. Similarly, programs developed by you, the user, to be run more than once may also be stored in auxiliary memory. The procedure for storing in auxiliary memory is discussed in Appendix B.

COMPUTER TERMINAL.   It was previously stated that an input/output device associated with timesharing computer systems is called a

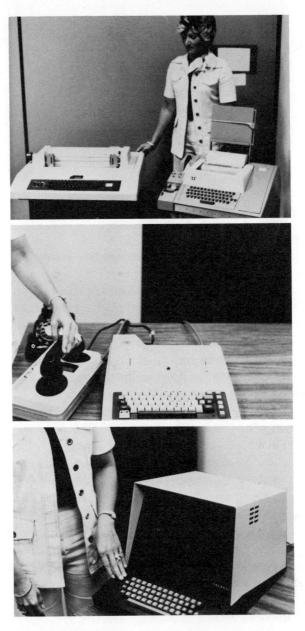

FIGURE 3.15   Computer terminals.

FIGURE 3.16   Acoustic couplers.

terminal. Two different kinds of terminals are in wide use today: (1) those that print information on paper and (2) those that display information on a screen. Those of the first kind are generally called *printers* and those of the second kind *video display units* (VDU). Figure 3.15 shows some computer terminals currently available. Figure 3.15a and b show printers, while Figure 3.15c shows a VDU. Notice that all of them have keyboards (the input part of the terminal) and a place for computer-generated information to appear, either on paper or on a screen (the output part of the terminal). Most keyboards are quite similar in appearance. Letters are arranged in the same positions as they are on any standard typewriter. Other characters, including the decimal digits, may appear in different locations on different terminals.

ACOUSTIC COUPLER.   Computers and computer terminals produce electrical pulses called *digital* signals. You will recall from the earlier discussion of timesharing systems that often telephone lines are used to connect terminals to the central processors. Telephone equipment is made to handle a different kind of electrical signal than digital signals. Its signals are called *analog* signals. Because of this difference in signals, an electronic device called an *acoustic coupler* is needed to convert digital signals to analog signals and analog signals to digital ones. Figure 3.16 shows some acoustic couplers. Figures 3.16a and b show two models of couplers, while Figure 3.16c shows a telephone receiver properly placed in the cradle of an acoustic coupler. Once the telephone receiver is in position on an acoustic coupler, and the telephone/coupler is also in place at the other end of the cable, then communication is established between the terminal and the central processor. Figure 3.17 further illustrates the concept just described. Typically, at the central-processor end of the line there would be many couplers, one for each terminal connected to it. These couplers at the central processor would not be acoustic couplers. The telephone wires would be directly connected to the couplers and the couplers to the central processor. Such a coupler is said to be "hard wired," implying that the link is more permanent than when the telephone receiver is placed in the cradle of an acoustic coupler.

TERMINAL KEYBOARD.   Before leaving the discussion of the hardware aspects of a timesharing computer system, we examine some of the details of a typical terminal keyboard. Figure 3.18 shows one version of a terminal keyboard. Most of the characters needed by a beginning programmer are clearly identifiable. There are three keys, however, whose significance is not obvious. These are the following: (1) uppercase O (left-pointing arrow); (2) uppercase N (upward arrow); and (3) LINE FEED. We call the left-pointing arrow the correction symbol and the upward arrow the exponentiation symbol.

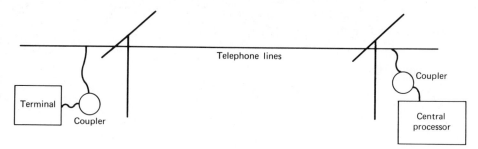

FIGURE 3.17   Computer communications system.

The correction symbol is used whenever a mistake has been made in the keying of a program statement. Suppose you were keying the characters in a program line that was to contain the PRINT instruction but you struck the "M" key rather than the "N" key and you recognized the error as soon as it was made. Here is how the correction symbol could be used:

100   PRIM←NT A,B,C

The correction symbol causes the computer to ignore the M (which was keyed by mistake) and continue processing with the N immediately following the correction symbol. The result is that the computer processes line 100 as if it had been keyed

100   PRINT A,B,C

which is a correct statement. If you do not recognize the error until you have keyed more characters, key the correction symbol as many times as needed to eliminate

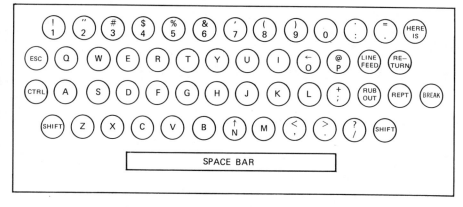

FIGURE 3.18   Teletype keyboard.

the wrong character and then proceed with the correct characters. For example, suppose you had keyed

100   PRENT A

before you recognized the incorrect letter E. To correct it you would key the correction symbol five times (to replace ENT A) and continue with the correct characters. Here is what your line would look like:

100   PRENT A←←←←←INT A,B,C

The computer would process this line as if it had originally been keyed as

100   PRINT A,B,C

The exponentiation symbol is used to indicate the arithmetic operation of "raising to a power." For example, suppose you wanted to compute the cube of the number stored in variable A. One way to communicate this to the computer is by keying in the expression

A↑3

at the appropriate place in a program statement. Note that the exponentiation symbol is keyed immediately following the variable (or constant) that is to be raised to a power. The power itself (called the exponent) is keyed immediately after the exponentiation symbol. More will be said about this in the section on arithmetic operations in BASIC.

Arithmetic Operations in BASIC

Now we continue our consideration of BASIC. The symbols designating the arithmetic operations in BASIC are:

ADD	+
SUBTRACT	−
MULTIPLY	*
DIVIDE	/
EXPONENTIATION	↑

To represent the sum of the contents of variables A and B, write A+B. Similarly their difference is A−B, their product is A*B, and their quotient is A/B. The square of the contents of variable A could be represented by A↑2. It is possible, of course, to indicate the performance of several operations one after the other as in the expression

A*B/(C−3)

Here multiplication, division, and subtraction are indicated. It is important to notice the use of parentheses in the sample expression. As shown, the meaning of this expression is "the product of A and B divided by the difference of C and 3." If the parentheses had been omitted, the expression would have been

A*B/C−3

and would mean "the product of A and B divided by C then 3 subtracted from that result." Note that the two end results are not identical. There is a built-in order in which the arithmetic operations are performed unless parentheses are used to specify the order. This built-in order is first, exponentiation; second, multiplication and division in order from left to right, and third, addition and subtraction in order from left to right. Consider some examples:

BASIC Expression	Mathematical Interpretation
A+B/C*2	$A + \dfrac{B*2}{C}$
R*S*T↑3−X	$R*S*T^3 - X$
(A+B)/(C*2)	$\dfrac{A+B}{C*2}$

Note that parentheses may always be used to specify a particular order of operations. If there are two or more levels of parentheses (parentheses within parentheses) the operations in the innermost parentheses are performed first. This use of parentheses is the same as that in mathematics.

    LET STATEMENT.   The BASIC statement that uses the arithmetic-operation symbols is the LET statement. Here is a sample:

    10   LET X=B*C↑2/N

Like all statements it must have a line number. Following the line number is the word LET after which any variable could appear. The character immediately to the right of the variable must be the equals sign. To the right of the equals sign may be written any BASIC arithmetic expression as described in the preceding section. The sample LET statement is interpreted as follows: "compute the product of B and the square of C, divide that result by N, and store the final quotient in variable X." Only the line number, the word LET, and a single variable may appear to the left of the equals sign. All arithmetic operations must be in the expression on the right of the equals sign.

Although the LET statement is the usual means for accomplishing arithmetic operations it is possible to do so directly in the PRINT statement. For example, the statements

```
10   READ A,B
20   DATA 2,5
30   PRINT A*B, 3*(A+B)
```

would produce this line of output

```
10        21
```

In other words, if the arithmetic you want done is no more complicated than can be achieved in a single arithmetic expression like 3*(A+B) then it is unnecessary to use a LET statement. The arithmetic may be performed right in the PRINT statement.

Changing the Natural Order in which Statements Are Executed

Recall from an earlier discussion of line numbers that the BASIC compiler processes statements in ascending order of line number. Regardless of the physical order in which statements appear in the program they are translated and executed in the order of their line numbers. Sometimes, however, it is not desirable that the program be followed line for line. When this is the case programmers will use either the GO TO statement or the IF-THEN statement.

GO TO STATEMENT. This statement is called an unconditional transfer statement because it requires transfer of control, regardless of conditions, to the statement whose line number is specified. For example,

```
50   GO TO 75
```

means that regardless of any statements between 50 and 75, they must be skipped and line 75 must be executed. In a GO TO statement no test is made to determine whether or not transfer occurs. Transfer *always* occurs. An example of the use of this statement in a program is considered in the next section.

IF-THEN STATEMENT.   Many times a programmer wants the natural order of statement execution to be changed only under certain conditions. If those conditions do not exist the statement execution order should not be changed. That is, execution should then continue in the natural order. The BASIC statement that accomplishes this goal is the IF-THEN statement. Here is an example:

30   IF A=X↑2−7*Y THEN 100

Note the position of the special words IF and THEN. The characters between those two words specify the condition that must exist if transfer is to take place; that is, if something other than the natural order of executing statements is to occur. In the example, if the value of X^2-7Y equals A, then line 100 (the number following the word THEN) is the next statement to be executed. Of course, the number following THEN must be a line number that exists in the program, but it need not be larger than the line number of the IF-THEN (30 in the example). Therefore, transfer *can* occur to a line previous to the IF-THEN statement.

In the example, the symbol of comparison used was the equals sign (=). There are five other symbols available for use in an IF-THEN statement:
    < less than
    > greater than
    <= less than or equal
    >= greater than or equal
    <> not equal
Note that the last three symbols require that two keys be consecutively depressed. For example, to obtain the "less than or equal" symbol requires that the "less than" key be pressed followed by the "equals" key is.

Except that their meanings differ from the equals symbol, these five symbols are used in the same way as the equals symbol. That is, if the relationship expressed between the words IF and THEN is true, the next statement to be executed is the one whose line number follows THEN. If the relationship is false, the next statement executed is the one whose line number is next larger in size to the line number of the IF-THEN statement.

Because the IF-THEN statement results in a transfer only under specified conditions it is called a conditional transfer. Together with the GO TO statement it makes reuse of certain statements in one's program possible. The student may wonder why it would ever be desirable to reuse statements. Suppose the problem were to input 10 numbers and find their sum. If it were not possible to reuse any statements, the program to accomplish this would probably be something like this:

```
10   REM FINDS SUM OF TEN NUMBERS
20   READ X1,X2,X3,X4,X5,X6,X7,X8,X9,X0
30   DATA 2,4,6,8,1,3,5,7,12,32
40   LET S=X1+X2+X3+X4+X5+X6+X7+X8+X9+X0
50   PRINT S
60   END
```

This is not a particularly long program so there is no real reason to try to shorten it, although lines 20 and 40 seem unusually long. Suppose, however that 30 numbers were to be read into the computer's memory and summed. In this case, the method used in the previous example might result in the following program:

```
10   REM FINDS SUM OF THIRTY NUMBERS
20   READ X1,X2,X3,X4,X5,X6,X7,X8,X9,X0
30   READ Y1,Y2,Y3,Y4,Y5,Y6,Y7,Y8,Y9,Y0
40   READ Z1,Z2,Z3,Z4,Z5,Z6,Z7,Z8,Z9,Z0
50   DATA 2,4,6,8,10,12,14,16,18,20,22,24,26,28,30
60   DATA 32,34,36,38,40,42,44,46,48,50,52,54,56,58,60
70   LET S1=X1+X2+X3+X4+X5+X6+X7+X8+X9+X0
80   LET S2=Y1+Y2+Y3+Y4+Y5+Y6+Y7+Y8+Y9+Y0
90   LET S3=Z1+Z2+Z3+Z4+Z5+Z6+Z7+Z8+Z9+Z0
100  LET S=S1+S2+S3
110  PRINT S
120  END
```

Again, the size of this program may not seem unduly large, but writing it is tedious. Note also that no statements were reused in either program.

Now let us rewrite the first program, this time using transfer statements.

```
10   REM FINDS SUM OF TEN NUMBERS
20   LET S=0
30   LET T=0
40   READ X
50   LET S=S+X
60   LET T=T+1
```

```
70   IF T=10 THEN 90
80   GO TO 40
90   PRINT S
100  DATA 2,4,6,8,1,3,5,7,12,32
110  END
```

This version of a program to find the sum of 10 numbers contains more lines than the previous program performing the same task, but each line is now very short so that the total program length is about the same as for the first program.

By changing only one digit in one line, this latest program can also find the sum of 30 numbers. (Of course, the DATA statement was changed to include 30 numbers.) Here it is:

```
10   REM FINDS SUM OF THIRTY NUMBERS
20   LET S=0
30   LET T=0
40   READ X
50   LET S=S+X
60   LET T=T+1
70   IF T=30 THEN 90
80   GO TO 40
90   PRINT S
100  DATA 2,4,6,8,10,12,14,16,18,20,22,24,26,28,30
110  DATA 32,34,36,38,40,42,44,46,48,50,52,54,56,58,60
120  END
```

You will notice that only line 70 has been changed (plus appropriate changes in DATA statements) yet this latter program finds the sum of 30 numbers rather than 10. Clearly, this same program could be used to find the sum of 100 numbers by changing line 70 to

```
70   IF T=100 THEN 90
```

and appropriately changing DATA statements. In fact, the same program could be used to find the sum of any number of numbers by appropriately changing line 70 and DATA statements.

A set of instructions executed repeatedly, such as lines 40 through 80 in the last example, is called a *loop.* Transfer statements such as IF-THEN and GO TO make the writing of loops possible, and the use of loops usually makes programs much shorter.

Before this study of BASIC programming is concluded, we present two problems and the programs used to solve these problems.

Problem 1

Produce a table showing the simple interest earned in one year by investing principals of $100,$150,$200,$250, and $350 each at annual rates of 4%, 4.5%, 5%, 5.5%, and 6%. A BASIC program to accomplish this follows:

```
10   REM PRINTS TABLE OF INTEREST EARNED
20   PRINT "PRINCIPAL", "RATE", "INTEREST"
30   LET P=100
50   LET R=.04
70   LET I=P*R
80   PRINT P,R,I
99   IF R>=.06 THEN 120
100  LET R=R+.005
110  GO TO 70
120  IF P=350 THEN 150
130  LET P=P+50
140  GO TO 50
150  END
```

This program contains two loops. One of them consists of lines 70 through 110; the second one is defined by lines 50 through 140. Notice that one loop is completely contained within the other in the sense that all statements in the smaller loop (lines 70 through 110) are also statements in the larger loop. Such a situation is called *nested loops*. That is, one loop is nested within the other. Notice that this program has no READ statements, yet it will produce numeric output. Not all programs require input data.

Problem 2

Write a BASIC program to input student name and four test scores for each student. Continue reading names until the two words "THE END" are read as a name. From the input data select those students who earned at least one test score of 100 and produce a list of such students. Print the heading "STU-DENTS HAVING AT LEAST ONE PERFECT TEST".

Following is a BASIC program that accomplishes this task.

```
10   REM PROGRAM FOR SELECTING STUDENTS
15   REM WITH PERFECT TESTS
20   PRINT "STUDENTS HAVING AT LEAST ONE PERFECT TEST"
30   READ N$, T1, T2, T3, T4
40   IF N$ = "THE END" THEN 150
50   IF T1 = 100 THEN 90
60   IF T2 = 100 THEN 90
70   IF T3 = 100 THEN 90
80   IF T4 = 100 THEN 30
90   PRINT N $
100  GO TO 30
110  DATA "JOHN PETERSON",82,95,89,78,"MARY SMITH"
115  DATA 88,90,100,95
120  DATA"KIM COLE",70,82,79,80,"JOE LARSON",100,88,95,100
130  DATA "PAT JONES", 82,79,75,81, "LEE SAMSON", 85,90,90,100
140  DATA "GLEN AMES",68,72,80,75,"THE END",0,0,0,0
150  END
```

You are urged to enter the programs given for Problems 1 and 2 into the computer to which you have access. Study the input data and the output produced, making sure you understand the relationship between them and the program statements.

The BASIC programming given in this chapter is just an introduction. It should be enough to provide you with a realistic impression of how to get a computer to perform useful work. However, you would be wise not to claim that you are now a computer programmer. In fact you are not even a BASIC programmer because that language has many features not mentioned here. The interested student is encouraged to obtain one of the books on BASIC listed in the Selected References at the end of this chapter.

EXERCISES

3.1 Make a diagram of a twelve-bit computer word in which is stored the binary integer 11010.

3.2 List some common devices that maintain either of two stable conditions and therefore could be used as storage media for binary digits.

3.3 Suppose a computer has words whose length is 32 binary digits. Using Table

3.1 for reference, make a diagram showing how the name JOHN AMES would appear in ASCII code in three adjacent computer words.

3.4 Describe the function of acoustic couplers in a timesharing computer system.

3.5 Explain why COBOL and FORTRAN are called problem-oriented languages.

3.6 Identify the following statements as being true of machine language or of problem-oriented languages:

> (a) it is entirely numeric
> (b) it must be translated before the computer produces desired results
> (c) it consists of words and symbols associated with the area of application
> (d) it is troublesome to use because all memory locations must be identified by numeric address

3.7 Match each item in the left column with the appropriate item in the right column.

(1) compiler	(a) FORTRAN
(2) address	(b) identification of a
(3) computer function	computer word
(4) computer language	(c) COBOL
for business	(d) memory
(5) computer language	(e) translator for problem-
for scientists	oriented language

3.8 Identify the following as being correct or incorrect BASIC variables:

(a) A1	(d) R	(g) N$
(b) AB	(e) PAY	(h) A2$
(c) 1X	(f) X1	(i) B23

3.9 Identify the following as being correct or incorrect BASIC constants:

(a) 3*10	(d) 14.93
(b) 2E3	(e) .0000625
(c) 376	(f) 1.67E-5

3.10 Identify the following as being correct or incorrect BASIC statements:

> (a) 10   READ X and Y
> (b) 20   INPUT R,S,T
> (c) 375   PRINT A,B, "CITY OF RESIDENCE"
> (d) 461235 LET T=75*A
> (e) 130 LET C↑2=A↑2+B↑2
> (f) 5 GO TO END
> (g) 100 END
> (h) DATA 15,20,7, "TUESDAY"
> (i) 30 READ A,B,C,D
> (j) 40 REM X=A+(2+B)

3.11 Consider this BASIC program:

```
 5  LET N=0
10  READ A,B
20  PRINT A,B,A↑2,B↑2,A*B
30  LET N=N+1
40  IF N=3 THEN 70
50  GO TO 10
60  DATA 2,3,4,5,6,7
70  END
```

(a) How many lines of output are produced by this program?

(b) What is the first line of output?

(c) Does this program contain any loops?

3.12 Consider this BASIC program:

```
10  READ A,B,C,D,E$,F$,G
20  DATA 1,2,3,4,"DIAMETER","ALTITUDE",15.2
30  PRINT A*B,E$
40  PRINT C+D,F$
50  END
```

What would be the output of this program?

3.13 Consider this BASIC program:

```
10  READ N1,N2,N3
20  DATA 2,4,5
30  PRINT "FIRST NUMBER IS ";N1,
40  PRINT "SECOND NUMBER IS ";N2
50  PRINT 2*N3
60  END
```

What would be the output of this program?

3.14 Write a BASIC program to accomplish the following: Input the name, social security number, number of hours worked, and rate of pay per hour for each of 10 employees. Compute the gross wages for each employee and print out a table with the headings

        S.S.NUMBER   NAME   GROSS WAGES

having 10 lines, one for each employee, as specified by the headings.

3.15 Write a BASIC program to input 10 sets of three numbers per set calling them A,B, and C. For each set of A,B, and C compute a quantity D equal to the square of B minus the product of 4, A, and C. If D is positive output the message "ROOTS ARE REAL AND UNEQUAL". If D is zero, output the message "ROOTS ARE REAL AND EQUAL". If D is negative, output the message "ROOTS ARE COM-

PLEX''. Your program should produce 10 lines of output, one for each set of A,B, and C.

3.16 Write a BASIC program to input 25 numbers, find their sum, and their arithmetic mean. Output the sum and mean.

3.17 Write a BASIC program to solve the problem of inputting for each employee the social security number, the hourly rate of pay, the number of hours worked, and a tax-deduction multiplier applied to gross wages to determine withholding tax. For hours worked through 40, the employee gets regular pay. For any hours over 40, the rate is 1.50 times the regular rate. The output for each employee is social security number, gross wages, and take-home pay. A dummy social security number of 999999999 is used to signal the end of processing.

3.18 Write a BASIC program that determines which three-digit numbers are such that the number has the same value as the sum of the cubes of the digits in that number.

SELECTED REFERENCES

BOOKS

Barnett, Eugene H., *Programming Time-Shared Computers in BASIC,* Wiley-Interscience, New York, 1972.

De Rossi, Claude J., *Learning BASIC Fast,* Reston Publishing, Reston, Va., 1974.

Gottfried, Byron S., *Programming with BASIC,* McGraw-Hill, New York, 1975.

Gruenberger, Fred, *Computing with the BASIC Language,* Canfield Press, San Francisco, 1972.

Hare, Van Court, *BASIC Programming,* Harcourt Brace Jovanovich, New York, 1970.

Maratek, Samuel L., *BASIC,* Academic Press, New York, 1975.

Murrill, Paul W. and Cecil W. Smith, *BASIC Programming,* Intext, Scranton, 1971.

Nolan, Richard L., *Introduction to Computing through the BASIC Language,* Holt, Rhinehart and Winston, New York, 1974.

Pavlovich, Joseph P. and Thomas E. Tahan, *Computer Programming in BASIC,* Holden-Day, San Francisco, 1971.

Sack, John and Judith Meadows, *Entering BASIC,* SRA, Chicago, 1973.

Sharpe, William F., *BASIC An Introduction to Computer Programming Using the BASIC Language,* The Free Press, New York, 1971.

Spencer, Donald D., *A Guide to BASIC Programming: A Time-Sharing Language,* Addison-Wesley, Reading, 1970.

Wu, Nesa L'Abbe, *BASIC: The Time-Sharing Language,* Wm. C. Brown, Dubuque, 1975.

PERIODICALS

Sammet, Jean E., "More People Should Learn the Basics of Computers," *The Office,* January 1975, p. 64.

4
COMPUTERS IN THE EDUCATIONAL ENVIRONMENT

A major objective of the book up to this time has been to make you feel comfortable about the computer. Comfortable in the sense that you recognize the computer as a very ingenious machine, but nevertheless, a machine. In Chapters 1 and 2 you learned that the computer was developed over a long period of time through the efforts of many people throughout the world. It did not mysteriously appear and insidiously begin assuming the countless tasks that it now performs. *People* thought of the ideas that evolved into a computer. *People* make it possible for computers to be useful to society. *People* determine what jobs are programmed for computers, and *people* develop the programs that control computers. Furthermore, *people* have brought about the growing role played by computers in our lives. So it falls to all of us to become aware of some of the more important ways in which people are using computers to influence other people.

No one can dispute the fact that computers have had an impact on education, and they will be sources of even greater changes in the future. Many educators who are familiar with computerized instruction are pleased with the results.

ADMINISTRATIVE APPLICATIONS OF THE COMPUTER

One of the first and persistently growing applications of computers to education has been in record-keeping. As you know, all important institutions of society must keep numerous records, and education is no exception. In fact, even in this time of extreme concern over personal privacy, the importance of keeping accurate records of the academic pursuits of its people is well recognized by society. Whether completely valid or not, prospective employers continue to use a person's academic performance as a basis for offering employment. How extremely important that the record of that performance be correct.

86

Along with scholastic records, educational institutions must maintain many of the same kinds of records as businesses use. For instance, all employees of an educational institution, as of a business, must be paid salaries. Income taxes must be withheld, government reports made, purchases and payments processed, fringe benefits recorded, and all the other aspects of an on-going business handled. Among people in education, the record-keeping and business functions are referred to as *administrative functions*. Educational administrators early recognized that these necessary but sometimes tedious jobs could best be handled by computers, and they began looking for ways to acquire computer capability and human expertise to bring it about.

MANAGEMENT INFORMATION SYSTEM

In recent years, a concept called the management information system (MIS) has evolved in the business world. MIS's have been adapted to handling administrative functions in education. We now examine the features of a management information system as they apply to education. The name, management information system, is used to denote an integrated collection of sets of information that help management make decisions. Such systems did not come upon the scene instantly. Portions were developed and used, then other parts were created, and little by little people recognized the wisdom of tying it all together as one integrated system. We look now at the constituent parts of a MIS.

Data Base

It is certainly not true that a computer is essential for the functioning of a MIS. However, the most effective systems have used computers, and by far most such systems today depend on computers for their operation, so we shall assume a computerized MIS. The foundation of a MIS is the *data base*. A data base is a collection of information (data) organized into various pieces, called *files*. The files, in turn, are organized into smaller pieces called *records,* and records consist of information facts called *data elements,* which are the smallest units of information in the data base. Figure 4.1 shows the relationships between the pieces of information that make up a data base. Note that different space allocations for files in Figure 4.1 are intended to show that the sizes of the files in a data base may be different; that is, one file may have more records than another. Similarly a record in File 1 may have less data elements than a record in File 2. In fact, records within the same file *may* have different numbers of data elements, although many MIS's require that the format of all records within a given file be identical.

What kinds of information make up the various files? How are the data collected in the first place? How are data bases organized for education? In our

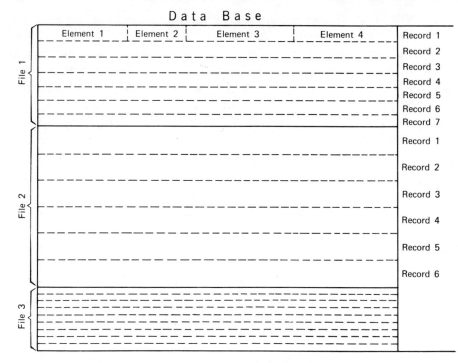

FIGURE 4.1   Diagram of the parts of a data base.

discussion of a data base, let us consider a typical school district. All states of the United States require that school censuses be taken to gather information about students and prospective students in each school district. Figure 4.2 shows one such school census questionnaire. As you can see, some facts requested are parent's name and address, student's name and birthdate, code for the school the student is attending, grade in school, reason for not attending school if that is the case, and sometimes other facts. To gather these data, people in some way talk to all of the families residing in the district. Each household contacted is typically assigned a unique number called the family number as a convenient and accurate means of associating students with their families. Similarly, a unique number is usually assigned to each student in the family. This number is simply an accurate way to identify each family, it does not depersonalize relationships between school districts and families. When family members are referred to in reports, letters, and so forth, their *names* are used, not the family number or the student number. A document like the Census Report Form used by the census enumerator is usually called a *source document* with reference to the whole MIS. Any document used for recording data that will later be processed by a computer is called a source document.

CENSUS REPORT FORM

Enumerator _____ Date _____

Items of Information

 1-14 Child's Last Name _____ 15-24 First Name _____ 25 Middle Initial _____
26-29 House Number _____ 30-44 Street Name _____
45-46 Area Code _____47 Sex, Race Code _____ 48 Handicap Code _____
49-54 Birth Date _____ 55-56 School Attending _____
             Month   Day   Year

57-58 School Planning to Attend _____ 59-60 Grade _____
61   Reason Non-attending Code _____ 62-63 Number of Children in Family _____
64-77 Parent or Guardian's Last Name _____
78-79 Parent's initials _____
80   Card Number

FIGURE 4.2   School census form.

The next step is to present the source documents to someone who can prepare the data for entry to a computer. This process, called *data entry,* usually involves the use of a keypunch machine (Figure 4.3), a key-to-tape machine (Figure 4.4), or a key-to-disk machine (Figure 4.5).

A keypunch machine produces holes in specially designed cards, and the resulting punched cards contain data in *machine-readable* form; that is, in a form that can be sensed by a device (card reader) which is a part of a computer system. The operator of a keypunch machine keys the data, character-by-character, on a keyboard similar to a typewriter keyboard, reading the information from the source document. If the data entry is done on a key-to-tape machine, the information is recorded as magnetized spots on magnetic tape (similar to the magnetic tape used in music or voice recorders) in a form that can be sensed by a device (tape reader) which is a part of a computer system. If the data entry operator uses a key-to-disk machine, the information ends up as magnetized spots on a magnetic disk, in a form that can be sensed by still another device (disk unit) which is a part of a computer system. A magnetic disk consists of many steel platters (like phonograph records) fastened to the same central core (see Figure 4.6). The flat surfaces of the platters are coated with an iron oxide material similar to that used in coating the plastic used in magnetic tape. Particles in this material respond to magnetic fields produced by the recording and sensing device (read-write head).

FIGURE 4.3   Keypunch machine (courtesy IBM).

Although we have taken a very short look at the physical form that school data might have as it goes to a computer, we are more concerned right now about the logical organization of the data base. The file of information collected in a school census might well be referred to as the *census file,* and each record in that file contains the information on one family. The file would contain as many records as there are families, each identifiable by the unique family number.

Another file of information likely to be a part of a school's data base would be the *activity file.* Each record on this file deals with an activity in which a student may participate, such as a course, a laboratory period, a study period, or a lunch period. Each record is likely to contain a unique number (activity number), the

FIGURE 4.4   Key-to-tape machine.

FIGURE 4.5   Key-to-disk machine (courtesy DATA 100).

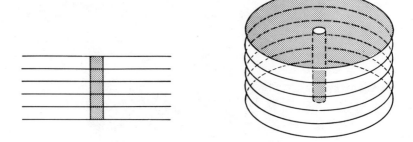

FIGURE 4.6   Two views of a magnetic disk.

name of the activity, time of meeting, days of meeting, place, identification number of the teacher involved, number of credits (if any), department responsible for the activity, and so on. The activity file would have as many records as there are activities.

A third file in a typical school data base would be a *student file.* Each record in the student file would contain a student number and an activity number and grade (if any) for each activity in which the student was involved. There would be as many records as there were students.

A file containing information about all school employees would also be useful, and it would surely be a part of a school's data base. Such a file is usually called the *personnel file.* Each record would contain an employee identification number, social security number, name, address, home phone, office phone, date of employment, previous experience, education, and possibly other data. The personnel file would contain as many records as there are employees.

In addition to these student/teacher-related files, a complete data base would have other files, such as a *receipts file,* and *expenditure file,* a *purchases file,* a *budgets file,* and maybe others.

We must emphasize that any given item of information should be stored in only one file if possible. For example, a student's name should appear only in the census file and not also in the student file. The information from both files would be tied together by the student number, which is stored in both files. Similarly, the name of an activity should be stored only on the activity file and not also on the student file. The bridge between these two files would be the activity number, stored on both files. As you can see, it is necessary that some information be stored on two or more files in order to be able to associate data from one file with that in another. Usually these crossover data are small numbers, which require less storage space than alphabetic information, such as names or activity titles.

Now let's see how we use some of the files in this data base to produce useful reports. Suppose we want a list of students registered in each of the classes.

Such lists are commonly called class lists. The computer program would use the activity number as the key for accessing the activity file, retrieving from it the course name, teacher identification number, and place of meeting. Course name, meeting room, and teacher name would logically be used as headings for the class lists. Then, using the activity number as a basis for comparison, the student file would be read record by record, comparing activity numbers in each record with the activity number of the course for which the class list is being produced. Whenever those

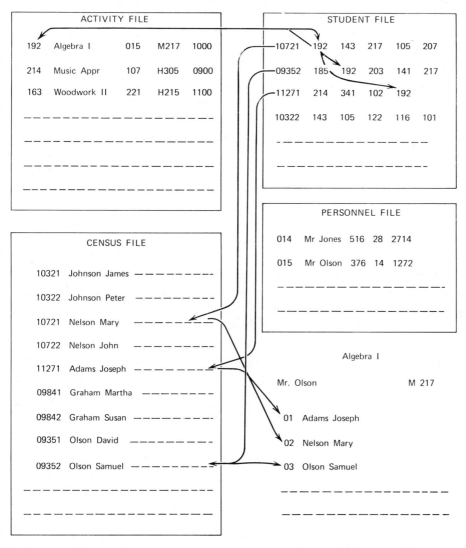

FIGURE 4.7   **Use of files to produce class list.**

activity numbers were identical, the corresponding student number in the activity file would be compared with student numbers in the census file until an identical one was found. Then the student name corresponding to that student number would be made ready for printing on the class list.

As you read this paragraph refer to Figure 4.7 and you will have a better understanding of the process. In the example shown in Figure 4.7, the class list for activity 192, Algebra I, is being generated. Its activity number, 192, is first compared with activity numbers associated with student number 10721 in the student file, and one of these numbers is 192. Then the census file is searched for student number 10721, yielding the name Nelson Mary, which is then stored in a work storage space later to be sorted in alphabetical order with other names. Similarly, the student file is searched for other students having 192 among the activity numbers. Each time a match occurs, the corresponding student number from the student file is used to search student numbers in the census file. Again, whenever a match occurs, the corresponding name is stored in a work storage space. This process continues until all records in the student file have been searched for activity number 192. When this task is completed, all student names associated with activity 192 should be in the work storage space. From there they are sorted in alphabetical order and printed, yielding the class list for Algebra I taught by Mr. Olson in room M217.

This appears to be a complicated process for generating something as relatively simple as a class list. But remember that these files are stored in a computer system where each "look" at a data element takes one hundred-thousandth of a second, or less. By having the information organized into files as previously described many other kinds of reports are easily produced. The variety of lists or reports that can be generated is much greater when several files, each containing related collections of data, are stored than when all the information is stored in one file. The information thus stored is used by decision makers (management) to help make their actions more effective. Hence the name Management Information Systems. Such systems are being widely applied in educational units (school districts, colleges, universities) to aid school administrators in making the best possible use of finances, teachers, and physical facilities to give students the best possible education. An added benefit is the fact that a MIS lends itself so well to the preparation of reports. Today, when many public officials are keenly aware of the need to account for their administrative decisions to the public, an information system that makes it relatively easy to provide meaningful reports about the educational system is welcomed by conscientious administrators.

Only the example of producing class lists has been given, but information systems like this are used by schools to prepare payrolls, pay for purchases, maintain supply and equipment inventories, prepare student schedules, develop bus schedules, evaluate classroom utilization and faculty work loads, analyze costs for operating the various departments, compute grades and prepare grade lists, prepare reports for state and federal agencies, make enrollment studies, especially projections of future enrollments, and on and on goes the list. As you can well imagine, being able to turn to a machine for so many functions has made more time available to the school administrator for doing the kinds of things only *people* can do. For example, administrators can help a student who has an unusual home situation, or deal with personality problems among the faculty, or do some creative thinking about completely new ways of teaching, or study the characteristics needed in a proposed building. And not only have administrators been relieved of some of the drudgery they formerly had to contend with, but many record-keeping functions of the classroom teacher have been shortened or completely eliminated. The net result of all of this has been to make more time available for educators to be as innovative, yet effective, as they can possibly be.

JOINT VENTURES IN EDUCATIONAL COMPUTING

A data base like the one we have just discussed almost certainly requires a computer system on which to operate. The storage and retrieval of thousands, even millions, of pieces of information would be impossible by any means other than a computer system with appropriate programs. Although the cost of many components in a computer system has decreased substantially since the Univac I, a computer capable of the storage, speed, and output needed for a MIS would be relatively costly. In fact, only the largest and wealthiest institutions could afford such a system. Consequently, smaller school districts, colleges, and universities have joined in cooperative ventures to acquire adequate computing facilities.

One of the first such efforts took place in the twin cities of Minneapolis and St. Paul, Minnesota. There a number of the school districts surrounding the Twin Cities formed an organization called Total Information Educational Systems (TIES), hired a director and staff, and set about acquiring the necessary computer equipment and developing the software to do administrative functions. The cost of such a project would have been prohibitive for any of the cooperating districts alone. By dividing costs among some 19 districts the financial burden was made bearable, and unexpected benefits began to appear both in the area of administrative activities as well as in instructional computing (a topic yet to be discussed in this chapter). TIES has grown to include more than the original participants and has served as a model for many other schools. TIES frequently hosts visiting teams from other parts of the United States or from distant nations. The project has been most successful at the elementary-secondary level of education and merits imitation.

A number of computer networks have also been developed for use at the college/university level. The first such programs received significant financial assistance from the National Science Foundation (NSF), an agency of the United States government. As was the case with elementary and secondary schools, many colleges and universities could not individually afford an adequate computer system. In addition a computer system meeting the necessary requirements for storage and peripheral equipment was of such speed that any single institution could not utilize the full capacity of the central processor. However, many institutions of higher education felt the need to have some kind of input and output equipment on site so as to have faster response from the computer. Therefore, cooperative efforts at this level of education tended to be designed around networks of computing equipment as illustrated in Figure 4.8. This concept differs from that displayed in Figure 3.14 in that the input device considered would probably be a card-reading device or a magnetic tape unit instead of a keyboard device. The output device would typically be a printer, which can produce between 300 and 1100 lines of 132 characters each minute. In this system, the output produced by the central processor is not returned to the output device immediately. Information coming to the central processor is handled in the same order as it is received. Some data takes longer to process than other data, and sometimes there is more material to process than at other times. All of this affects the time elapsed between submission of a program and related data, and the printing of desired results.

As we discussed in Chapter 3, in a timesharing system the input/output

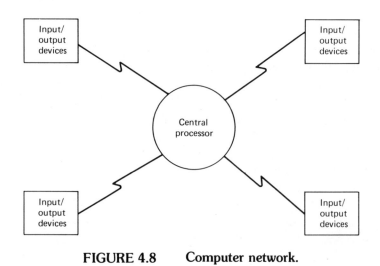

FIGURE 4.8   **Computer network.**

devices located in a given room are referred to as terminals. The devices described in this chapter, however, are properly called remote batch terminals or remote-job-entry (RJE) terminals. The word "batch" is probably derived from the fact that when such devices were first used, several programs with appropriate data (a *batch* of punched cards) were entered at a specific time. The terminal is called "remote" because it is always some distance from the central processor; it may be a number of feet (for example, in the adjoining room) or thousands of miles away. Furthermore, to many people who work with computers, the word "batch" connotes that such terminals typically transmit much larger quantities of information both to and from the central processor than is characteristic of timesharing terminals.

In this course concerned with the social impact of computers, yet another type of cooperative venture is of interest. In the United States, the state governments have the greatest responsibility for funding education at all levels. Adequate computing power is a costly but productive resource for education, and much of the money to support it comes from state taxes. Therefore, it would seem prudent to establish an organization at the state level that would help all of education use its computer dollars most effectively. Such a system was established in May 1973, when an agreement was signed by representatives of the Minnesota Department of Education, the Community College System, the State University System, the University of Minnesota, and the Department of Administration (the agency responsible for handling all state funds in Minnesota). The agreement provided for the establishment of the Minnesota Educational Computing Consortium (MECC), which would coordinate all educational computing activities in Minnesota supported by public funds. For the first time in any significantly large geographical area, one agency was charged with seeing to it that *all* levels of public education, from kindergarten through graduate school, make the best use of funds allocated for computer support. Such an all-inclusive task brought with it massive problems, but the concept seemed well worth pursuing. The operation of MECC is supervised by its Executive Director, and all agencies participating in the agreement are represented in policy decisions. MECC is still a new venture and is being carefully watched by people from other states and countries who are concerned about the coordination of educational computing resources in their own geographical areas. If MECC succeeds in significantly improving education through the increased availability of computing power, it must be applauded for its role. By the fall of 1976, MECC and Sperry Univac had brought into existence the largest timesharing computer system in the world. This system, consisting of dual Univac 1110 central processors with much related computer equipment, will be able to process data from 440 terminals simultaneously when it is fully operational. Users will be able to process programs in a variety of programming languages like BASIC, FORTRAN, and COBOL. Centrally stored programs may be accessed by any user, provided the developers of the programs have agreed to make them available. This concept has especially far-reaching implications to instructional (or academic) computing. Many other aspects of MECC bear watching by any person concerned with the effects of computers on education. An especially important result of the MECC concept is access to computer facilities is not limited by a school's geographical location. The state bears most of the costs associated with telephone lines and other equipment needed to be able to communicate with a distantly located computer.

INSTRUCTIONAL APPLICATIONS OF THE COMPUTER

We have learned that computers help schools perform record-keeping functions, but they also have *instructional* or *academic* applications; that is, they are used in the teaching/learning process. The computer assumes some of the functions normally accomplished by the teacher or by the out-of-class work done by the student. In one of its early educational applications, the computer provided drill and practice experience for the student.

Drill and Practice

In a drill-and-practice situation, the computer is programmed to display simple exercises to which the student responds. The responses are examined by the computer for correctness, and appropriate comments made by the computer provide immediate feedback to the student. The student is given some positive reinforcement if his/her answer is correct and some encouragement to try again if it is wrong. Under certain conditions, the computer can analyze the incorrect answers in such a way that the student is given remedial exercises. Perhaps an actual drill-and-practice program should be introduced now to help you see how it works.

Program 4.1

```
10 REMARK A PROGRAM FOR ADDITION PRACTICE
15 LET K=1
20 PRINT "AFTER THE QUESTION-MARK"
25 PRINT "PLEASE TYPE YOUR NAME."
30 PRINT "REMEMBER TO PRESS CARRIAGE RETURN"
35 PRINT "AFTER YOUR NAME."
40 INPUT N$
50 PRINT "HI, ";N$;", I HOPE WE'LL HAVE SOME FUN TOGETHER."
60 PRINT "WE'RE GOING TO PRACTICE ADDITION."
```

```
70 PRINT "AFTER THE QUESTION-MARK, TYPE 1, 2, OR 3."
80 PRINT "THIS WILL TELL ME HOW MANY DIGITS TO USE "
90 PRINT "IN THE NUMBERS I PUT IN THE PROBLEMS."
95 PRINT "DON'T FORGET TO PRESS RETURN"
98 PRINT "AFTER YOU TYPE A NUMBER."
100 INPUT D
110 PRINT "I WILL PRINT THE PROBLEMS."
120 PRINT "YOUR JOB IS TO TYPE THE ANSWER"
130 PRINT "RIGHT AFTER THE QUESTION-MARK."
140 PRINT "REMEMBER TO PRESS RETURN AFTER EACH ANSWER."
145 PRINT "WHEN YOU DON'T WANT ANY MORE EXERCISES,"
148 PRINT "TYPE THE NUMBER 99999 AS IF IT WERE THE ANSWER."
150 LET U=INT (RND(-1)* 10↑D+1)
160 LET L=INT (RND(-1) * 10↑D+1)
170 PRINT U;"+ ";L;"=";
180 INPUT A
190 IF A=99999 THEN 350
195 IF A <> U+L THEN 230
200 READ A$
210 PRINT A$
212 LET K=K+1
214 IF K < 13 THEN 150
216 RESTORE
218 LET K=0
220 GO TO 150
230 PRINT "SORRY, THAT'S NOT RIGHT."
240 PRINT "HERE, TRY AGAIN."
250 PRINT U;"+ ";L;"=";
255 INPUT A
260 IF A <> U+L THEN 290
270 PRINT "GOOD. NOW HERE'S ANOTHER ONE."
280 GO TO 150
290 PRINT "TOO BAD. I CAN'T GIVE YOU MORE THAN 2 TRIES."
300 PRINT "WE HAD BETTER TRY AN EASIER PROBLEM."
310 IF D<> 1 THEN 320
312 PRINT "ON SECOND THOUGHT."
313 PRINT "THAT WAS AS EASY AS I CAN BE."
314 GO TO 150
320 LET U=INT(RND(-1)*10↑(D-1)+1)
330 LET L=INT(RND(-1)*10↑(D-1)+1)
```

```
340 GO TO 170
341 DATA "ALL RIGHT", "FINE", "SUPER", "OK"
342 DATA "RIGHT ON", "TERRIFIC", "WOW"
343 DATA "YOU BET", "STRAIGHT AHEAD",
344 DATA "KEEP IT UP", "YOU'RE REALLY HOT",
345 DATA "GO, MAN", "KEEP TRUCKIN' "
350 PRINT "THANKS FOR THE FUN, ";N$;". GOODBYE."
360 END
```

Here is a sample of what the output from Program 4.1 looks like (underlined characters are the student's responses.)

```
AFTER THE QUESTION-MARK
PLEASE TYPE YOUR NAME.
REMEMBER TO PRESS CARRIAGE
RETURN AFTER YOUR NAME.
?PETE
HI, PETE, I HOPE WE'LL HAVE SOME FUN TOGETHER.
WE'RE GOING TO PRACTICE ADDITION.
AFTER THE QUESTION-MARK, TYPE 1, 2, OR 3.
THIS WILL TELL ME HOW MANY DIGITS TO USE
IN THE NUMBERS I PUT IN THE PROBLEMS.
DON'T FORGET TO PRESS RETURN
AFTER YOU TYPE A NUMBER.
?2
I WILL PRINT THE PROBLEMS.
YOUR JOB IS TO TYPE THE ANSWER
RIGHT AFTER THE QUESTION-MARK.
REMEMBER TO PRESS RETURN AFTER EACH ANSWER.
WHEN YOU DON'T WANT ANY MORE EXERCISES,
TYPE THE NUMBER 99999 AS IF IT WERE THE ANSWER.
15 + 37 = ?52
ALL RIGHT
43 + 64 = ?117
SORRY, THAT'S NOT RIGHT.
HERE, TRY AGAIN.
43 + 64 = ?107
GOOD. NOW HERE'S ANOTHER ONE.
25 + 18 = ?33
SORRY, THAT'S NOT RIGHT.
HERE, TRY AGAIN.
25 + 18 = ?44
TOO BAD. I CAN'T GIVE YOU MORE THAN 2 TRIES.
```

WE HAD BETTER TRY AN EASIER PROBLEM.
9 + 4 = ?<u>13</u>
FINE
23 + 11 = ?<u>34</u>
SUPER
69 + 7 = ?<u>99999</u>
THANKS FOR THE FUN, PETE. GOODBYE.

Let's discuss Program 4.1 and its output. The first two lines of output were produced by statements 20 and 30, respectively. Line 40 causes the question mark that appears in the third line of output, following which the student using the program types "PETE". The next six lines of output are produced by lines 50 through 95. The INPUT statement in line 100 causes a question mark to be printed in the tenth line of output. The student types "2", after which the next six lines of output are the result of lines 110 through 148. Line 170 in the program causes the first drill exercise to be printed. The numbers 15 and 37 in that exercise are computed by lines 150 and 160, respectively.

Lines 150 and 160 use two symbols not yet introduced—the three-letter words INT and RND. These two words refer to two members of a collection of frequently used programs called *library functions*. A library function is a computer program always stored in a computer's memory so it is available for any user of the BASIC language. INT refers to a program called the *greatest integer function*. This special program determines the greatest integer that is less than or equal to whatever number is computed within the set of parentheses to the right of the word INT. For example, the statement

100 LET U = INT(15.8)

would cause the integer 15 to be stored in the location named U. The statements

120 LET A = 9.8
130 PRINT INT(2*A+1)

would result in the printing of the integer 20 because 2 times 9.8 is 19.6, and 1 added to that is 20.6. Finally, the greatest integer less than or equal to 20.6 is 20, so 20 is printed.

The word RND refers to a special program called the *random number function*. This program causes the computer to generate a random number between zero and one. In the case of the sample output, a number between .14 and .15 must have been produced, because when it is multiplied by 100 (the second power of 10) and the number 1 added to that product, the result is a number between 15 and 16, so that the greatest integer applied to that number results in 15. A similar explanation could be given for the number 37 in the output.

Note that the use of the RND function guarantees that each drill problem given by the computer is different from all others. The numbers are generated as if they were selected in a random manner. For more information on random numbers see one of the references on statistics listed at the end of this chapter.

Returning to a discussion of Program 4.1 and its output, we note that the comment

ALL RIGHT

follows the first drill exercise to which the student responded 52. Of course, the comment ALL RIGHT is suitable because 52 is indeed the sum of 15 and 37. The program statements that produce that comment are lines 200 and 210, where line 200 reads the string ALL RIGHT from the DATA statement, line 341, storing it in location A$. Then line 210 causes the string stored at A$ to be printed. An examination of lines 341 through 345 reveals the comments that the program will use as positive reinforcement to the student's correct answers. If so many exercises are done correctly by the student that all comments are used, line 216 in the program, the RESTORE statement, causes any subsequent use of a READ statement to take data from the first DATA statement again. Thus, the comments are repeated. That is, the RESTORE statement resets the data pointer back to the beginning of any DATA statement in the program. Its form is simply

50 RESTORE

Just the line number and the word RESTORE make up the entire statement. The resetting of the data pointer occurs whenever the RESTORE statement is encountered. Here is a short program to illustrate further what it does:

```
10 READ A,B,N$
20 DATA 3,5,"EDIE"
30 RESTORE
40 READ X,Y
50 PRINT B,A,X,Y,N$
60 END
```

The output of this program would be

5   3   3   5   EDIE

A little study of the preceding program should make clear the function of the RESTORE statement.

If you look again at lines 190 and 195 in Program 4.1, you will see how the student's response to an exercise is tested, first against 99999 (the signal to stop the drill-and-practice session), and then against the correct answer. If the response is 99999, line 190 causes a transfer to line 350 which prints the computer's "good-bye", after which the END line is encountered. If the response was not 99999, line 195 compares it to the correct sum. If the response matches the correct sum, a positively reinforcing comment is printed. If the response does not match the correct sum, line 195 causes a transfer to line 230 which prints the line

SORRY, THAT'S NOT RIGHT

and the student is given a second chance. Line 260 checks the second answer given by the student. If that also does not match the correct sum, statements 290 and 300 print appropriate statements. If it is correct, line 270 causes a positive comment. Line 310 checks to see if 1-digit numbers were requested by the student. If so, of course, no easier problems could be generated, but if not, lines 320 and 330 cause the next drill exercise printed to have numbers with at least one less digit in them than the one that the student could not answer correctly in two tries. In other words, the program attempts to provide a bit of remedial work for the student.

As you can imagine, the use of computers in drill-and-practice situations has proved extremely helpful. It seems to provide much greater motivation to learn than the familiar mimeographed sheets of drill problems. Apparently the key here is the appropriate comment printed by the computer program where certain conditions exist. The student feels as if he/she were getting more personal attention when the comments are produced as he/she works. Of course, from our study of Program 4.1, you know that the computer's comments were predetermined by the program developer and not intended especially for Pete Smith, or Mary Ames, or whoever uses the program. Neverthless, careful selection of the comments and the conditions under which they appear to the student can make the situation seem very personal to the student, and it has beneficial effects. Furthermore, a machine is not as threatening to many students as are some teachers. The computer cannot lose its temper or make comments not previously thought out, hence timid students tend to be more willing to give answers to it even if they are wrong.

You saw in Program 4.1 a small attempt to provide remedial help for the student who did not give the correct answer in two tries. The example is weak because it simply provides easier problems, but it is consistent with the level of programming expected in this course. It shouldn't be hard for you to imagine that instead of just providing easier addition problems, the program could have printed some instructional material about how to find sums. Maybe a review should have been given of the addition facts previously assigned to students for memorization. Or maybe some comments should have been made about the process of carrying digits from one column to the next. In any case, more remedial instruction could have been provided by the program had it been so designed. You can easily believe that developing a good drill-and-practice computer program is a time-consuming job, and generally requires that the developer be an experienced teacher. The human being designing the program must know the kinds of things to say to students to encourage learning and even inspire enthusiasm on the part of the learner.

Some Projects Using Drill-and-Practice in Education

Mathematics surely is not the only discipline to which computers have been applied. Computer-generated drill-and-practice in reading has been used since at least 1965. In that year Richard C. Atkinson and Duncan N. Hansen of Stanford University initiated a research project, called the Stanford Project, in which specially designed learning stations (essentially computer terminals) were used to access computer programs written to provide drill-and-practice in reading. (See article by Atkinson and Hansen in Vol. 2, 1966 issue of *Reading Research Quarterly* for further information.)

The Stanford Project was among the first to use the computer to teach reading. Since then many researchers have investigated a variety of ways to use the computer in education. Notable projects were conducted at the University of Michigan, the University of Texas, Pennsylvania State University, the University of Pittsburgh, the University of Minnesota, the University of Illinois (a project called PLATO) and the Mitre Corporation (the project called TICCIT). All of these projects have gone far beyond the drill-and-practice application of computers, and include the so-called tutorial mode as well as the use of computer simulations.

The Computer as a Tutor

When we say the computer is used in tutorial mode, we imply that the computer is doing some teaching, comparable to a human tutor. Of course, learning takes place in a drill-and-practice situation also, but drill-and-practice does not present new concepts, it simply provides practice in applying ideas and information obtained elsewhere. Although Program 4.1 would have to be classified as a drill-and-practice application, the weak provision in it for remedial exercises leans in the direction of being tutorial. But tutorial mode means much more than that. When concepts are presented by the computer program, illustrative examples given, and, in general, the kinds of learning stimuli provided by it that a human teacher would provide, then the computer is truly being used as a tutor.

There is no question that tutorial applications require much more time to develop than drill-and-practice ones, but this has not kept them from being produced. Some experts have estimated that it takes a skilled teacher and a computer programmer 100 hours to develop a tutorial program that provides one hour of teaching. The program developer must have enough experience teaching the subject to realize what kinds of errors in learning students typically make, and what activities usually straighten them out again. Because it is very difficult to find capable teachers in many disciplines who are also willing to learn computer programming, considerable effort has been devoted to designing programming languages that make it easy to write computerized courses. Commercial computer manufacturs have made such languages available; for example, IBM's Coursewriter II and Univac's ASET. University research projects have also produced some tutorial languages, such as the University of Illinois' PLATO, the University of Minnesota's MIL, and MITRE Corporation's TICCIT. It is hoped that these specialized languages will encourage good teachers to use computers in the teaching/learning process. Sometimes languages like these are called *CAI* (computer-assisted instruction) languages, or *author* languages. It is beyond the scope of this book to consider any such languages, but interested readers are urged to consult any of the references treating CAI languages listed at the end of this chapter.

Largely because teacher-oriented languages have been made readily available, a great deal of computer tutorial course work has been produced and classroom-tested. Because of the PLATO project, hundreds of courses are on the computer at the University of Illinois, ranging from elementary school science courses to college-level genetics courses. In addition to the University of Illinois, major contributors to the PLATO project have been the National Science Foundation and the Control Data Corporation (CDC). CDC's contribution has been the provision of a large timesharing computer system. Because of this involvement in the project, CDC has access to all the courses developed at PLATO and is currently modifying them to make them available to purchasers (or leasors) of CDC's Cyber 73 timesharing computer.

Other CAI language developers have also produced an impressive collection of computer programs. The Center for the Study of Human Learning at the University of Minnesota has available for university students complete one-year courses in several foriegn languages, in physics, in calculus, in hematology, and in several other subjects. Given access to appropriate equipment, students complete these courses at their own pace, can repeat whatever parts of them were troublesome, and can, in general, obtain a completely independent-study course. To many students, such courses mean accelerated programs of study and lead to college degrees sooner than otherwise possible.

Computer Simulations in the Educational Environment

Another use being made of computers in the field of education is in an area called computer simulations. What is a computer simulation? Before answering that question maybe it is worthwhile to answer a more fundamental one. What is a simulation? To most people, a simulation is an imitation, or a representation of something in a form different from the original. From that definition, you have undoubtedly used a simulation at some time in your life. For example, a road map of a state is a simulation of the system of roads in the state. A blueprint of a house is one form of a simulation of the house. Another simulation of a house would be an architectural model of it. A model airplane is a simulation of the real aircraft.

The examples of simulations given so far have been physical simulations of physical objects. A simulation can also be an abstract imitation of a physical object. For example, the equation

$$V = 4/3\ \pi\ r^3 \text{ cubic inches}$$

can be thought of as a simulation of the volume of a sphere (ball) of radius r inches. Or the equation

$$d = rt \text{ miles}$$

may be an abstract simulation of the distance traveled by an automobile moving r miles per hour for a period of t hours. From these examples of simulations it should be apparent that if enough equations were used it might be possible to simulate a ball moving through the air. Or by using different equations to represent the shape of the object (rather than those for a sphere) it would be possible to simulate an airplane in flight. And, of course, if it is possible to do that, given the equations for various chemical reactions, it should be possible to put several such equations together to simulate the digestion of, say, bread.

By now you're getting the idea of simulations. To sharpen our definition a bit, let's say that a simulation is a model, physical or abstract, of some system, where "system" refers to a collection of interrelated physical or abstract objects. If that model is in the form of a set of computer instructions that produce information about the system, we call it a *computer simulation*. A very simple computer simulation would be a computer program that calculates the distances from a starting point attained every quarter hour by an object moving at the rate of 55 miles per hour. If the simulation is to cover a period of six hours, here is such a simulation:

Program 4.2

```
10 LET T = 0
15 PRINT "HOURS ELAPSED", "DISTANCE"
20 PRINT T, 55*T
30 IF T = 6 THEN 100
40 LET T = T + .25
50 GO TO 20
100 END
```

Clearly, the output from this simulation consists of two columns of numbers with a heading for each column, like this:

HOURS ELAPSED	DISTANCE
0	0
.25	13.75
.50	27.5
.75	41.25
1.	55.
1.25	68.75
.	.
.	.
.	.
6.	330.

If, instead of supplying a table, the computer printed a graph consisting of points plotted on a two-axis coordinate system (one axis representing hours elapsed, the other representing distance), the computer program might be an even more useful representation of a moving object. Or, if the points were to show up as illuminated spots on a video display unit, the simulation might be still more effective in studying the moving object.

Science teachers have found computer simulations extremely useful in teaching concepts such as the motion of freely falling bodies, the interaction of chemicals, the interrelationship of heavenly bodies on each others' orbits, the laws of genetics, and the laws of magnetism. Sociology teachers have developed computer simulations embodying some of the numerous aspects of human population centers and have been able to demonstrate the effects on populations caused by things like widespread illness, changing birth rates, changing food supplies, and improved medical care. Business teachers have been able to clarify concepts related to principles of management by using computer simulations of businesses in competition with each other. Students are allowed to make management decisions regarding various aspects of the business, then the computer simulation follows established business principles to determine the effects of the decisions of such things as sales, inventory, and profits. In effect, computer simulations make it possible for the student to test specific situations without incurring the costs and/or dangers often accompanying laboratory experimentation. Sometimes computer simulations make it possible to study situations otherwise not even open for serious consideration in the classroom. For example, a long-term study of the effects of various economic forces on the overall economy is impossible in any economics course. Yet by preparing an accurate computer simulation of the nation's economy and varying the extent of the several influences being studied, the student can usually see quite readily the effects caused by these influences.

Many computer simulations designed to teach certain concepts are available from several sources. A widely used collection of such simulations was developed under the auspices of the Huntington II Computer Project in New York. The following list will give you an idea of some of the educational simulations that can be obtained.

PROGRAM NAME	DESCRIPTION
CHARGE	**A simulation of the Millikan oil drop experiment (physics).**
GENE 1	**A simulation of the inheritance of genetic traits according to Mendel's laws (biology).**
LOCKEY	**A simulation of the lock and key model of enzymes (biology).**
MARKET	**Simulates the competition between two companies selling the same type of product (business, social studies).**
POLICY	**A socioeconomic simulation of American society (government, political science, urban studies).**

POLSYS	Simulates the democratic processes whereby an individual attempts to influence city hall (government).
POLUT	A simulation of an ecological model of the interaction between water and waste.
POP	A simulation of some of the forces interacting in a community when a population undergoes change (government, political science).
STERL	Simulates pest control and makes it possible to test certain theories of pest control.

Copies of student workbooks, teachers' guides, resource handbooks, and program listings for these simulations are available from

> Software Distribution Center
> Digital Equipment Corporation
> Maynard, Mass. 01754.

Another well-known project for the development of computer-oriented curriculum materials is Relevant Educational Applications of Computer Technology (REACT). REACT materials were prepared by the Northwest Regional Educational Laboratory, headquartered at the University of Oregon. Further information about REACT may be obtained by writing to

> Northwest Regional Educational Laboratory
> 500 Lindsay Bldg.
> 710 S.W. Second Avenue
> Portland, Oregon 97204

Other aids, or even complete courses, may be obtained by contacting any of the organizations for educational computing listed at the end of this chapter.

EXERCISES

4.1   What is included in the term "administrative functions" when discussing computer applications to education?

4.2   Provide suitable responses to the following questions about a management information system:

   (a)   What is its purpose?
   (b)   What is the relationship between a data element, a record, and a file?
   (c)   What is a data base?
   (d)   What area of human activity developed the MIS?

4.3   Define the following terms:
   (a)   data entry
   (b)   source document
   (c)   keypunch machine
   (d)   key-to-tape machine
   (e)   key-to-disk machine
   (f)   machine readable

4.4   How is information stored on:
   (a)   data processing cards:
   (b)   magnetic tape?
   (c)   magnetic disk?

4.5   What are some advantages of storing information organized into a data base?

4.6   Identify at least one organization of educational institutions established to make computing capability available for education.

4.7   Distinguish between "drill-and-practice" and "tutorial" uses of computers in education.

4.8   Enter Program 4.1 into a timesharing computer (if you have access to one) and try to make some changes in it to make it a more effective teaching aid.

4.9   Define each of the following:
   (a)   library function
   (b)   CAI
   (c)   computer simulation

4.10   Write a program in which, after it prints some introductory remarks, the computer asks some questions to which the user can respond yes (by typing 1) or no (by typing 0). The program should examine the responses and make appropriate comments. After completing this exercise, you should better understand how interactive computer programs are designed.

4.11   Write a program requiring the computer user to type five numbers. Then have the computer print the following output:

> **THE NUMBERS YOU GAVE ME WERE** ___ ___ ___ ___ ___
> **THEIR SUM IS** _____
> **THEIR PRODUCT IS** _____
> **AT THE END OF THIS RUN YOU CAN SEE THE AMOUNT OF TIME**
> **IT TOOK ME TO DO THIS.**

4.12   Write a program that inputs for each of 10 students an identification number and four test scores (percentage numbers like 85, 63, etc.). Your program then finds the average score for each student and assigns grades as follows:

90 – 100 = A	70 – 79 = C	Below 60 = F
80 – 89 = B	60 – 69 = D	

The output is to be two columns; the first column gives the student identification numbers, and the second column provides the corresponding grades.

4.13   Write a program that will teach long and short vowel sounds. Your program should print some explanatory information about how the student is to respond to the computer. You might also have your program print an example of what the computer will print and how the student is to respond. Your program should provide drill with at least 10 words. That is, you will likely have your program print a one-syllable word and ask the student for a response of "1" or "2" to indicate short or long vowel sound, then check the student's answer for correctness and print an appropriate comment.

4.14   Write a paper on the use of computers to improve the educational level of children in depressed areas of the country.

4.15   Write a paper on the use of computers as tutors. Especially fruitful areas of application have been foreign languages, medicine, mathematics, physics, and other sciences.

4.16   Write a paper on the University of Illinois PLATO project.

4.17   Write a paper on the MITRE Corporation's TICCIT project.

4.18   Prepare a teaching lesson based on one of the Huntington II simulation programs. If your school has access to these programs on a computer, do some runs of the program you select for your teaching lesson and include them in the lesson outline.

4.19   Do some research on other projects designed to use computers in education, and write a paper on your research.

SELECTED REFERENCES

BOOKS

Albrecht, Robert L. Eric Lindberg, and Walter Mara, *Computer Methods in Mathematics*, Addison-Wesley, Reading, Mass., 1969.

American Association of School Administrators, *Administrative Technology and the School Executive,* Amer. Assoc. of School Adm., Washington, D.C., 1969.

Amstutz, Arnold E., *Computer Simulation of Competitive Market Response,* MIT Press, Cambridge, 1967.

Anderson, A.E., ed. *Minds and Machines,* Prentice-Hall, Englewood Cliffs, N.J., 1964.

Association for Educational Data Systems, *Layman's Guide to the Use of Computers,* Assoc. for Educ. Data Systems, Washington, D.C., 1971.

Bushnell, Don and Allen Dwight, *The Computer in American Education,* John Wiley & Sons, New York, 1967.

Charp, Sylvia, *Computers in General Education,* Pennsylvania Dept. of Public Instruction, Harrisburg, 1967.

Data Processing Horizons, *The Directory of Data Processing Education, Second Edition,* Data Processing Horizons, Diamond Bar, Cal if., 1973.

Department of Computer Science, Univ. of Oregon, *Computers in Education Resource Book,* Dept. of Comp. Sci., Univ. of Oregon, Eugene, 1974.

Edwards, Judith B., *Computer Instruction—Planning and Practice,* Northwest Regional Educational Laboratory, Portland, Oregon, 1969.

Ellis, Allen, *The Use and Misuse of Computers in Education,* McGraw-Hill, New York, 1974.

Gerard, Ralph, "Shaping the Mind: Computers in Education," *Applied Science and Technological Progress,* a report to the Committee on Science and Astronautics, U.S. House of Representatives, by the National Academy of Sciences, 1968.

Greenberger, Martin, Julius Aronofsky, James McKenney, and William Massey, *Networks for Research and Education,* MIT Press, Cambridge, 1974.

Goodlad, John, John O'Toole, and Louise Tyler, *Computers and Information Systems in Education,* Harcourt, Brace, & World, New York, 1966.

Hayward, Paul R., *ELIZA: Scriptwriter's Manual,* Educational Research Center MIT, Cambridge, 1968.

Loughary, John, *Man-Machine Systems in Education,* Harper & Row, New York, 1966.

McLuhan, Marshall, *Understanding Media,* McGraw-Hill, New York, 1964.

National Council of Teachers of Mathematics, *Computer-Assisted Instruction and the Teaching of Mathematics,* Nat'l Council of Teachers of Math., Washington, D.C., 1969.

Spiegel, Murray R., *Statistics,* Schaum's Outline Series, McGraw-Hill, New York, 1961.

Suppes, Patrick, Max Jerman, and David Brian, *Computer-Assisted Instruction at Stanford: The 1965—66* Arithmetic Drill-and-Practice Program, Academic Press, New York, 1968.

Whitlock, James, *Automatic Data Processing in Education,* Macmillan, New York, 1964.

PERIODICALS

Atkinson, Richard, and Duncan Hansen, "Computer-Assisted Instruction in Initial Reading: The Stanford Project", *Reading Research Quarterly,* 2, 1966.

Datamation, Entire Issue, September 1968.

Feldhusen, John F., and Michael Szabo, "A Review of Developments in Computer-Assisted Instruction," *Educational Technology,* April 1969.

Grosswirth, Marvin, "Leachim the Teaching Robot," *Datamation,* August 1974.

Peters, Harold J., "The Electronic Aristotle," *Computer Decisions,* July 1976.

Suppes, Patrick, "Computer Technology and the Future of Education," *Phi Kappa Deltan,* April 1968.

Suppes, Patrick, "How Far Have We Come? What's Just Ahead?," *Nation's Schools,* October 1968.

Swets, John, and Wallace Feurzeig, "Computer-Aided Instruction," *Science,* October 29, 1965.

JOURNALS PUBLISHING ABOUT COMPUTERS AND EDUCATION

Computers and the Humanities

Data Processing for Education

EDU

Educational Technology

Educom

Journal of Educational Data Processing

People's Computer Company

ORGANIZATIONS

CONDUIT
   Write to: Director, CONDUIT/Central, Box 388,
   Iowa City, Iowa 52240

LOCAL
   Write to: Project LOCAL, 44 School Street,
   Westwood, Massachusetts 02090

Minnesota Educational Computing Consortium
   Write to: Executive Director, MECC,
   2520 Broadway Drive, Lauderdale, Minnesota 55113

Northwest Regional Educational Laboratory
   Write to: NREL, 500 Lindsay Building,
   710 S.W. Second Avenue, Portland, Oregon 97204

PLATO
   Write to: PLATO, University of Illinois,
   Urbana, Illinois 61801

TICCIT
   Write to: TICCIT, Mitre Corporation, Burlington Road,
   Bedford, Massachusetts 01730

Total Information Educational System
   Write to: TIES, 1925 West County Rd B2,
   St. Paul, Minnesota 55113

5 COMPUTERS IN BUSINESS AND INDUSTRY

Univac I and other early computers intended for the marketplace were designed mainly to handle record-keeping functions for large companies. Only very large companies could afford machines that cost as much as those first computers did. Recall that Univac I alone cost about $12 million to design and construct. Because of the need to justify their cost, computers were first programmed to take over the accounting functions of large businesses. In those applications computers did the work of enough people to pay for themselves over a period of time. More importantly, they made it possible to obtain information for management never before possible.

ACCOUNTING APPLICATIONS

Among the very first business tasks programmed on a computer was the computation of a payroll. This application was a natural for a computer because it was an easily defined task requiring repetitions of virtually the same sequence of instructions for each employee. That is, once the program did the job correctly for one person, only the wages per hour, number of hours worked, withholding tax data, and similar information needed to be varied to make the same program compute payroll data for every other employee. Today, managers of business operations often consider acquiring computers simply to handle the payroll and the many related record-keeping functions.

Here is a BASIC program that performs a very simple payroll operation

Program 5.1

```
10   REM FUNDAMENTAL PAYROLL PROGRAM
12   LET T1=0
```

```
13   LET T2=0
14   LET T3=0
15   PRINT "SOC SEC NO", "NAME", "GROSS WAGES",
16   PRINT "AMT WITHHELD", "NET WAGES"
17   READ X
18   DATA .3
19   READ S$,N$,R,H,D
20   IF S$="999999999" THEN 100
30   LET G=H*R
40   LET W=(G*X)/D
50   LET N=G-W
60   LET T1 = T1+G
80   LET T2=T2+W
90   LET T3=T3+N
95   PRINT S$,N$,G,W,N
98   GO TO 18
100   PRINT " ", "TOTALS", T1, T2, T3
105   DATA "123456787","JOHN SMITH", 3.10, 40, 4
106   DATA "234567890","MARY AMES", 3.25, 42, 2
107   DATA "999999999","NOBODY", 0, 0, 0
110   END
```

Although Program 5.1 is not very long, it can do a job that would take a human being a long time to complete. Even using some sort of calculator, making sure all computations are correct, writing the results on paper, keeping individual payroll data and cumulative information separate, and, finally, writing the cumulative totals would take at least five minutes per person. If the payroll consisted of 200 people, the process would take almost 17 hours. Of course, that amount of time saved could not justify purchasing or leasing a computer, but several such applications could. Notice also that the human being is freed from a routine, uninteresting task. Relieved of tedious jobs, the person would have time to think of ways to extract information that would result in management decisions making the company more productive without using more resources.

Completely Computerized Accounting Systems

Computerizing payrolls is probably the most widely used application of computers to the business world. In addition, entire computerized accounting systems have been established that initiate and maintain journals and ledgers. Accounts in various ledgers are queried to produce an endless variety of reports. And even computerized auditing systems have been developed. Although logically such auto-mated systems would result in a reduction in the accounting staff, the truth is that this does not usually happen. Why not, especially when it is true that many tasks are done so much better and faster by the computer? One reason is that when management realizes the relative ease with which timely information can be ob-tained from a computerized record-keeping system, it requests more reports than it ever did before. More reports mean more people-time is required, and the end result is that employees are not laid off but their tasks are redefined and their time utilized to generate more and more management reports. As stated previously, such management aids unquestionably increase business efficiency, resulting in overall resource conservation. Given our concern with the wise use of *all* resources, more timely information is a desirable goal.

Another force that presses for more reports is the government. Because of laws, for example, that insist on equal treatment for both sexes and for all races, governmental agencies must monitor and report on the treatment given the various groups in order to determine compliance with the law. Many of the reports now required would have been virtually impossible without computers because large masses of information have to be searched to yield desired facts. Computers make the task fairly easy, provided the source information is already available in the computer. Of course, *people* have to develop the computer programs to produce any kind of report, so the staff functions lost to the computer are replaced by the need to have staff prepare additional programs. Thus as a rule, no reduction in staff occurs, although it may be necessary to retrain some staff.

With widespread use of computers have come entirely new concepts of information processing. In Chapter 4 we considered management information sys-tems (MIS). In a MIS, the results of activities traditionally associated with accounting tasks would be stored in a file typically called the financial file. This would be one of several files, including, the personnel file, the inventory file, and the facilities file. Recall that such files are organized into records, which, in turn, consist of data elements. The entire collection of files is called a data base. Programs are written to extract specific information from the data base, and to process it to produce numerous reports on the status of company activity. These programs, together with the data base, constitute the MIS.

Management reports, that is, reports on virtually all aspects of a business, have long been available to the management of firms that had good accounting departments. However, in the past, it was not essential to have the information so soon after it was generated as seems to be the case now. A weekly report was good enough for the Board of Directors to make wise policy decisions regarding the company's activities. Today, however, a time lag of more than a day can be devastating to a firm's profits, and the only way to meet that sort of deadline is to

STATION FILE COPY

FARMERS UNION GRAIN TERMINAL ASSOCIATION

STD. FORM ELEV. 100-M

SALES RECEIPT TICKET

No. 0088100

| LOCATION | TRANS. CODE | ELEVATOR NO. | DATE |
| MOORHEAD, MINNESOTA | 400 | 0613 | |

NAME

SPECIAL ACCOUNT CODE

ADDRESS

CUST. NO.

TRANS. CODE	DESCRIPTION	COMM CODE	PRICE	QUANTITY	AMOUNT
401	FOR				
401	GRAIN SALES				
401	USE FIRST FOUR				
401	LINES ONLY				
401	FOR				
401	MERCHANDISE				
401	COMMODITIES				
401	AND				
401	SERVICES				
401	USE				
401	THIS				
401	AREA				
401					
401					

GRAIN

BUSHEL
01 SP WHT
02 WTR WHT
03 DURUM
04 FLAX
05 RYE
06 BARLEY
07 OATS
08 SOYBEANS
09 CORN
10 MILO
24 MIXED WHT

POUND
20 FLAX SCREENINGS
21 SCREENINGS
11 MILLET
12 SUNFLOWER
13 SAFFLOWER

MERCHANDISE

40 FEED SALT & SHELLS LB
46 FERTILIZER DRY LB
46 FERTILIZER LIQ LB
48 COMMERCIAL SEEDS LB
49 SEED WHEAT BU
50 SEED DURUM BU
51 SEED CORN BU
52 SEED FLAX BU
53 SEED SOYBEANS BU

54 SEED BARLEY RYE BU
55 SEED OATS BU
56 TWINE LB
59 COAL LB
66 FLOUR LB
66 WEED SPRAY LIQ GAL
66 WEED SPRAY DRY LB
66 PANOGEN GAL
66 DRINOX GAL
66 OTHER MERCHANDISE

SVCS

88 REIMBURSEMENTS
90 DRYING
91 CLEANING TREATING
97 GRINDING

94 STORAGE & HANDLING
98 SPREADING
99 WEIGHING

DELIVERY CHARGE	
SALES TAX	
TOTAL	
CASH RECEIVED →	
CHARGE SALE	
PREV. BALANCE	
CREDIT TO ACCOUNT	
NEW BALANCE	

I ACKNOWLEDGE RECEIPT OF THE ABOVE AND ALSO RECEIPT OF A COPY OF THIS SALES TICKET AND AGREE TO THE TERMS AND CONDITIONS ON THE REVERSE SIDE.

BUYER

MANAGER

FIGURE 5.1 Sales slip designed to serve as data entry document (courtesy GTA, Moorhead, Minnesota).

118

FARMERS UNION GRAIN TERMINAL ASSOCIATION

STD. FORM ELEV. 100-M

SALES RECEIPT TICKET

No. 0088100

LOCATION	TRANS. CODE	ELEVATOR NO.				
MOORHEAD, MINNESOTA	400	0613	DATE	0 / 0 7 7 6		

NAME PETERSON JOHN J

SPECIAL ACCOUNT CODE

ADDRESS 809 18TH AVE, MOORHEAD, MN

CUST. NO. 0 0 1 3 5 0

TRANS. CODE	DESCRIPTION	COMM CODE	PRICE	QUANTITY	AMOUNT
401	KENTUCKY BLUEGRASS	3 2	8 5	3 5 0	2 9 8
401	LAWN FERTILIZER	6 5	3 0	2 0 0 0	6 0 0
401	VEG FERTILIZER	6 6	2 8	2 0 0 0	5 6 0
401					
401					
401					
401					
401					
401					
401					
401					
401					
401					
401					

GRAIN

BUSHEL		POUND	
01 SP WHT	07 OATS	20 FLAX SCREENINGS	
02 WTR WHT	08 SOYBEANS	21 SCREENINGS	
03 DURUM	09 CORN		
04 FLAX	10 MILO	11 MILLET	
05 RYE		12 SUNFLOWER	
06 BARLEY	24 MIXED WHT	13 SAFFLOWER	

MERCHANDISE

40 FEED SALT & SHELLS LB	54 SEED BARLEY RYE BU	
46 FERTILIZER DRY LB	55 SEED OATS BU	
46 FERTILIZER LIQ LB	56 TWINE LB	
48 COMMERCIAL SEEDS LB	59 COAL LB	
49 SEED WHEAT BU	66 FLOUR LB	
50 SEED DURUM BU	66 WEED SPRAY LIQ GAL	
51 SEED CORN BU	66 WEED SPRAY DRY LB	
52 SEED FLAX BU	66 PANOGEN GAL	
53 SEED SOYBEANS BU	66 DRINOX GAL	
	66 OTHER MERCHANDISE	

SVCS

88 REIMBURSEMENTS	
90 DRYING	94 STORAGE & HANDLING
91 CLEANING TREATING	98 SPREADING
97 GRINDING	99 WEIGHING

DELIVERY CHARGE	
SALES TAX	
TOTAL	1 4 5 8
CASH RECEIVED →	1 4 5 8
CHARGE SALE	
PREV. BALANCE	
CREDIT TO ACCOUNT	
NEW BALANCE	

I ACKNOWLEDGE RECEIPT OF THE ABOVE AND ALSO RECEIPT OF A COPY OF THIS SALES TICKET AND AGREE TO THE TERMS AND CONDITIONS ON THE REVERSE SIDE.

BUYER

MANAGER

FIGURE 5.2 Sales-slip data for entry to a computer (courtesy GTA, Moorhead, Minnesota).

use computers. By so doing, it is possible to produce during the night summary reports of the previous day's activities. When managers come to their offices in the mornings, the reports they need are on their desks.

Sales Records and Invoicing

Besides making available accurate reports of the financial status of a company, it is very important to let customers know how much they owe for goods or services received. Generally, the sooner people are notified, the sooner they pay their bills, and the money becomes available to the firm to use in the best possible way to generate more income. An accurate, up-to-date record of sales and customers is the key to a timely invoicing plan. A very effective way to make such a plan operational is to use a computer.

The starting point for a computerized invoicing system would very likely be the redesign of a company's sales document (sales slip, invoice, etc.) to conform to computer-oriented data entry procedures. Figure 5.1 shows a sales slip from which data can be entered onto a machine-readable medium (punched cards, paper tape, magnetic tape, or magnetic disk). Notice the exact spacing designated for date, invoice number, customer number, name, street address, city, zip code, item number (of item purchased) and price per item. Once this information is in a form that can be read by a computer input device, it is a simple matter to write a program to post the information to an accounts receivable account, then generate an invoice from that account. Let's follow the procedure from the writing of the sales slip to the inclusion of those data in a program that generates a computer-stored account and finally prints an invoice. Figure 5.2 shows the sales slip data.

SUBSCRIPTED VARIABLES

Before proceeding to a BASIC program designed to process sales data, let us examine a feature of BASIC that greatly simplifies the handling of collections of data. In connection with the sales-slip application, for example, it might be very useful to be able to refer to all item numbers on the sales slip by the group name I. The item number of the first article on the sales slip could be referred to as I_1. The item number of the second article could be I_2, and so on for all articles listed on the sales slip. Similarly, the quantity of each of the articles sold might conveniently be called by the group name Q. The quantity sold of the first article could then be designated by Q_1, the quantity sold of the second article by Q_2, and so on for all articles. A situation similar to item number and quantity could be defined for the price of articles where P might be the group name for "price" and P_1, P_2, and so forth, the prices for articles 1, 2, and so on, respectively. Names like I_1, I_2, Q_1, Q_2

P_1, and P_2 are commonly called subscripted variables, where the small number below and to the right of each letter is the subscript. Such notation is widely used in mathematics and statistics and is extremely useful.

In BASIC, the notation for subscripted variables requires the use of parentheses. For example, the mathematical notation P_1 would be written P(1) in BASIC. As is apparent, in BASIC the subscript is written in parentheses just to the right of the group name. In BASIC a variable like P(1) is called a subscripted variable. Since such notation violates the rules for naming variables (parentheses are not allowed in the name of a nonsubscripted variable), a special BASIC instruction is used to tell the computer that P(1) is a valid variable name. That special instruction is the DIMENSION statement, or more commonly the DIM statement. Here is a sample of a DIM statement:

10 DIM I(10),Q(20),P(30)

Here, the line number is followed by the word DIM after which are listed any group names and the number of members in the group. In this example, there are to be 10 members of the group I, 20 members of Q, and 30 members of P. This means that elsewhere in the program it would be legitimate to use variable names such as I(1), I(10), Q(1), Q(5), Q(20), P(1), P(15), P(21), and P(30). It would *not* be valid to use I(11), or Q(21), or P(31) since these subscripts exceed the number specified in the DIM statement.

In other words, the appearance of a DIM statement in a BASIC program causes the computer to set aside as many memory locations as indicated for each variable listed. Referring again to the previous example, that statement would cause 10 locations to be allocated for the use of I(1) through I(10); 20 locations allocated for Q(1) through Q(20); and 30 locations for P(1) through P(30). Note that no information is placed in storage by a DIM statement. Subscripted variables like I, Q, and P here described are also called *arrays*. Thus "array" is another name for a subscripted variable.

With this introduction to subscripted variables you will be able to follow more clearly the logic of the next program.

Program 5.2 processes the data shown in Figure 5.2.

Program 5.2

```
10    DIM I(10),Q(10),P(10),T(10)
15    LET S2=0
20    READ D,V,C1,L$,F$,M$,S$,C$,A$
```

```
30    DATA 010776,081826,001350,"PETERSON"
40    DATA "JOHN","J","809 18TH AVE","MOORHEAD"
50    DATA "MN"
55    DATA 3
60    DATA 32,3.5,.85
70    DATA 65,20.0,.30
80    DATA 66,20.0,.28
85    READ N
90    LET K=1
100   READ I(K),Q(K),P(K)
110   LET T(K)=Q(K)*P(K)
120   LET S2=S2+T(K)
130   IF K=N THEN 160
140   LET K=K+1
150   GO TO 100
160   PRINT D,V,C1
170   PRINT F$; " ";M$;" ";L$
180   PRINT S$
190   PRINT C$;",";A$
200   PRINT "ITEM NO.","PRICE","QUANTITY","TOTAL"
210   LET K=1
220   PRINT I(K),P(K),Q(K),T(K)
230   IF K=N THEN 260
240   LET K=K+1
250   GO TO 220
260   PRINT " "," ","TOTAL OWED", S2
270   END
```

Just a few comments about Program 5.2 will clarify some matters. The DIM statement (line 10) causes 10 locations to be allocated for each of the variables I, Q, P, and T. Line 20 causes the reading into memory of date (D), invoice number (V), customer number (C1), last name (L$), first name (F$), middle initial (M$), street address (S$), city (C$), and state (A$). Lines 30 through 50 provide those data. Line 55 provides the number of purchases (N) by this customer. Lines 60 through 80 provide the item number (I), price per unit (P), and quantity purchased (Q) for each of the different items sold. Line 85 stores in location N the number from line 55. Lines 90 through 150 cause the reading of sales data, the computation of total cost for each different item sold, and the total cost of all items sold (S2). Lines 160 through 200 print invoice identification information and column headings. Finally, lines 210 through 260 print itemized sales data and total cost of all items purchased.

The actual printed output would be as follows:

010776	081826	001350

JOHN J PETERSON
809 18TH AVE
MOORHEAD, MN

ITEM NO.	PRICE	QUANTITY	TOTAL
32	3. 5	.85	2.975
65	20.	.30	6.00
66	20.	.28	5.60
		TOTAL OWED	14.575

If only a single sales slip were to be processed, using a computer would be foolish; it would be better to do the whole invoicing process by hand. However, once Program 5.2 is written, only minor changes would be necessary to have it process any number of sales-slip data. Furthermore, if the program were written in, say, COBOL there would be instructions available that would make it possible to store the sales data on magnetic tape or disk. Then these stored data could be accessed each time an invoice is produced to include any unpaid balances on the statement. Thus a permanent, computer-readable accounts-receivable ledger could be maintained very easily. In fact, using a computer to store such historical data opens up a variety of other uses; for example to keep track of the time elapsed between sale and receipt of payment for that sale. Accountants call this "aging accounts receivable."

INVENTORY MANAGEMENT

A very important aspect of any business established for the purpose of selling goods is the supply of merchandise kept on hand. If too much money is tied up in merchandise inventory, the firm may be losing money because funds are not available for other purposes, thus possibly forcing the borrowing of money on which interest would have to be paid. And, of course, any money invested in inventory cannot be earning interest in any other investment, so care must be taken not to have too much of the company's resources so assigned.

On the other hand, if the inventory is allowed to become too small, customers must be turned away. Whenever that happens, the firm runs the risk of losing customers permanently. It is important that every business that sells goods know which items customers are willing to place an order for and accept a delay in delivery, and which ones customers insist on obtaining immediately. That kind of knowledge comes from experience in the business, not from a computer. But just being aware of such peculiarities of the business does not guarantee good inventory management. An up-to-date record of all merchandise on hand, its cost, its current value, its present location in the company, as well as complete knowledge of what items have been ordered, when they will be available for customers, and their cost, are essential to any system designed to maintain an optimum inventory.

That's where computers enter the picture. As you know by now, a computer can store large quantities of information. If appropriate programs are written, that information can be retrieved and used to generate reports of the type needed for inventory control. In fact, the state of the art is now such that cash registers are often much more than just cash registers, they are really computer terminals. When the salesperson keys into the "cash register" the required data, usually including a unique item number, the number of items sold, and the selling price, the information is immediately transmitted to a computer where its stored information is modified to show the effects of the sale just made. In particular, the "number of items on hand" for the items just sold would be decreased to reflect the sale. In a system like this, an accurate inventory record is continually available upon request. More will be said about such systems in the next section because not only do they provide a good inventory record, but they also affect many other aspects of marketing.

It must be stated that even using the highly automatic inventory system just described does not eliminate the need to actually count items on hand. You understand that occasionally an item can be placed in the wrong location, that is, in a place different from the one indicated in the records. Therefore, the records may show that bin 35 contains 15 shirts of a specific kind when in reality it has only 14, because one has been mistakenly placed elsewhere. Similarly, the records can show one less shirt in a bin than is actually there. Of course, errors of this kind do occur, and it is very important to make periodic physical checks of items on hand so that the inventory record reflects the true number of items on hand. Thus the inventory record reflects the true physical situation. Nevertheless, if people handling the merchandise train themselves to exercise care, an automated system can reduce significantly the number of actual item counts required.

Although the preceding discussion on inventory control emphasized marketing firms (like retail stores or wholesale distributors), a very similar approach would hold for a manufacturing business. In that situation it would be essential to have on hand the necessary raw materials, the proper parts for assembling at a given time, and enough (but not too many) spare parts to supply customers having purchased the end product. As you can surmise, the inventory problem for a manufacturer is not much different from that of the marketing firm.

COMPUTERS IN MARKETING

In this section we consider some direct applications of the computer in the marketing process. In marketing the ability to show a profit is often simply a matter of having the right information or the right product at the right time. In fact, many of the considerations of a good inventory-control system apply without change to a profitable marketing system.

A major concern of marketing people is knowledge of where an item can be obtained and how long delivery will take. To help alleviate this concern, many larger firms have installed networks of equipment attached to computers, which, together with appropriate computer programs, constitute a parts-ordering system. Figure 5.3 is a diagram of the hardware involved in such a system. As you can see, the hardware system shown is not unlike the timesharing system of Chapter 3. In some ways this is true, but in the sense of how it is used, there is very little similarity. The only device in the diagram with which you are not already familiar is the *multiplexer*. This piece of equipment receives electrical signals from many sources and transmits them in proper sequence to a computer. When the computer has information to send back to a specific terminal, the multiplexer must send the signals to the appropriate terminal. Only five dealer terminals are shown in Figure 5.3, but in reality thousands of terminals, all accessing the same computer and its stored information, may be part of the system.

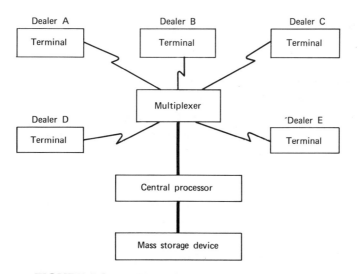

FIGURE 5.3   Typical parts-ordering system.

FIGURE 5.4   An airlines reservation system (courtesy Northwest Orient Airlines).

Besides having the right hardware, a parts-ordering system is greatly dependent on the software (programs) which processes the parts-availability information. A good system would take into consideration the location of the terminal that originated the parts order when it returns information about the delivery schedule. For example, if a firm has two major warehouses, one in Chicago and one in Denver, with smaller warehouses in Fargo, Minneapolis, Omaha, and St. Louis, a request for a part from a terminal in Fergus Falls, Minnesota, should be handled by the Fargo warehouse (the closest one) if the part is available there. If a part is not in stock at the closest warehouse, the next closest place where it is available should be directed by the system to handle the order. And, of course, the underlying goal of the whole system must be to provide accurate information and timely service to the customer.

Although commercial airlines do not sell merchandise, the seats on specific airlines flights have almost all of the properties of goods for sale. Accurate, easily available, up-to-date information about those seats must be available if customers are to be well served and airlines are to optimize their ticket sales. It should not surprise you that computers have been the means whereby those goals have been achieved. Typical hardware systems for airlines reservations are nearly identical to the one just described for parts ordering. The software systems also would be very similar to that just discussed. Essentially, the system must increase the number of available seats on a given flight whenever cancellations occur. It must also store the names of passengers assigned seats on a given flight in case it should be necessary to contact them. Since all ticket offices for a particular airlines are connected to the same computer, the same files of information are accessed both for finding out what seats are available and for changing the number of seats yet unsold. Therefore, accurate information is provided to all terminal users. Figure 5.4 shows the computer hardware necessary to handle one airline's reservation system.

Point-of-Sale Terminals

We turn our attention now to a situation related in several ways to all of what has been said thus far in this chapter. The circumstances being referred to are those associated with retailing. A retail merchant has need to do accounting, invoicing, and inventory management. A means has been devised whereby a computer can be used in conjunction with cash registers to accomplish these functions almost automatically. The key to this system is a special "cash register" technically called a point-of-sale terminal. Such a terminal has most of the features of a regular cash register, such as a keyboard (although a greatly modified one), a cash drawer, and a place for printing a paper tape record of the transactions (to be given to the customer). Figure 5.5 shows one point-of-sale (POS) terminal. As you can see, it resembles any modern cash register, but its function is much more complex. Each POS terminal is connected by cable to a computer, or to a device that records all information from the POS terminals on magnetic tape, later processed by a computer. We shall assume the situation where each POS terminal is attached directly to a computer system.

   Systems using POS terminals display varying degrees of sophistication; we shall consider one of the more sophisticated systems. Before any data from a POS terminal are entered, the computer would have been programmed to recognize data from such a terminal. In addition, the computer would have stored in it a wide array of data associated with each item in stock. Typically, stored data would include a unique item number, brief item description, current number on hand, optimum number to have on hand, description of item, supplier of the item together with supplier's address, actual cost and replacement cost, and current selling price of the item. We shall assume that the computer has an internal clock and calendar available. Note that one of the stored facts is the current selling price of the

FIGURE 5.5   Point-of-sale terminal (courtesy NCR).

item. This price can be updated every night if desired, so that the very latest price is always the one stored. In fact, if an item goes on temporary sale, the sale price can be stored in the computer.

Now let's consider what happens when an item is sold, and keyed into the system. All that the salesperson would have to key into the POS terminal would be the unique item number and the number of items purchased. With that information entered into the computer it would have enough stored information to list on the paper tape (to be given to the customer) the item description, cost per item, and total cost (product of cost per item and number of items purchased) for each different item purchased. When all item numbers have been entered, the salesperson would press a "TOTAL" key, and the total cost of all purchases would be printed on the tape as well as displayed on a visible register for both customer and salesperson to see. The amount paid by the customer would be entered and the correct change computed and displayed, and the transaction would be complete.

So far the POS terminal has done very little more than any cash register, except that it computed total cost when two or more of the same item were purchased. This difference should not be minimized, however, because it does ensure more accurate billing. Using a standard cash register, such a multiple purchase would have required that at least the "enter transaction" key be depressed for each of the like items purchased. Eliminating that step has eliminated a place for potential error. Furthermore, if the buying public could be provided with a satisfactory method of obtaining the price of an item even though the item was not individually marked, then the feature of having the item price stored in the computer would be necessary to the check-out system. In that case, a standard cash register would be useless; only the POS terminal could do the job.

But now let's investigate some features that make a sales-record system using POS terminals and a computer decidedly superior. As the item number is entered, indicating a sale of one or more of those items, the computer record of the number on hand is reduced by as many as the number of that item sold. Thus the information in the computer's memory always includes the current number on hand of each item stocked as well as how many were sold during any given day. Given the appropriate program, those data are all the computer would need to provide detailed inventory and sales reports.

The POS-terminal computerized system can also be applied to the ordering process of the firm. As stated earlier, the *minimum number to have on hand* of each item stocked is stored in computer memory. As soon as the *current number on hand* is reduced to the *minimum number to have on hand,* a signal is given to a special order-writing program to produce an order. The number of items to be ordered could be determined by the computer by referring to the *optimum number to have on hand* figure, also stored in the computer's memory. Since the supplier's name and address are also stored in the computer, everything is available to print a complete order for merchandise. Of course, any properly run business would have the computer-printed orders reviewed by a knowledgeable human being to check for gross errors that might result from hardware or software malfunction. But it is not hard to imagine the human time saved by having such automatically printed orders. In fact, such constant surveillance of the stock of goods on hand and on order would almost certainly increase sales, because a given item would less often be out of stock. Furthermore, the chances of being overstocked would be minimized because the computer would have instantly available to it the several numbers related to an ideal stock of merchandise on hand.

Universal Grocery Product Code

About the same time the POS terminals came into use the Universal Grocery Product Code (UGPC) was developed. Figure 5.6 shows some examples of the UGPC as it is appearing on the packaging of more and more merchandise, espe-

FIGURE 5.6   Examples of Universal Grocery Product Code.

FIGURE 5.7   Railroad bar code (left center) (reprinted with permission of DATAMATION, copyright 1975 by Technical Publishing Co., Greenwich, Connecticut).

130

FIGURE 5.8   Variety of bar codes in use (reprinted with permission DATAMATION, Copyright 1975 by Technical Publishing Co., Greenwich, Connecticut).

cially the items found in supermarkets. The UGPC is a particular configuration of a bar code. Bar codes were first used by the Association of American Railroads to identify freight cars (see Figure 5.7). The railroad association in 1967 adopted a bar code that measures 10½ by 22 inches and contains 13 digits identifying the type of railroad car, the owner, and the serial number. Special optical sensing devices can scan these codes on cars going by at speeds of up to 80 miles per hour. The object of this procedure is to make it possible for railroad companies to keep track of their equipment and thus make more effective use of it. All but a small percentage of the approximately 1,800,000 freight cars in the United States now have the bar code painted on them, but the number of scanning devices is still much below the minimum number believed necessary to keep an accurate record of equipment locations. Consequently, many railroad companies still do not know where all their freight cars are at any given time. But the technology has proved beneficial. One railroad company, the Illinois Central, uses both railside and roadside scanners because their piggyback trailers as well as their railroad cars are marked. This company credits the bar code system with increasing freight car utilization by 9 percent and reducing personnel costs by 11 percent. Obviously the system is worthwhile.

Since its adoption by the Association of American Railroads, many other businesses have devised applications of bar codes, in many cases adapting the railroad code to their own needs. Figure 5.8 shows various bar codes now in use. Depending on the application, several different kinds of scanners are available to automatically read the codes. Figures 5.9 and 5.10 display three different code scanners in current use. One of these codes is the 10-digit UGPC code, which identifies any product on sale in a supermarket. It was adopted in 1973 by the grocery industry as its standard code, and since that time has been appearing on more and more of the items on supermarket shelves. One of the reasons for

FIGURE 5.9   Scanners for bar codes (reprinted with permission of DATA-MATION, Copyright 1975 by Technical Publishing Co., Greenwich, Connecticut).

adopting the UGPC was to increase the speed and accuracy of procedures at the check-out counter.

    If you think back on the various things said about POS terminals, and assume that the terminal also has an optical scanner feeding information directly to a computer, you can easily see how the system benefits both customer and merchant. As you probably know, the code for an item is printed on the container by the manufacturer or processor, so the retail merchant has no package marking to do. As stated previously, the price for any given item is stored in the computer. As the scanning device is passed over the UGPC code on the package, a signal transmitter to the computer identifies the item, and the computer's memory is searched for the item price, which is instantly displayed on the POS terminal. If multiple purchases are made of any item, the scanner is simply passed over each item and the appropriate total is produced by the computer for display and paper-tape printing on the POS terminal. All of the aspects of inventory control and sales data mentioned in the section on POS terminals would, of course, be applicable to a terminal that had the optical scanner. As you can surmise, the use of UGPC

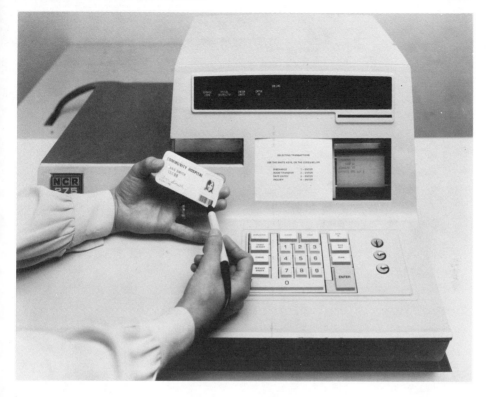

codes, optical scanners, and POS terminals virtually eliminates errors in check-out, speeds up the process for the customer, and reduces the number of employees the supermarket needs. The main objection to such a system has been that prices do not appear on individual items. Prices could not be printed by the manufacturer because merchants in different locations charge different prices. Of course, merchants could always stamp prices on items as they have done for years, but costs would be much lower if that did not have to be done. One solution would be to mark *shelves* on which items are stored, and from those markings the customer could determine item costs. There are drawbacks to this plan; if an item were placed on the wrong shelf, the price marked on the shelf would not be correct. Another solution might be to install in shopping carts a device, similar to that shown in Figure 5.10, designed to display the price when the UGPC code is scanned. This solution might be too costly, however, and thus cancel the cost-saving benefits of a bar code/POS-terminal system. Perhaps the cost benefit will be so great to the buying public that it will accept the system without any special concessions. In any case, check-out systems utilizing computers, POS terminals, and UGPC codes are sure to be prevalent in the very near future.

FIGURE 5.10   Portable scanner for bar codes (reprinted with permission of DATAMATION, Copyright 1975 by Technical Publishing Co., Greenwich, Connecticut).

ELECTRONIC FUNDS TRANSFER (EFT)

The nearly automatic check-out system just described is similar to a system used in banking. The system that has developed, in all its numerous variations, has come to be called electronic funds transfer (EFT). Like the check-out system, EFT makes use of a computer and a terminal. This terminal is more like the standard VDU terminal described in Chapter 3 than the POS terminal. Instead of the optical scanner of the check-out system, EFT usually makes use of a special plastic card not unlike a credit card. In an EFT system, item numbers give way to customer account numbers. Figure 5.11 shows a typical EFT terminal being used.

In its experimental stages, EFT has enabled a person to go to one of the special terminals and, in effect, have 24-hour-a-day banking service. The person who wants this service is issued a plastic card by his/her bank on which is stamped the person's name, bank identification number, person's checking-account number, and the date the card expires. At the time of receiving the card, the person is also given a unique four-digit code number to remember. Suppose the customer

FIGURE 5.11   EFT terminal in use (Courtesy NCR).

now wants to use the service to obtain $50. He/she finds one of the special terminals, inserts the plastic card as designated on the terminal, keys into the terminal keyboard the four-digit code number and the transaction amount of $50, and presses the key indicating that this transaction is a withdrawal of funds. These actions cause signals to be sent to a computer, which then verifies with data in its memory that the customer is legitimate and that the account balance is large enough to permit a $50 withdrawal. If these conditions are met, the computer signals the terminal to release $50 in cash from the supply stored in the terminal, stores in its memory a record of the transaction, modifies account balances as needed, and closes the transaction. A similar procedure would be followed to deposit funds into one's account.

As you can tell, if the EFT system were no more than that just described, its only benefit would be to make banking services available at any time. Worthwhile as that goal is, it would probably not justify the cost of installing the system. The ultimate goal of EFT systems is to make cash or checks unnecessary. In order to do this, the cooperation must be obtained of all merchants and banking institutions in the area in which the system is to be used. Every merchant would have at least one EFT terminal on the premises, which would be used to transfer funds from the customer's bank account to the merchant's account. As a customer finished shopping, he/she would go to the POS terminal and determine the total amount owed the merchant. At this point, the sales person and the customer would go to the EFT terminal (probably located beside the POS terminal) and each would key in data to cause the transfer of funds from the customer's account to the store's account. No money or checks would ever be handled. The store would know immediately whether the customer had enough funds in the bank to cover the purchase. With this system customers should enjoy reduced prices because merchants will lose less money because of bad checks, and because money will be instantly available to the merchant's account, reducing the merchant's need to borrow money. The customer should also benefit from savings to the banks resulting from no check nor money handling. This should make it possible for banks to reduce the costs of their services.

The motivation for proceeding to EFT systems from standard check-and-money systems is the tremendous increase in the number of checks. Each year a significantly larger number of checks must be processed by banks than the preceding year. Not only is the cost of personnel to process the checks a problem, but the sheer volume of checks makes it difficult to handle them within a reasonable time period. Furthermore, the expenditure of paper needed for producing checks violates today's concern for preserving natural resources. It seems likely that the time is very near when EFT will become the prevailing method for handling funds.

Another interesting aspect of EFT systems is that employees would no

Numerically—controlled machines are capable of following instructions previously recorded in the form of numbers on paper or magnetic tape.

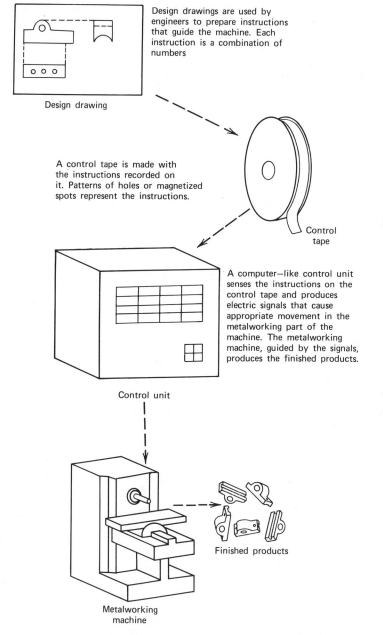

Design drawings are used by engineers to prepare instructions that guide the machine. Each instruction is a combination of numbers

Design drawing

A control tape is made with the instructions recorded on it. Patterns of holes or magnetized spots represent the instructions.

Control tape

A computer—like control unit senses the instructions on the control tape and produces electric signals that cause appropriate movement in the metalworking part of the machine. The metalworking machine, guided by the signals, produces the finished products.

Control unit

Finished products

Metalworking machine

FIGURE 5.12   Numerically controlled machine.

137

longer receive paychecks. In their place the employer would probably issue something corresponding to today's payroll-check stub. That is, the employee would receive a paper record of what funds would have been transferred where. The equivalent of the check itself would be the electronic transfer of funds from the employer's account to that of the employee.

COMPUTERS IN THE FACTORY

Computers have affected business and industry in yet another way; they have made the manufacturing process more automatic. For many years manufacturers have used parts-making machines that are "numerically controlled" by punched paper tape or punched cards in much the same way that a player piano is controlled by a roll of punched paper (see Figure 5.12). Today, an even more complex process, controlling virtually every aspect of many manufacturing operations, is available. For example, those industries in which one continuous process yields the completed product, such as in the refining of oil products from crude oil, the production of sugar products from sugar beets, the manufacture of steel from iron ore, the creation of various glass products from sand, and the processing of fertilizers from minerals, all lend themselves to computerization. The manufacturing process itself is essentially dependent on the control of simple devices such as valves or heating mechanisms. These devices must be accurately controlled within relatively narrow ranges, but aside from that the processes are very simple. Thus there are entire factories whose many functions are controlled by a computer (see Figure 5.13).

　　　　Human beings are needed only to supervise the overall operation to ensure that no gross problems develop. Properly programmed computers controlling factories in that way would allow for necessary slowdowns in the procedure and adjust related operations accordingly. Of course, appropriate sensing devices would monitor conditions all along the production line, feeding their information to the computer. The computer would coordinate all activities by sending the necessary signals to control devices. For example, if in a fertilizer plant some machine failure occurred in the packaging operation, sensors should detect the pile-up of processed fertilizer, relay the information to the computer, which would stop the conveyer belts supplying the raw minerals.

　　　　In noncontinuous manufacturing situations (like the separate manufacturing of the thousands of parts that go into an airplane), computers are most effective in controlling the factory's resources and in scheduling the production of parts so that they are ready for incorporation into the major product at the appropriate time. In such manufacturing situations (sometimes called "batch production") the following reasons have been given for computerizing the factory processes:

1. To reduce the price of the product.

2. To increase the uniformity of the quality of the product.

3. To increase job satisfaction.

The last of these reasons is somewhat surprising, but it is related to the need for people to supervise operations, program the machines, and manage the various aspects of manufacturing rather than perform the hopelessly dull and routine tasks often associated with mass-production factories. Here is what one expert, Dr. Robert H. Anderson of the University of Southern California, says about computers in manufacturing:

> *Probably the fastest-growing application of information sciences during the next decade will be computer-based automation of the manufacturing process. All aspects of manufacture—design, prototyping, production*

FIGURE 5.13   Computer for controlling a bakery (courtesy Honeywell).

engineering, part forming, assembling, inspection, material transfer and storage—will increasingly become directly controlled by computers. Furthermore, computer control will bring a new flexibility to automation; the machines that perform manufacturing operations will be programmable, allowing one machine to perform a variety of manufacturing steps. This capability, combined with complete computer-based scheduling and allocation of resources, will result in a major increase in manufacturing productivity, especially in the important area of batch production and job shop operations. In addition, most of the dull and demeaning jobs within a manufacturing facility will be replaced by more interesting and challenging tasks such as programming and system maintenance.*

Whether or not Anderson is correct in his analysis of computers in the factory, there are significant indications of a growth in the use of computers for this purpose.

SOME CONCERNS OF THE THOUGHTFUL CITIZEN

From the topics discussed in this chapter there would seem to arise some serious questions, among them the following:

1. Because of the increased demand for accurate reports, will all accounting procedures be computerized? Will the traditional training for accountants be adequate in that situation?

2. Is there some way to decrease the demands of all levels of government for reporting of the businessman's activities?

3. Will computerized retailing operations cause massive unemployment among retail clerks?

4. Will EFT result in an even more impersonal relationship between customer and banker, between employer and employee, and between merchant and customer?

5. Is the average work week likely to be cut to 32 hours in the near future? If so, will productivity remain high enough that salaries need not be decreased accordingly?

*Robert H. Anderson, "Programmable Automation: The Bright Future of Computers in Manufacturing," *Datamation*, December 1972.

These and other questions might well have crossed your mind as you have read this chapter. There is no easy answer to any of them, if indeed any answer is possible. However, let's consider some responses as we conclude this chapter.

The first question with its two parts would seem to be most easily answered. From some knowledge of the computer as well as of accounting objectives, we can conclude that most, if not all, accounting procedures will gradually be done by computer. Human beings who know accounting processes well will design computerized systems, but the routine work now performed by accountants will be relegated to computers. This may necessitate some changes in the training presently given at many accounting schools.

Regarding the demands of government for more reports, perhaps two trends need to be reversed if there is to be a reduction in the time businesses spend generating required reports. The first trend is the increasing dependency by many businesses on government money in the form of government contracts or at least government-arranged contracts. The second trend is the desire on the part of an ever-increasing number of bureaucratic agencies to be reported to by the people, and especially by businesses. Unless these trends change, even greater use of computers seems inevitable.

The last three questions are more closely related so our discussion of them will include references to all three. If past records are any indication of the future, one must conclude that it is not likely that large numbers of retail clerks will become unemployed because of computers. This is because the use of computers in retailing has raised the level of productivity to the extent that it is quite possible that the work week for people in the retailing business could be lowered to 32 hours. Whether the interpersonal relationships between the several categories of people mentioned in the question can be made more meaningful depends entirely on the people involved.

Without a doubt, computers have irreversibly affected business and industry. Probably most results have been good. The one nagging question is related to the replacement of people by computers, but in the great majority of such cases, people have been released from jobs they found most distasteful. The problem remains as to how those people can obtain the income they lost. Retraining plans and shorter work weeks seem to merit thoughtful consideration by those who plan for the future of our society.

EXERCISES

5.1 What technique is used in Program 5.1 to stop the reading of employee data?

5.2 Prepare Program 5.1 for entry into a computer. Supply your own data at lines 105 and following, then run the program to produce output.

5.3 What reasons can be given for the ever-increasing need for business firms to produce reports of their business activities?

5.4 List some likely reasons for the increased use of computers in accounting applications.

5.5 Describe the steps involved in a computerized sales record and billing system.

5.6 Prepare Program 5.2 for entry into a computer, then run your program to verify that the output described in the chapter is the actual output of the program.

5.7 What advantage was there to using the subscripted variables I, Q, P, and T in this program?

5.8 Describe some features of a computerized inventory system.

5.9 Discuss the place of computers in a parts-ordering system and an airlines reservation system.

5.10 List the steps involved in modifying a store's inventory record if the store uses POS terminals connected to a computer. Start with the selection of articles purchased by the customer.

5.11 In what ways is a POS terminal similar to a cash register? How is it different?

5.12 What is the Universal Grocery Product Code?

5.13 List some advantages and disadvantages of using the UGPC.

5.14 List some benefits and dangers associated with the widespread use of EFT.

5.15 What forces in society are virtually dictating the acceptance of EFT?

5.16 Identify at least two applications of computers to manufacturing processes.

5.17 Give three reasons for the management of a factory to decide to computerize as many functions as possible.

5.18 Write a BASIC program that uses four subscripted variables to read five of each of the following: name, street address, city, and state. Then print three-line addresses for each person named such that the first line contains the name, second line the street address, and third line the city and state.

5.19 Write a BASIC program that does the following:
    (a) establishes expense accounts by reading 10 pairs of numbers; where the first of each pair is a four-digit account number and the second is the starting balance of that account;
    (b) updates expense-account balances by reading pairs of numbers, where the first of each pair is again a four-digit account number, and the second is a number to be added to the previous account balance;
    (c) prints a list of the 10 account numbers and balances. You will need to use subscripted variables for the account numbers and account balances. Write your program so that when an account number of 9999 is

read, the program will produce the output and then stop. Use the following data to test your program:

Account Number	Starting Balance
1234	210.50
1235	82.40
1236	25.00
1237	175.00
1238	165.50
1239	109.25
1240	75.00
1241	82.45
1242	16.50
1243	35.10

Account Number	Amount to Be Added
1237	25.00
1234	10.00
1239	6.50
1235	15.50
1241	3.50
1234	17.00
1243	5.50
9999	0.00

5.20 Write a short paper on your feelings toward a supermarket that does not price individual items but posts prices on shelves, and where the check-out is done using an optical scanner. In your paper discuss possible benefits you might derive from such a supermarket, as well as aspects you would not like about it.

5.21 Describe a manufacturing operation that is completely computer-controlled.

SELECTED REFERENCES

BOOKS

Davis, Gordon B., *Management Information Systems: Conceptual Foundations, Structure, and Development*, McGraw-Hill, New York, 1974.

Gore, Marvin and J. Stubbe, *Elements of Systems Analysis*, Wm. C. Brown, Dubuque, 1975.

Sanders, Donald H. *Computers in Business,* McGraw-Hill, New York, 1975.

Silver, Gerald A. and Joan B. Silver, *Data Processing for Business,* Harcourt Brace Jovanovich, New York, 1973.

PERIODICALS

Anderson, Robert H., "Programmable Automation: The Bright Future of Computers in Manufacturing," *Datamation,* November 1974.

Barr, David A., "GM's Parts Ordering System," *Datamation,* November 1974.

Davis, Ruth M., "The Computer Serves, The Consumer Relishes," *Computer Decisions,* May 1975.

Feidelman, Lawrance A., "The Automation of the Supermarket," *Modern Data,* March 1974.

Flynn, Robert L., "A Brief History of Data Base Management," *Datamation,* August 1974.

Fried, Louis, "When Is The Right Time To Computerize?," *The Office,* September 1973.

Hoffman, Gerald M., "MIS Can Stem the Flood of Paperwork," *The Office,* January 1974.

Huhn, Gerald E., "The Data Base in a Critical On-Line Business Environment," *Datamation,* September 1974.

Kemper, Robert L., "Bank Automation Improves Service to Customers," *The Office,* January 1974.

Kimes, Terry J., "Computer Utilization for Accountants," *The Office,* January 1974.

NASA, "NASA Computer Program Aids Automative Industry," NASA News Release No. 71-221, November 4, 1971.

Nolan, Richard L., and K. Eric Knutson, "The Computerization of the ABC Widget Co.," *Datamation,* April 1974.

Reside, Kenneth D., and T.J. Seiter, "The Evolution of an Integrated Data Base," *Datamation,* September 1974.

Rickert, Jerome P., "On-Line Support for Manufacturing," *Datamation,* July 1975.

Schubert, Richard F. "Directions in Data Base Management Technology," *Datamation,* September 1974.

Sobczak, Thomas C., "Universal Product Coding: Who Profits and Who Loses?," *Computers and People,* February 1976.

Wasserman, Joseph J., "Computer Systems Must Be Audited," *The Office,* August 1974.

Yasoki, Edward K., "Bar Codes For Data Entry," *Datamation,* May 1975.

Yasoki, Edward K., "Toward the Automated Office," *Datamation,* February 1975.

6 COMPUTERS, POLITICS, AND GOVERNMENT

Two areas of society that would appear to be impervious to computer application are politics and government. In this chapter you will discover a number of ways in which ingenious people have put the computer to work in politics and government service.

COMPUTERS IN POLITICAL CAMPAIGNS

The lifeblood of political campaigns is humanpower. Any candidate who has large numbers of volunteers contacting voters on his/her behalf, or sufficient funds to reach voters through the mass media, is almost sure to win an election. One of the most successful methods of contacting people for contributions of either money or time is computer-generated mailings. It's not that the computer does a better job of producing mailing labels than volunteer party workers, but it completely outclasses human beings when it comes to the number of names and addresses it can generate in a given amount of time. Not only is the computer many times faster than a small army of the party's faithful but it can keep a much greater number of contacts in its electronic memory than could be conceived of when noncomputer techniques are used. For example, it was reported that during the 1972 presidential campaign Senator George McGovern sent seventeen million pieces of mail. Here's what that volume of mail means in terms of human power. If we assume that the letters are already prepared and stuffed into envelopes by other people, then only the addressing of the envelopes remains to be considered. To address 17 million envelopes 50 people would have to work eight-hour days for two months solid, and *each* would have to complete almost 1000 envelopes each hour. Can you imagine addressing 16 envelopes every minute for two months? That's the kind of human effort it would take to match the computer mailings done by McGovern's campaign committee. The letters *were* successful in raising funds, although not as successful in garnering votes.

But the Nixon campaign went even further. That effort saw 27 million pieces of mail sent. Not only were those letters addressed by computer but they were computer-composed. That is, the contents of each letter was geared to the individual receiving it. How was that possible? Well, certain information about each of the 27 million people was collected and stored; such information might include their political affiliations, their occupations, and their positions on some of the major political issues. Based on those stored facts, many different letters were written.

Did you realize that if 10 different facts are available 1022 different letters can be developed using those facts! No wonder voters get the impression that their letter was written by the candidate specifically to them. Then if the machine-produced signature is done in water-soluble ink so that it smears when a little moisture happens to hit it, the letter seems even more personal.

Lest you immediately condemn this use of computers you should recall that for political candidates to give the impression that they understand the individual voters' concerns is nothing new. When the country was less populous, it was the mark of a good (and successful, it might be added) politician that he could respond to the unique concerns of many of his constituents. That capacity was lost because of the sheer number of voters. Now by means of the computer it is again within the realm of possibility.

To help you comprehend how a computer can be used in the way just described, here is a program written by a college student whose major was political science. You must realize that this is a first attempt at such an application, and is tremendously simple compared to the polished product of the professional political consultant. It does, however, create a "personal" letter for each voter depending on the facts available on him/her.

Program 6.1

```
20   DIM L$(4), K(4,5)
25   REM LINES 30-58 READ IN NAMES AND CODES
30   LET I=1
35   READ L$(I),K(I,1),K(I,2),K(I,3)
40   LET I=I+1
45   IF I=4 THEN 70
50   GO TO 35
52   DATA "MR. TRUITT", 1,2,1
54   DATA "MR. MONEY", 1,4,2
56   DATA "MS. HAPPY", 2,3,1
```

```
58    DATA "MS. COOL", 2,1,2
70    REM LINES 80—415 PRINT THE LETTER
80    LET I=1
90    PRINT "FROM THE OFFICE OF SENATOR JOE SNORKLE"
100   PRINT "263 WASHINGTON STREET"
110   PRINT "MINNEAPOLIS, MINNESOTA 55103"
120   PRINT
130   PRINT
140   PRINT "DEAR"; L$(I)
150   PRINT "AS THIS FALL'S ELECTION NEARS"
155   PRINT "I SINCERELY HOPE THAT YOU WILL"
160   IF K(I,1)=1 THEN 200
165   PRINT "PLEASE GIVE ME YOUR SUPPORT IN MY"
170   PRINT "GOAL OF CREATING A RESPONSIVE GOVERNMENT."
180   GO TO 210
200   PRINT "AGAIN GIVE ME YOUR SUPPORT AS YOU"
205   PRINT "DID IN MY LAST BID FOR ELECTION."
210   PRINT "TODAY THIS COUNTRY FACES AN"
215   PRINT "ENERGY CRISIS, HIGH UNEMPLOYMENT,"
220   PRINT "WORLD TENSION, AND INFLATION"
225   PRINT "TOGETHER WITH RECESSION."
230   IF K(I,2)=1 THEN 260
235   IF K(I,2)=2 THEN 270
240   IF K(I,2)=3 THEN 280
245   IF K(I,2)=4 THEN 290
250   PRINT "MOST WORKING MEN STILL FEAR LAYOFFS"
255   GO TO 300
260   PRINT "STUDENTS ARE IN A FINANCIAL CRUNCH"
265   GO TO 300
270   PRINT "AGRICULTURE HAS BEEN HIT THE HARDEST"
275   GO TO 300
280   PRINT "THE COST OF RAISING A FAMILY SOARS"
285   GO TO 300
290   PRINT "FEWER BUSINESSES ARE MAKING PROFITS"
300   PRINT "SINCE LITTLE HAS BEEN DONE YET"
305   PRINT "TO HELP THE ECONOMIC SITUATION."
310   IF K(I,3)=2 THEN 340
320   PRINT "        I HAVE ADVOCATED STRONG RE-"
325   PRINT "FORM MEASURES ON THE ISSUE OF"
330   PRINT "DEFENSE SPENDING."
```

```
335   GO TO 360
340   PRINT "          I HAVE ADVOCATED STRONG CON-"
345   PRINT "SERVATIVE MEASURES ON THE ISSUE"
350   PRINT "OF ABORTION."
360   PRINT "          CERTAINLY NOT ALL OF THE ISSUES"
365   PRINT "HAVE BEEN DISCUSSED IN THIS LETTER."
370   PRINT "HOWEVER, I HOPE I HAVE TOUCHED ON"
375   PRINT "ENOUGH OF THEM TO CONVINCE YOU"
380   PRINT "THAT YOU SHOULD SUPPORT ME. I"
385   PRINT "REALLY APPRECIATE YOUR TAKING TIME"
390   PRINT "TO READ THIS."
400   PRINT "              SINCERELY,"
410   PRINT
415   PRINT "              JOE SNORKLE"
420   IF I=4 THEN 440
425   LET I=I+1
430   GO TO 90
440   END
```

Program 6.1 has only three places where different statements could be printed:

1. line 160 tests for the voter's previous support code;

2. lines 230—245 test for occupation code;

3. line 310 tests for liberal/conservative code, assuming liberals want less defense spending and conservatives want strong measures against abortion.

Obviously this program is a simple attempt at computerized letter writing, but it does provide you with a fairly easy-to-follow example. You are urged to prepare it for computer processing and try it out.

COMPUTERS AND THE ELECTORAL PROCESS

The standard voting medium for as long as this country has existed has been the paper ballot. Within recent years the voting machine has replaced the paper ballots, especially in the more heavily populated areas. Still more recently, computerized methods have replaced the others in some specially selected cities. When voting is computerized, the citizen usually designates his/her choice of candidate on a computer card, hence this method is most often called punched-card voting. The cards given to the voter have perforated spots on them which can be punched out easily with any device like a small nail or a special tool. Figure 6.1 shows what such a card might look like. Notice the dotted rectangles indicating perforations that must be punched out by the voter. When such ballots are used, upon closing a polling place the ballot cards are taken to a location where a computer capable of reading punched cards and properly programmed for the process stands ready to tabulate the votes.

Records indicate that for the United States elections of 1974, the various voting methods used are distributed as follows:

voting machines	60% of the polling places
paper ballots	20% of the polling places
punched-cards	10% of the polling places
other methods	10% of the polling places

It is interesting to note the significant percentage of places already using punched-card voting. In a talk given at a 1975 computer conference, David L. Dunbar stated that the use of punched-card voting is growing at a rate of 2 to 3 percent each year. Mr. Dunbar said further that as of October 1975 there were 150,000 punched-card vote recording machines in the United States. The "other methods" listed in the chart above include some experimental machines that serve as computer terminals.

```
            OFFICIAL BALLOT — District 5
                 November 2, 1976

                 Republican              Democrat

State Senator    [] Peter R. Bogs        [] John Q. Snort
(vote for one)

State Representative  [] Mary R. Dogood   [] James C. Doting
(vote for one)

County Commissioner   [] Josef Ball      [] Mark T. Downs
(vote for two)

                 [] John R. Nobody        [] Ellen P. Rose
```

FIGURE 6.1   Ballot for punched-card voting.

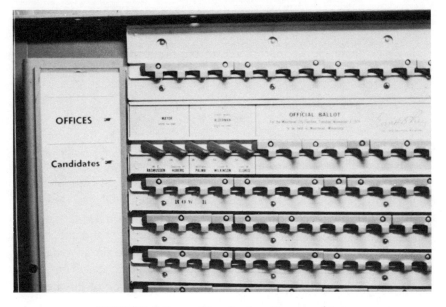

FIGURE 6.2   Standard voting machine.

That is, instead of having the voter punch a ballot card, then pass the card through a machine for tabulation, the voter presses certain keys on a device connected directly to a computer by way of telephone lines. Such voting terminals are definitely in the experimental stage yet, but with the ever-increasing use of point-of-sale (POS) terminals and electronic fund transfer terminals (see Chapter 5) in the business world, it would seem that voting terminals are not far in the future. After all, tabulating votes is a process not unlike tabulating items sold. Having studied POS terminals in Chapter 5, it should not be difficult to imagine how a system of voting terminals would function.

Some experts in the use of computers in voting believe that computer terminals intended for voting purposes should be designed to operate as much like presently used voting machines as possible. Voters are familiar with such machines, and evidence indicates that they represent good human engineering. It is certainly possible to design computer voting terminals that resemble voting machines with all their levers (see Figure 6.2). However, no manufacturer has yet developed such a machine. Computerized voting systems, other than those using punched cards, have thus far used standard computer terminals like those discussed in Chapter 3.

What are the advantages and disadvantages of a voting process involving computers? Before we consider the answer, maybe we should think about the question, "What is the goal of any electoral process?" It would seem that any response to the latter question would include statements like the following:

1. to determine the true will of the majority of the voters;

2. to obtain an accurate count of the number of voters favoring each candidate and issue;

3. tabulate votes as quickly as possible.

Undoubtedly other factors could be mentioned, but quite likely they could all be condensed into these phrases: accurate, fast tabulation used by many eligible voters. If these are the goals of a free election process, then computerization is certainly worth considering. Provided the voting medium (punched card or voting terminal) is familiar to voters and easy to use, computerization is apt to be accurate and widely used. The accuracy depends on how tamper-proof and understandable a method is, and either punched cards or voting-machine-like terminals can be made tamper-proof and understandable. Getting voters to actually vote is likely to be a problem unless they can do it from their homes. None of the methods yet discussed allow for that possibility, but at least punched-card ballots and voting terminals would not keep people *away* from the polls.

Very little needs to be said about the goal of fast tabulation because speed is one of the computer's greatest advantages. Assuming programs have been prepared to tabulate votes and print summary reports, once votes have been entered into the computer, results are almost instantly available. The punched-card process is slower than the terminal process because it takes time to physically pass cards through a card reader, while terminal-voting places data immediately in the computer.

Are there any disadvantages to computerizing the voting process? Certainly. There are probably many citizens who would hesitate to vote if they thought the procedure would be hard for them. Thus a carefully developed plan for informing voters about any new procedure would be required. Such an information campaign would cost money. Authorities would have to examine the costs and benefits associated with all proposed election systems and select the one deemed most desirable by all criteria.

If votes are cast on special terminals, it is necessary to create a traceable record of votes. Any such system would have to provide for a means of recount (that is, an audit trail must be created). The computer can easily be programmed to retabulate votes in a manner defined by the voting district. However, the conscientious citizen must be convinced that the authorities who make the decisions about the voting process have insisted on the inclusion of procedures that protect the voters' rights.

It is not at all clear that the old paper-ballot method guaranteed all the rights we thought it did. Very restrictive regulations for validating paper ballots have almost certainly prevented the will of the majority from being carried out in some past elections. Furthermore, recounts of paper ballots sometimes yield different results each time the recount is done, which must say something about the accuracy of paper ballots. The point is that if computerized voting is to be introduced, knowledgeable citizens must be involved in the development process to see that individual and societal rights are protected.

Computers and Election Results

Aside from the actual election process itself, computers are being used in the reporting of election results. Undoubtedly you have watched election returns on television; the rapidly changing numbers that appear on the screen indicating the current tabulation of votes correlated by computer. The broadcasting networks are doing what they consider the best possible job of reporting to the nation the returns from the day's election. People selected by the networks report to a central location (e.g., the television studio) the tabulations from each of the voting districts. These reports are keyed into a computer as quickly as they are received, and the computer is programmed to output summary reports of various kinds.

Perhaps more mysterious is the use of computers to project final results

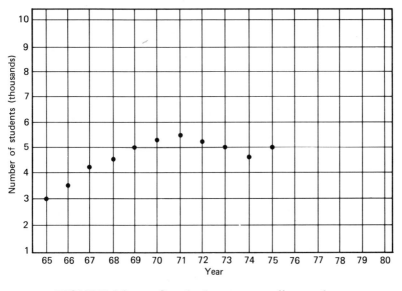

FIGURE 6.3   Graph showing enrollment data.

before all votes have been cast. How is that possible? Let's try to answer that question by considering some simple graphical data. Figure 6.3 is a graph of school enrollment. It shows that in 1965 the school to which these figures pertain had 3000 students. In 1966 there were about 3500 students, in 1967 about 4200, and so on. Now suppose that in 1975 school administrators wanted to estimate as accurately as possible the enrollment for 1976, 1977, 1978, 1979, and 1980. Using the information in the graph, how could they do this? One method might be to draw a straight line through the plotted points that, to the eye of the observer, comes closer to fitting all points plotted than any other straight line. The result might resemble Figure 6.4, where the dotted portion of the line represents the approximate enrollments for future years. As previously stated, the procedure for determining which line to draw was an "eyeballing" procedure and hence probably not very accurate in any mathematical sense. And yet, if no other information were available, one could look at Figure 6.4 and make a prediction about future enrollments which ought surely to be better than any figures generated by pure chance. For example, the line in Figure 6.4 shows that enrollment for 1980 would be about 8000 students. The dotted portion of the line is called a *projection* because it approximates data not yet available.

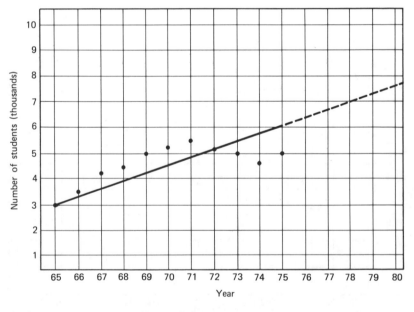

FIGURE 6.4   Enrollment data approximated by a straight line.

There are precise mathematical procedures for fitting straight lines and curves to any data available. Such procedures can be built into computer programs and relatively accurate projections obtained. Similarly, if more than two categories (such as years and numbers of students in Figure 6.4) of data are involved, mathematical procedures exist to fit a curve to those data in the "best" way (where "best" must be defined) so that projections can be made.

Let's reconsider how election results are projected. If the voting records of selected precincts are available and other factors that affect elections are known (e.g., unemployment rate, consumer price index, military problems), it is possible to use a computer to fit a curve to those data and project the total votes for a specific candidate knowing only the votes obtained in those selected precincts. The procedures are complex both from the viewpoint of mathematics and that of political science. But perhaps the example in Figure 6.4 removes some of the mystery associated with these kinds of projections.

LAW MAKING AND COMPUTERS

We turn now to the use of computers in the actual law-making process. Here, as in elections, the need is to obtain accurately and quickly a tabulation of the lawmakers' votes on the various bills they consider.

In the spring of 1973, the U.S. House of Representatives put into operation an automated voting system. Because individual terminals could not be provided for each member of congress, personalized vote-identification cards were provided for each representative. Then 44 (an arbitrary number) chairs in the House chamber were equipped with a vote card slot and buttons to indicate a person's vote (see Figure 6.5). When a vote is taken for a given bill, each member of congress wanting to vote must go to one of the 44 chairs and register his/her vote within the specified time period. Four display panels (see Figure 6.6) mounted over the press gallery show how each representative has voted. Beside each name is a small green light (vote of yea), a red light (nay), and an amber light (present but abstaining from the vote). Thus the press has knowledge of any vote cast as soon as it is registered. Also, two accumulating panels, mounted on the ledges of the east and west galleries, display the totals for the three kinds of votes (yea, nay, and present), an abbreviated identification of the bill being voted on, and the time remaining for congressmen to vote (see Figure 6.7). Because of this computerized voting, less time is wasted by House members in the voting process, and better information is available to everyone interested in the progress of House bills.

Several state legislatures have installed computerized systems that provide

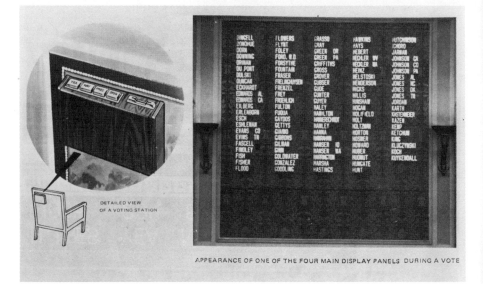

DETAILED VIEW OF A VOTING STATION

APPEARANCE OF ONE OF THE FOUR MAIN DISPLAY PANELS DURING A VOTE

FIGURE 6.5 House of Representatives voting station (courtesy House Administration Committee of the U.S. House of Representatives).

FIGURE 6.6 One of the voting display panels (courtesy House Administration Committee of the U.S. House of Representatives).

an almost continuous progress report on the status of bills. Typical of such systems is a daily report showing at a glance the step at which each law introduced in either house is currently being processed. The report includes a brief statement of the contents of each measure, as well as an estimate of when it will be reported out of committee onto the floor of the legislative chamber for action. The more sophisticated systems provide terminal access to the computer, so that legislators may obtain up-to-the-minute status reports at any time.

A few state legislatures have funded the development of computerized bill-drafting systems. Nebraska, for example, has used such a system since 1971. During the 1971 session 1226 bills were drafted, for an average of 10 minutes per bill. In previous sessions the average time had been 24 hours per bill. The system provides for the use of eight VDU terminals into which typists enter the text of each law, together with instructions for formatting it. The computer program then takes over to produce a copy of each bill in the format specified so as to make it as easy as possible to deal with all facets of the proposed law. Such systems undoubtedly save the lawmakers clerical time and may even result in better laws because all aspects of a measure can be dealt with easily.

FIGURE 6.7   House of Representatives voting accumulation panel (courtesy House Administration Committee of the U.S. House of Representatives).

COMPUTERS AND THE TAXPAYER

All United States taxpayers are aware that for some years now the Internal Revenue Service (IRS) has been building computer-readable files of income tax reports. Every IRS region has magnetic tape and disk files on all federal taxpayers in the region (Figure 6.8). Essential data from these files are transmitted to a computer system with massive storage capacity located in West Virginia (see Figure 6.9).

There, the data are processed by programs that check for errors in arithmetic and call attention to items in the return that deviate considerably from the norm. For example, if a tax return shows more than 10 percent of the gross income as itemized contributions, a printed message might appear that instructs a human being to examine the return more carefully. It may even call for a complete audit of the report by IRS agents. Similar responses may be given by the computerized system if the refund specified by the taxpayer is greater than some average amount, or if the number of dependents claimed is unusually large, or if the depreciation claimed by the taxpayer exceeds some average amount.

FIGURE 6.8   An IRS regional computer (courtesy IRS).

FIGURE 6.9   The National IRS Computer Center (Courtesy IRS).

Ideally, the honest taxpayer should benefit from a computerized tax reporting system because it has more ways of detecting fraudulent returns. As a practical result, more taxes are likely to be collected without increasing tax rates. You see, all employers are required to submit to the IRS reports of all salaries paid. All banks and savings institutions are required to report to the IRS any interest paid and to whom it was paid. All businesses and industries paying shareholders dividends are required to report to the IRS all such dividends paid and to whom they were paid. With all that information being provided to the IRS, every income tax return can now be checked by computer for errors. Whether errors of omission as far as reporting all income are deliberate or accidental can probably be known only by the individual taxpayer. But the knowledge that quick, accurate checks of our returns are now possible has the tendency to make us more honest.

COMPUTER SIMULATIONS AND ECONOMIC CONTROL

A major concern of every United States president and governmental leader has been with the country's economic condition. Special economic consultants are constantly available to advise the president and cabinet on economic measures that might be taken to control various aspects of the economy. One of the most useful tools available to today's economists is the computer simulation. You read something about simulations in Chapter 4. There you learned that a computer simulation is really a mathematical model of whatever is being simulated. Thus an economic model of the United States is a collection of many statistics and interrelationships expressed in a way that provides information about the actual economy. Of course, any economic system is complex, and it can be only partially understood. Therefore, a simulation of it can only include those aspects that people understand, hence, at its very best, it is faulty. Nevertheless computer simulations of local, regional, and national economics have greatly helped economists.

Here is a BASIC program of a greatly simplified computer simulation of the U.S. economy. This program was developed more as an aid to the understanding of various aspects of economics than it was to generate ideas for the control of the nation's economy. However, it has some value in helping achieve the latter goal as well. It is not intended that your level of programming knowledge will enable you to understand every aspect of the program, but much of it ought to be comprehensible to you. We include it here so that you can see an actual simulation, and if your interest is aroused, you can enter the program into a computer and run it.

```
1     DIM P(17,16),D(17),E(17),F(17)
2     PRINT "INSTRUCTIONS NEEDED? TYPE ZERO, ELSE 1."
3     INPUT A
4     IF A=0 THEN 7
5     GO TO 11
7     GOSUB 600
11    LET J=1
12    LET E(1)=0
13    FOR X = 1 TO 16
14    READ D(X)
15    NEXT X
16    DATA 128.2,128.4,129.3,129.6,130.2,130.2,131.3,131.4
17    DATA 131.7,131.9,132.6,133.0,137.0,141.0,144.2,146.3
20    FOR X=1 TO 16
22    READ F(X)
24    NEXT X
25    DATA 0, .002, .002, .009, .003, .005, .006, .011, .002
26    DATA .003, .002, .007, .004, .04,.04,.032
30    LET P(1,1)=1000
35    LET P(1,2)=154
40    LET P(1,3)=180
45    LET P(1,4)=-20
```

```
50     LET P(1,5)=.2
55     LET P(1,6)=665
60     LET P(1,7)=180
65     LET P(1,8)=26
70     LET P(1,9)=220
75     LET P(1,10)=80
80     LET P(1,11)=5.88
85     LET P(1,12)=6.03
90     LET P(1,13)=5
95     LET P(1,14)=48.2
100    LET P(1,15)=49.2
105    LET P(1,16)=1
110    LET U6=85
130    PRINT
140    PRINT "THE ORIGINAL TAX EQUATION IS T = −20 + .2 (GNP)"
150    PRINT
160    PRINT "ORIGINAL VALUES FOR THE SYSTEM ARE:"
163    PRINT
165    GOSUB 500
170    LET J=J+1
175    IF J>=17 THEN 990
180    PRINT
183    LET L=J−1
185    PRINT "INPUT DATA FOR QUARTER";L
190    PRINT "GOVERNMENT SPENDING";
195    INPUT P(J,2)
200    IF P(J,2) < 0 THEN 990
205    PRINT "MONEY SUPPLY";
210    INPUT P(J,9)
215    PRINT "AUTONOMOUS TAXES";
220    INPUT P(J,4)
225    PRINT "MARGINAL RATE OF TAXATION;"
230    INPUT P(J,5)
235    PRINT "IF ABOVE INFO IS CORRECT, TYPE A ONE,"
237    PRINT "ELSE TYPE ZERO."
240    INPUT A
245    IF A=0 THEN 180
250    REM GNP COMPUTATIONS
255    LET K=0
265    LET Y=.79 − .74*P(J,5)
```

```
266    LET M=L−1
267    IF M=0 THEN 270
268    LET M=1
270    LET G=P(J,2)−P(L,2)−.74*(P(J,4)−P(L,4) )
271    LET H=4*(P(L,13)−P(M,13) )
272    LET E(J)=G−H
275    LET E(J)=E(J)−F(L)
280    IF J=2 THEN 315
285    FOR Z=2 to L
290    LET Y1=J−Z
295    LET K=K+Y↑Y1*E(Z)
300    NEXT Z
305    LET P(J,1)=P(L,1)+K
310    GO TO 320
315    LET P(J,1)=P(L,1)+E(J)
320    REM TAX REVENUE COMPUTATIONS
325    LET P(J,3)=P(J,4)+P(J,5)*P(J,1)
330    REM CONSUMPTION COMPUTATIONS
335    LET P(J,6)=50+.75*(P(J,1)−P(J,3))
340    REM INVESTMENT COMPUTATIONS
345    LET P(J,7)=150+.05*P(J,1)−4*P(L,13)
350    REM SURPLUS COMPUTATIONS
355    LET P(J,8)=P(J,3)−P(J,2)
360    REM EMPLOYMENT COMPUTATIONS
370    LET P(J,10)=75+.0051*P(J,1)
375    REM EMPLOYMENT COMPUTATIONS
380    LET U6=U6+.05
385    LET P(J,11)=(U6−P(J,10))*(100/U6)
390    REM INFLATION COMPUTATIONS
395    (LET P(J,12)=3+16/P(J,11)+(.015−.001*(P(J,9)−P(L,9)))
400    REM INTEREST RATE COMPUTATIONS
405    LET P(J,13)=2−P(J,9)/10 + .025*P(J,1)
410    IF P(J,13)<9.5 THEN 420
415    LET P(J,13)=9.5
420    REM IMPORT COMPUTATIONS
425    LET P(J,14)=40+.01*(P(J,1)−P(J,3))
430    REM EXPORT COMPUTATIONS
435    LET X=0
440    FOR Z=1 TO L
445    LET X=X+.25*P(Z,12)
```

```
450   NEXT Z
455   LET P(J,15)=49.35-.01*(X+143-D(L))
460   REM BALANCE OF TRADE COMPUTATIONS
465   LET P(J,16)=P(J,15)-P(J,14)
470   GOSUB 500
475   GO TO 170
500   REM THIS IS THE ROUTINE FOR PRINTING
505   PRINT "GNP=";P(J,1)
510   PRINT "GOVT SPENDING=";P(J,2)
515   PRINT "TAX REVENUE=";P(J,3)
520   PRINT "AUTONOMOUS TAXES=";P(J,4)
530   PRINT "MARGINAL TAX RATE=";P(J,5)
535   PRINT "CONSUMPTION=";P(J,6)
540   PRINT "INVESTMENT=";P(J,7)
545   PRINT "SURPLUS=";P(J,8)
550   PRINT "MONEY SUPPLY=";P(J,9)
555   PRINT "EMPLOYMENT=";P(J,10)
560   PRINT "UNEMPLOYMENT RATE=";P(J,11)
565   PRINT "RATE OF INFLATION=";P(J,12)
570   PRINT "INTEREST RATE=";P(J,13)
575   PRINT "IMPORTS=";P(J,14)
580   PRINT "EXPORTS=";P(J,15)
585   PRINT "TRADE BALANCE=";P(J,16)
590   RETURN
600   REM THIS IS THE ROUTINE FOR PRINTING INSTRUCTIONS
605   PRINT
610   PRINT "THESE ARE THE INSTRUCTIONS."
611   PRINT "YOU ARE TO DIRECT THE ECONOMY"
612   PRINT "FOR SIXTEEN QUARTERS"
613   PRINT "USING THE FISCAL AND MONETARY"
614   PRINT "TOOLS OF THE FEDERAL"
615   PRINT "GOVERNMENT AND THE FEDERAL RESERVE SYSTEM."
618   PRINT "EACH QUARTER THE PROGRAM WILL REQUEST"
619   PRINT "THE NEW LEVELS"
620   PRINT "OF GOVERNMENT SPENDING,"
621   PRINT "THE MONEY SUPPLY, THE AUTONOMOUS"
622   PRINT "COMPONENT OF THE TAX EQUATION AND THE"
624   PRINT "MARGINAL RATE OF TAXATION. IN ADDITION, YOU"
625   PRINT "CAN CONTROL THE BALANCE"
628   PRINT "OF TRADE BY CONTROLLING INFLATION."
```

```
635   PRINT
640   PRINT "IF YOU SHOULD WISH TO STOP THE PROGRAM"
645   PRINT "SIMPLY INPUT A MINUS NUMBER"
646   PRINT "FOR GOVT SPENDING."
649   PRINT
650   RETURN
700   REM THIS IS THE ROUTINE TO PRINT ALL 16 QUARTERS
704   PRINT
705   PRINT "THESE ARE THE TOTALS FOR";L;"QUARTERS."
710   PRINT "QTR","GNP","GOVT","TAX REV","AUT TAX"
715   FOR X=2 TO J
720   PRINT X-1,P(X,1),P(X,2),P(X,3),P(X,4)
725   NEXT X
730   PRINT
735   PRINT "QTR","TAX RATE","CONS","INVEST","SURPLUS"
740   FOR X=2 TO J
745   PRINT X-1,P(X,5),P(X,6),P(X,7),P(X,8)
645   PRINT "SIMPLY INPUT A MINUS NUMBER"
646   PRINT "FOR GOVT SPENDING."
750   NEXT X
752   PRINT
755   PRINT "QTR","MONEY","EMPLY","UNEMP","INFLA"
760   FOR X = 2 to J
765   PRINT X-1,P(X,9),P(X,10),P(X,11),P(X,12)
768   NEXT X
769   PRINT
780   PRINT "QTR","INT RATE","IMPORT","EXPORT","BALANCE"
785   FOR X = 2 TO J
788   PRINT X-1,P(X,13),P(X,14),P(X,15),P(X,16)
789   NEXT X
790   RETURN
990   PRINT "IF A";L;"QUARTER TABLE"
991   PRINT "OF THE TOTALS IS DESIRED"
992   PRINT "TYPE IN A ONE IF NOT TYPE IN A ZERO."
995   INPUT A
997   IF A=0 THEN 999
998   GOSUB 700
999   END
```

An economic simulation makes possible the testing of certain proposed situations. For example, in the program just presented, if you wanted to find out what effects would be produced if the Federal Reserve Bank were to make more money available, you would only need to input the appropriate amount of money made available. When the program was run, this data would produce output indicating the effect of that move on all the other economic factors. A careful examination of those factors would help you decide if increasing the amount of money available is wise. The cost to society for learning the results would have been limited to the cost of the computer time required to execute the program. If the decision to increase amount of money available were made without using a simulation, the effects might be disastrous to the economy, and the decision, of course, is irreversible.

URBAN PROBLEMS AND COMPUTERS

Politicians, sociologists, economists, business people, and nearly all thinking members of society are concerned about the difficult problems facing urban areas, especially the very large cities. Problems such as unemployment, distribution of welfare funds, health care, businesses that exploit the citizens, and bankrupt businesses are demanding solutions. The computer has been helpful in finding solutions to some of these problems.

For example, an accurate record of all jobs available in an area and the skills required for those jobs, and an equally accurate list of all people looking for jobs together with their qualifications, have been incorporated into employment-related computer programs. In fact, not only have such computer programs been used in certain regions to help people find suitable jobs, but the United States Department of Labor is developing such a program on a nationwide basis. Now, with the large storage capacity of modern computers, it really is possible to have all jobs and all potential employees checked against each other for possible matching. The effects should be obvious. Provided people are willing and able to relocate, more of them should be able to find jobs to their liking.

Many states presently handle the distribution of welfare funds by computer. With the increasing number of old people needing assistance and the growing number of mothers left with dependent children, the total number of people needing welfare aid has reached the point where some machine assistance is absolutely essential. Without it, welfare workers would be busy all of the time with the clerical work associated with the disbursement of funds. By using well-designed computer programs, the welfare worker need only provide certain basic facts, such as amount of income, number of people in the family and their ages, and health conditions of the family, and the computer program will calculate the appropriate amount of welfare to be granted. The computer is also often used to actually print the checks in a form ready for distribution, whether by mail or in person.

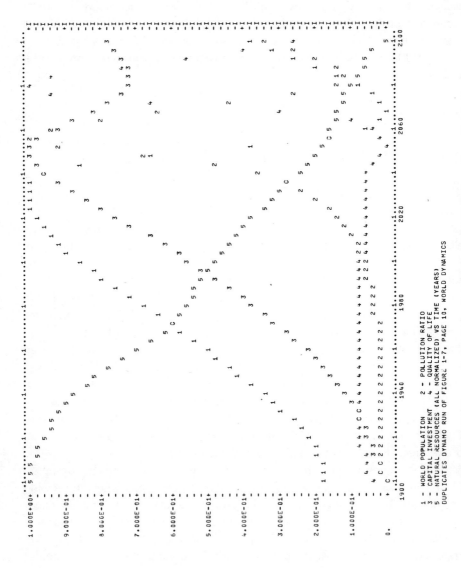

1 – WORLD POPULATION   2 – POLLUTION RATIO
3 – CAPITAL INVESTMENT   4 – QUALITY OF LIFE
5 – NATURAL RESOURCES (ALL NORMALIZED) VS TIME (YEARS)
DUPLICATES DYNAMO RUN OF FIGURE 1-7, PAGE 10, WORLD DYNAMICS

FIGURE 6.10   Sample output from World Dynamics simulation.

166

Some people seem to think the use of a computer to determine amounts of welfare aid is a cold and unfeeling way to handle people in need. The truth is that by relegating such tasks to machines, social workers have more time to deal with the personal needs of their clients, needs that could never be handled by computers. Furthermore, the guidelines used by the computer program to determine the amount of welfare aid for a given person have been specified by the social workers. All the computer does is to print results based on data and processing instructions.

One of the most recent uses of computers related to solving urban problems is in the simulation of as many aspects of an urban area as possible. That is, economic conditions, housing conditions, health conditions, employment data, and any other quantifiable aspects of urban society are built into the simulation. When the computer simulation can provide a reasonable representation of reality, data related to a specific aspect of society can be modified and the effects studied by executing the computer simulation several times, each time with different input data. The output from these computer runs would probably reveal actions that could alleviate some of society's problems.

Computer simulations are also being used to study ecological systems. Many social and natural scientists are studying the interaction between humans and their creations and nature. One of their goals is to discover how human beings can modify their behavior within acceptable limits so they can live happy and comfortable lives without destroying the beauty and natural resources around them. Some computer simulations of the environment have become famous because of the doomsday predictions they have produced. Among such simulations is the so-called Club of Rome simulation, which is based on concepts presented by Jay Forrester in his book *World Dynamics*. This simulation considers human population growth, food production, use of natural resources, industrialization, and many other activities that affect humanity's ability to survive on the earth (see Figure 6.10). Among other conclusions reached with this particular simulation is that humanity cannot survive much beyond the year 2000. Such startling discoveries do indeed generate wide attention. Not all experts agree with the assumptions inherent in the Club-of-Rome model but its results cannot be ignored. Society must recognize that many natural resources *are* being depleted and begin to take strong corrective measures. Perhaps computer simulations can help.

SOME THINGS TO THINK ABOUT

In this chapter, we have seen some of the beneficial applications of computers in politics and government, but we must also discuss some potential problems. One problem is the matter of a right to privacy. With an ever-increasing number of governmental agencies effectively using computerized data files, the possibility of consolidating the various files becomes a matter of concern. Did you know that the U.S. Department of Health, Education and Welfare (HEW) alone has set up over 3000 different data files on people! Apparently, all these files are needed for the many functions carried on by HEW. But this is just one governmental agency. The Justice Department, the Treasury Department, the Department of the Interior, the Department of Agriculture, and many agencies also utilize computerized data files. The possibility of linking all government files poses a serious threat to the citizen's right to privacy.

How could such files be consolidated? If, whenever a file were established for a given person, the same identifying data element were always used for records associated with the person, then a computer program could easily be written to search all files for records containing that identifying data element. For example, almost every time we are asked to provide information to a governmental agency, our social security number must be given. That number, unique to each person, could be the identifying data element. A data element used as an identifier for many different files is called a *universal identifier.*

Congress has recognized this problem of privacy and has passed a law forbidding the use of one's social security number as a file identifier except by a very few governmental agencies. This law has not stopped the practice, however. A special HEW committee has recommended that a law should not only forbid the use of social security numbers as file identifiers, but it should also require that every file kept on a given person have a different identifier. Furthermore, the committee has recommended that the person on whom data are stored be notified about the fact, and be told the file identifier. Thus only the individual would know the identifiers for all files kept on him/her. The problem of keeping a dictionary of all file identifiers for all citizens has also been addressed. Reason tells us that there are critical situations where the citizen might be physically unable to provide a file identifier. At such times it might be a matter of life or death to obtain the identifier for a given file (maybe a health records file). It has been recommended that a computerized dictionary of all file identifiers for U.S. citizens be kept in a computer outside the jurisdiction of any U.S. government. That would make it possible to obtain a specific file identifier in a critical situation, but it would prevent any governmental agency from having access to *all* file identifiers. As you know, if such a dictionary were kept within the United States or any of its territories, a subpoena could be issued by a court of law to make the dictionary available. This sounds like we trust foreign governments more than our own. That is not true. Nevertheless, enough facts about several governmental agencies have come to light the past few years to make the suggestion a reasonable one. In any case, the matter of keeping computerized records private ought to be of real concern to everyone.

Reassuring to Americans concerned about the right to privacy of certain information is the fact that the Congress passed the Criminal Justice Information Control and Protection of Privacy Act of 1974. Enlightening information about some actual and potential misuses of computerized files are detailed in the record of the hearings held by the Judiciary Committee before that legislation was passed. (The record of these hearings is available from the U.S. Government Printing Office as documents 31-999 and 34-788 0.) In his statement opening these hearings, Senator Sam Ervin related a case in which a man was arrested and fingerprinted but later found to be innocent. By state laws, the local record had to be expunged. However, the fingerprints had been sent on to the FBI, and when the defendant requested that that record also be cleared, he was told that only the reporting police department could make such a request. Since the police department refused to do so, the man's fingerprints were on record with the FBI although he was innocent of any crime. Until the 1974 law was passed, the private citizen had no recourse in such a situation.

Another incident reviewed by Senator Ervin was one in which a service station operator was charged with maintaining an illegal gambling operation. It was later determined that one of his employees was the guilty person, running a numbers game without the knowledge of the service station operator. However, when the innocent operator asked that his arrest record be removed from the computer files, he was told (after considerable investigation) that if he paid a fee of $750 the record could be cleared. How unjust could matters be? The innocent man had to pay to have the record on himself cleared! Fortunately, the Privacy Act of 1974 has corrected that inequity.

But as Senator Ervin said, "It is not enough that we rely simply on assurances that these intelligence and investigative reports will not be abused. The time is long since passed for that. Before we permit computerization of these data, we must require rules to protect privacy at least as sophisticated as the ones we now propose for record information."

Just because legislation has been enacted that provides some protection of the individual's right to privacy is not enough to permit relaxation. Concerned citizens must constantly keep informed on this matter and take appropriate action to see that no further encroachments are made on individual privacy.

Citizens must also be concerned about the development of computerized systems that they are forced to use. For example, many things about Electronic Funds Transfer (EFT) systems are good, but not everything. As such systems are presently designed, once a customer makes a purchase, funds are transferred immediately from the customer's account to the seller's account. What if a customer later finds out that he/she had been swindled? The EFT has no feature comparable to the "stop payment" feature of checking accounts. Such a feature *could* easily be incorporated into any EFT system, but since they have been primarily designed without consumer input, features intended to preserve consumer rights are not always present. The old saying "the price of freedom is eternal vigilance" was never more true than today.

One last thought-provoking fact is related to the possibility of a computer terminal in every home. That possibility is the result of a federal law which requires that by 1977, every cable television system must be capable of two-way communication. This means that every customer of cable television, if he/she has an appropriate terminal, will be able to *send* information as well as receive it. Such a capability opens up a world of possibilities. Consumer surveys could be taken and people could respond right from their homes. Merchants could display their merchandise on television and customers could send in their orders from their homes. Whole new concepts of education would be possible. The potential for both good and evil of such a development are almost limitless. You are urged to keep abreast of developments, and make your feelings about them known to proper authorities.

EXERCISES

6.1 List at least three ways in which computers have been used in political campaigns.

6.2 Prepare Program 6.1 for entry to a computer, and provide your own data at lines 52 through 58. You will need to know the following codes:

Support code:
1 = supported candidate in previous election
2 = did not support in previous election
Occupation code:
1 = student   3 = wage-earner
2 = farmer   4 = professional
Liberal/conservative code:
1 = liberal   2 = conservative

6.3 Identify some problems that arise with each of these voting procedures: (1) paper ballots, (2) voting machines, and (3) punched-card voting.

6.4 Describe methods of computerized voting other than punched-card voting.

6.5 List some advantages and disadvantages of computerized tabulation and early reporting of election results.

6.6 Describe the process of projecting election results before actual results are known.

6.7 List at least three applications of computers to the law-making process.

6.8 List some advantages and disadvantages to the individual taxpayer of the use of computer files and information processing by the Internal Revenue Service.

6.9 Of what value are computer simulations of an economic system?

6.10 Describe your feelings about the use of computers in administering welfare programs.

6.11 List advantages and disadvantages of a national computerized employment service.

6.12 What are some problems associated with computer simulations for studying urban situations and ecological systems?

6.13 List advantages and disadvantages of making all computer data files maintained by the U.S. government accessible to a single governmental agency.

6.14 What is a universal identifier?

6.15 List some potential benefits and dangers of having computer access from every home in the nation.

SELECTED REFERENCES

BOOKS

Bushkin, Arthur A. and Samuel I. Shaen, *The Privacy Act of 1974: A Reference Manual for Compliance*, System Development Corporation, McLean, Va., 1976.

deSola Pool, Ithiel, Robert P. Abelson, and Samuel L. Popkin, *Candidates, Issues, and Strategies: A Computer Simulation of the 1960 Presidential Election*, M.I.T. Press, Cambridge, 1964.

Forrester, Jay, *World Dynamics*, Wright-Allen Press, Cambridge, 1971.

Freiberger, W.F. and W. Prager, *Applications of Digital Computers*, Ginn and Company, Boston, 1963.

Greenberger, Martin, *Computers, Communications, and the Public Interest*, Johns Hopkins Press, Baltimore, 1971.

Katzan, Harry, *Information Technology: The Human Use of Computers*, Petrocelli Books, New York, 1974.

Martin, James and Adrian R. D. Norman, *The Computerized Society*, Prentice-Hall, Englewood Cliffs, N.J., 1970.

Michael, D.S.N *Cybernation: The Silent Conquest,* The Center for the Study of Democratic Institutions, Santa Barbara, Calif., 1962.

Oettinger, Anthony G. and Selma Marks, *Run, Computer, Run,* Harvard University Press, Cambridge, 1969.

Rothman, Stanley and Charles Mosmann, *Computers and Society,* Science Research Associates, Chicago, 1972.

U.S. Dept. of H.E.W., *Records, Computers, and the Rights of Citizens,* U.S. Gov't Printing Office, Washington, D.C., 1973.

U.S. Senate Committee on the Judiciary, *Hearings Before the Subcommittee on Constitutional Rights, Volumes I and II,* U.S. Gov't Printing Office, Washington, D.C., 1974.

U.S. Senate Committee on the Judiciary, *Hearings Before the Subcommittee on Constitutional Rights,* #56-833 0, U.S. Gov't Printing Office, Washington, D.C., 1975.

PERIODICALS

Anonymous, "Computer Chase in New Welfare Plan," *U.S. News & World Report,* September 1, 1975.

Anonymous, "Governing the Computer Industry," *Computer Decisions,* September 1974.

Anonymous, "NBS Privacy Conference," *Computer Decisions,* June 1975.

Anonymous, "News Scene," *Datamation,* August 15, 1971.

Armer, Paul, "Computer Technology and Surveillance," *Computers and People,* September 1975.

Armer, Paul, "The Individual: His Privacy, Self Image, and Obsolescence," *Computers and People,* June 1975.

Associated Press, "Federal Data Banks Get Criticism on Two Fronts," *The Fargo Forum,* June 5, 1975.

Bemer, Robert W., "The Frictional Interface Between Computers and Society," *Computers and People,* January 1975.

Berkeley, Edmund C., "Networking," *Computers and People,* July 1974.

Berkeley, Edmund C., "The Almost Invisible Mountain," *Computers and People,* September 1974.

Drattell, Alan, "Electronic Voting System in Operation at House of Representatives," *Modern Data,* June 1973.

Elson, B.M., "Computer's Electronic War Role Growing," *Aviation Weekly,* March 3, 1975.

Farmer, James, "Computer Voting: Many Happy Returns." *Computer Decisions,* November 1974.

Farney, Dennis, "Machine Politics 1975," *Readers Digest,* January 1975.

Flato, Linda, "A Rose Among Thorns," *Computer Decisions,* June 1976.

Goodman, Glenn, "Information Systems for Better State Governments," *The Office,* January 1975.

Hurtado, Corydon D., "Automation Planning In Government," *Computer Decisions,* March 1975.

Kelly, Janice, "The Dossiers of American Citizens," *Computers and People,* March 1975.

Land, Thomas, "Sweden on Privacy," *Computers and People,* November 1974.

Mueller, George E., "Federal Government Data Processing: Considerations of Policy," *Computers and People,* September 1975.

Napier, Edward D., "Recommendations on Social and Political Issues," *Computers and People,* August 1975.

Pauly, D. and R. Thomas, "Through a Computer Darkly," *Newsweek,* February 24, 1975.

Price, Dennis G., "Automation in State and Local Government," *Datamation,* March 1967.

Royko, Mike, "It is Remarkable How Protective People Are About Their Own Privacy," *Chicago Daily News Service,* April 2, 1975.

Saltman, Roy G., "Guidelines for Reliable Use of Computers in Vote Tallying," *Report No. NSBIR 75-687, National Bureau of Standards,* Spring 1975.

Snow, C. P., "Science and the Advanced Society," *Computers and People,* April 1975.

Stanford Research Institute, "Automating the Monotonous Jobs," *Computers and People,* July 1974.

Sterling, Theodore D., "Information and Public Policy," panel discussion, *Proceedings of the Annual Conference, ACM '75,* October 1975.

Tomeski, Edward A., "Job Enrichment and the Computer: A Neglected Subject," *Computers and People,* November 1974.

Van Tassel, Dennie, "Daily Surveillance Sheet, 1987, from a Nationwide Data Bank," *Computers and People,* August 1975.

7 COMPUTERS AND CRIME

Of all the systems at work in any country, the one that every law-abiding citizen hopes works well even if all others start faltering is the criminal justice system. No one wants to be unjustly jailed or penalized, especially if such unjust treatment is the result of a breakdown in the system. It is very important, then, to know something about how information processing machines are being used by this far-reaching force in our society.

LAW ENFORCEMENT COMPUTER NETWORKS

It is understandable that if police departments are to effectively deal with violators of the law, accurate information must be available, and within as short a time period as possible. This implies the creation and utilization of computerized data files. Perhaps the most widely known of such operations is the FBI's National Crime Information Center (NCIC). This branch of the FBI began as a pilot project in January 1967 in cooperation with 16 law enforcement agencies throughout the United States. Figure 7.1 shows the computer center of the NCIC.

The NCIC was intended to be a means of recording wanted persons, stolen property, and criminal events in a way that would be most helpful to law enforcement personnel who needed such information. Participating law enforcement agencies, identified in the system by a seven-character code, enter into the computer's memory records on people, property, or events, using standard formats and abbreviations. Only the originating agency can change or delete a record. At the present time Alaska is the only state not tied into the network. Canada is also a cooperating partner in the venture.

In addition to the FBI's network, there is the Law Enforcement Assistance Administration's National Law Enforcement Teletype Network. The Law Enforce-

FIGURE 7.1   Computer center for the NCIC (courtesy FBI).

FIGURE 7.2   A local teletype connected to the NCIC teletype network (courtesy Law Enforcement Center, Moorhead, Minnesota).

176

FIGURE 7.3   Exterior of the Department of Justice data center (courtesy Department of Justice Photo Lab).

FIGURE 7.4   Computer Center, State of Minnesota Information Systems Division (courtesy ISD, State of Minnesota).

ment Assistance Administration (LEAA) was established under the federal government's Safe Streets Act of 1968 to administer funds allocated to the safe streets project. The Teletype Network is essentially a means whereby local law enforcement agencies can access a computerized central index of criminals and information on which police department has the complete record on each criminal. Then, via Teletype, the copy of the complete criminal history can be obtained (see Figures 7.2 and 7.3).

Besides these two *national* criminal data files, most states maintain their own State Police Department computerized files in which the actual criminal histories are usually kept. In some of the larger cities, city police records are also computerized. In many states, these criminal records are connected to the states' departments of motor vehicle registration records, and to the states' justice departments. Thus in most states there are at least five computerized data files on which data about a given citizen might be found.

How does a person's record get placed on one of these computerized files? Typically, if a citizen is arrested for any reason his/her record becomes part of the local arrest record and is accessible by any other part of the criminal justice computer networks tied to the local files. Of course, owning a motor vehicle or a driver's license will place your name in the motor vehicle department's file, and participation in any court action will get your record into the files of the state justice department (see Figure 7.4).

As you see, it is not very difficult for anyone to become a part of these computerized files. For all of that, there is nothing alarming about what has been said so far. In fact, it's rather reassuring to know that criminal records can be made immediately available to a law enforcement agency so that known criminals can be identified more accurately and in a shorter time. Furthermore, the ready availability of such data ought to make it possible to free an innocent suspect when correct information shows he/she could not possibly have been involved in the crime for which he/she was apprehended. However, the potential good of a system and the actual use made of it are two different things.

Faulty Maintenance of Criminal Records

One of the most difficult problems of any file is of keeping data in it current. This is especially true of computerized files because most of them contain so very many records. Often when computer files are created, too little thought and planning have gone into policies and procedures for updating the data in them. The emphasis has been on developing systems that result in faster and better procedures for apprehending criminals. The goal of many is an efficient system and that goal cannot be faulted. But efficiency at the expense of freedom? Fortunately, there are a number of law enforcement officials like Dr. Robert Gallati who heads the New York State Intelligence and Information System. When testifying before the Senate's Judiciary Committee in 1971 (at which time it was investigating data banks and the need for them), Dr. Gallati made the following statement:

> *The basic question is whether information processed and disseminated by data banks is reasonably related to advancing the general welfare of society. The maintenance of a free society is more important than any other argument for efficiency.*

The thoughtful reader will applaud Dr. Gallati's position. A very controversial issue before the American people at the present time is the matter of what extent personal files ought to be purged of information that is no longer relevant. And perhaps of more concern than irrelevant data is the fact that many criminal justice files do not contain the disposition of an arrest. That is, an arrest automatically gets a citizen's records into the data bank, but an acquittal does not necessarily get entered into the records. For example, suppose a person is charged with murder but the courts conclude that the act was a justifiable homicide committed in self-defense. The presence of the arrest record in the data bank could be very damaging to the person's reputation, whereas if the conclusion of the case were also there, the harm would be eliminated.

Law enforcement officials do not need to accept the full blame for the situation. Legislative bodies have often not provided enough funds to satisfactorily handle the whole job of maintaining the information systems that their laws so hastily create. Citizens react unfavorably to tax increases that will pay for staffing well-run information systems. All of us need to keep ourselves informed so that we will not sacrifice our freedom at the altar of low cost and efficiency.

There is no intention in this section to give the impression that criminal justice information systems should be eliminated. On the contrary, they are probably the only hope our society has for coping with the growing number of criminals. Probably only a national network of electronic machines powered by computers will make it possible for officials to apprehend real criminals. Our concern is that innocent citizens not be hurt in the process.

Juvenile Information Systems

In every society, those people especially vulnerable to the improper use of data banks are juveniles. Of course, a number of juvenile offenders deserve all the rigidity that access to a computerized data file makes possible. And society is far better off because of it. But there are young people whose records get placed in data banks who have done no more than run away from intolerable home situations, or stayed away from school, or refused to obey their parents. Whether or not you would say that such juveniles are right in what they do is not the point. What *is* pertinent is, "are they delinquents?" Probably not. Yet having their records in criminal justice files, with the implication that they are delinquents, would seem to be a real threat to their individual rights. Any record in the data bank is accessible (through a teletype at the police station) to any police officer, and such past records might only serve to prejudice the officer against the juvenile. The danger was pointed out by Dorothy Ellenberg, who led the fight to keep a Juvenile Information System out of Santa Clara County, California:

> *To give them (police officers) records, and place their (juveniles) names in the computer files would be tantamount to labelling them as anti-social kids, when their problems may not be of their own doing. We thought that was an inappropriate use of data, (and) that the disposition of the police officer should be based on information about the present situation, not on data from the past.*

As another member (Carol Guddal) of that Santa Clara group put it, "I never realized how profoundly a computer system can influence a community. They are not toys."

COMPUTERS AND THE COURTS

The two most vital components of the criminal justice system are the prosecution and the courts. Both depend on having accurate information available in a reasonably short time. We have already considered some of the benefits of computerized data files associated with the arrest of a criminal. For the prosecutor, a computerized case history file would be a real asset. Such a file would make it possible to more accurately match various aspects of the case with the defendant's criminal record. If it included data about court proceedings relative to the case (such as motions made, results of motions, trial dates, and arresting officer) and was readily available to the prosecutor (accessible by a terminal in his/her office), such a file could speed up greatly the handling of cases.

Regarding the benefits to the courts, it should first be stated that courts are often way behind in their trial schedules. An accused citizen who is unable to pay for bail must often stay locked up in jail for months before his/her case comes up for trial. One reason for this delay is the fact that a number of administrative details must be taken care of before a trial can begin. Using computers to schedule attorneys, provide files on the defendants, including data to help the judge determine which type of corrections program is likely to be most effective, provide an accurate record of current criminal cases in the court system, and select juries would greatly ease the burden on our courts. These applications of computers to the judicial process are only modifications of the administrative functions done by computers for management in business, but the courts are less willing to apply them to their situation. The time seems to have come when something like using computers is the only hope for making court procedures more efficient and making justice available in a more reasonable time.

COMPUTERS AND EMERGENCY CALLS FOR LOCAL POLICE

Probably the greatest drain on the time of local police officers is the emergency calls they get, the so-called "911 situations." That name comes from the fact that in more than 200 cities across the United States, the telephone number for police emergency calls is 911. Many of the larger cities have installed computer systems properly programmed to assist the police force in more effectively providing help where it is really needed (see Figure 7.5).

     Among the features of such a system are the following: (1) the names and locations of all the streets in the city; (2) all valid addresses; (3) the names of all schools, parks, buildings, and any other geographical features that might pinpoint the source of a call; and (4) the capability of detecting the telephone exchange from which the call originated (e.g., in New York City whether the call originated in Brooklyn or Manhattan).

     Suppose a 911 call comes in. Before the caller talks to anyone, the computer has determined that the phone is located in Brooklyn and switches the call to the Brooklyn emergency room. If phones there are busy, the computer switches the call to the emergency room of the police station close to Brooklyn, probably Queens. When the police operator answers, the caller may report gun shots heard at 809 West 59th Street in Brooklyn. The operator, who is seated by a computer terminal, keys this address into the terminal and immediately the response comes back from the computer that no such address exists. If the caller is still on the line, the operator might ask more questions to try to determine where the shots were fired. (Is there a factory or school nearby? Are you in an apartment building?) If, with the computer's help, the right address is determined, the operator would likely hit the hotline button to tell the police dispatcher about the call. Depending on what things are already going on, the dispatcher might give the gun shots at 829 West 59th Street top priority and get police officers to the scene as soon as possible.

FIGURE 7.5 Computer for New York City's Police Department (courtesy New York City Police Department).

If the operator could only get a name like Roosevelt as the address without any information as to whether it was a street, a park, or whatever, he/she could key information into the terminal asking the computer to provide any geographical objects with the name Roosevelt. Then, based on any other information given by the caller, a plausible location for the trouble might be determined.

The computer also keeps a record of the disposition of the calls received so that the dispatcher, who also sits by a computer terminal, can ask for a showing of calls handled during the previous hour in case some should be checked again.

This system has proved so effective that more and more cities are installing it. The states of New York and California have required that all major cities have such systems installed by specified dates.

COMPUTERS AND THE FBI

You have already read something about the Federal Bureau of Investigation (FBI) and its use of computers in the section on data files. Recall that the FBI began using its National Crime Information Center (NCIC) in 1967. By 1970 over 2000 law enforcement agencies were accessing the NCIC through state or local terminals. The NCIC was designed to be a record index on wanted persons, stolen property, and criminal events. By the end of the third year of operation 1,737,000 records were stored in the NCIC. Here is a table showing their distribution:

INFORMATION	NUMBER RECORDS	PERCENT
Boats	887	.05
Wanted persons	51,437	2.95
License plates	155,419	8.93
Guns	264,613	15.21
Vehicles	407,333	23.42
Securities	519,888	29.91
Other Articles	338,239	19.53

As you can see, objects rather than people occupied the giant share of the file. The NCIC has been directly responsible for the recovery of millions of dollars worth of stolen goods every year. It is difficult to place a dollar value on other benefits of the system. Benefits such as the saving of police officer's lives because of forewarning by information from the NCIC, improved rates of case solution, reduced investigation time, and prevention of crimes because professional criminals are apprehended and locked up, all help to improve the quality of life in our society.

Laboratory Applications by the FBI

A number of systems of computer-aided identification are used by the FBI. For example, if a gun is recovered, its various identifying characteristics are entered into a computer where sales records of all gun manufacturers are stored and the computer can tell quickly where it was sold. Or if an anonymous, typewritten letter is involved in an investigation, its characteristics are keyed into a computer. Previously stored in the computer is information provided by various typewriter manufacturers. By comparing characteristics it is often possible to determine the make and model typewriter used to type the letter, and eventually the specific typewriter itself can be located.

Another operation of the FBI is its PROCHECK program, a computerized file of information on professioanl bad-check passers. If any bad check case appears to be the work of a professional criminal, PROCHECK is called into use. Various aspects of the fraudulent check (such as writing style, unusual check-cashing procedures, or use of stolen blank checks) are given to a computer for

FIGURE 7.6   Computerized spectrophotometer.

comparison with modus operandis of known professional bad-check artists, which it has in its memory. In a matter of minutes, the computer provides a list of suspects from its files, and a laboratory expert can compare the fraudulent checks with samples of the work of those on the list.

Chemists have for some time used computers to compare the spectrophotometer charts of unknown substances with the charts of known substances, thus making it possible to identify the unknown substance. The FBI also makes extensive use of this procedure. Obviously, the computerized comparison of spectrophotometric charts is much faster than any other method. Figure 7.6 shows a computerized spectrophotometer.

Still another laboratory procedure utilizing computers includes the use of radioactive materials. The unknown material is subjected to high-intensity radiation after which it emits gamma rays. These emitted gamma rays are analyzed by a special device that feeds its measurements to a computer. Special programs in the computer check for the presence of certain features that will identify the composition of the unknown materials (see Figure 7.7).

Other Applications by the FBI

The FBI gets involved in almost every court case in which the U.S. government is a party. Consequently, the kinds of investigations it carries out are widely varied. For example, the FBI might investigate if a government contractor's bill exceeds the

FIGURE 7.7   Multichannel analyzer.

amount specified in the contract. Often such charges are legitimate because the governmental agency requested changes from the original specifications, but sometimes contractors deliberately try to defraud the government. At times, the FBI must use computers because interrelated companies can make such investigations very complex. That is, many large companies are either subsidiaries of some giant corporation or are such that a large share of the ownership can be traced back to some parent company. All such arrangements are, of course, legal, but difficult to discover. Why would the government be concerned? It would probably not be at all concerned if contracts were completed without resulting in overcharges. But far too often, firms which obtain government contracts are able to prepare what seem to be justifiable reasons for the overcharge; for example, a contractor may report that a subcontractor charged much more than could have been anticipated. Upon further investigation it is discovered that the subcontractor is owned by the firm that holds the contract, hence, the overcharge is questionable to say the least. The corporate intricacies are sometimes so carefully intertwined that only the searching of data by computer is able to reveal the truth. FBI computer investigations of this kind have saved millions of dollars of government funds.

The FBI is also called on to help government investigators prepare legal defenses against civil suits. As an example, there is on record a case in which the U.S. government was sued for damages caused to crops by a herbicide sprayed by planes hired by a government agency. The agency admitted liability but questioned the amounts of damages requested by some of the plaintiffs. In order to prove its point, the government had to analyze 300,000 sales invoices related to crops grown on 20 different farms over a period of five years. It was estimated that 100 trained people would have had to work full time for 30 days to do that analysis. Not only were there not 100 people available but there were less than 30 days to the trial. FBI computer experts were called in and were able to analyze the data in time to provide accurate information well before the trial to the U.S. attorney handling the case. During the trial some reanalysis was required but this was easily done using the program prepared before the trial. The entire investigation saved the government about $1,500,000.

FBI computers are often used to analyze checking accounts of several banks to try to uncover cases where worthless checks have been used to create checking accounts on which other checks have been drawn to open an account in yet another bank, and so on. Special computer programs can quickly search through the records of checking accounts and detect such illegal use of a bank's money.

COMPUTERS, THE CIA, AND THE IRS

As you read in Chapter 6, the Internal Revenue Service (IRS) maintains large files of data which it uses to report tax collections and make sure that the U.S. government gets its legal share of the citizens' money. Tax returns are sent to one of seven regional offices where information from them is transcribed to magnetic tapes. Computers at the regional offices check the returns for mathematical accuracy, issue bills and delinquency notices, select the returns to be audited, and prepare notices to taxpayers when adjustments are due. The data needed to update taxpayers' accounts are transmitted to the IRS National Computer Center at Martinsburg, West Virginia. Master tax files on every citizen who ever paid taxes are kept there. Besides keeping properly updated master files at Martinsburg, other computerized functions there include the preparation of data for collecting delinquent taxes, the preparation of refund information, the production of notices to taxpayers who have understated their income (by not including certain dividends, interest, royalties, etc.), and the generation of a directory of taxpayers.

Although the record of the IRS in its use of computerized files is, in general, good, recent investigations have brought to light some unfortunate activities. For example, it was discovered that from 1969 to 1973 a special branch within the IRS had compiled files on over 11,000 politically active individuals and organizations. The files were allegedly prepared in such a way as to give the impression that these individuals and groups were somehow likely to violate tax statutes or other laws.

These special files were compiled by using computers to compare the IRS master index of taxpayers against a computerized file of individuals considered civil disobedients maintained by the Justice Department. By selecting the tax returns of those people on the civil disobedience file and performing audits on them annually, the IRS actually harassed private citizens. As you can imagine, Congressional committees are agreeing with Senator Sam Ervin when he said "such tactics are a serious misuse of the tax power."

Another illegal use of IRS files was exposed in February 1975. In 1969 an operation within IRS called the Intelligence Gathering and Retrieval System (IGRS) began gathering information on citizens' sex lives, drinking habits, and political leanings. The IGRS justified this action by saying that such data were needed to identify potential tax violators. By January 1975, the names of more than 465,000 individuals and firms were stored in this special IRS file. Needless to say, such IRS misuse of computerized information has been stopped for now. But it is wise to recognize that as long as such vast amounts of information are available in easy-to-retrieve form, the probability of something similar happening again is rather high. Citizens must be constantly alert to the possibility of illegal use of computerized files by governmental agencies.

The CIA and Computer Files

The Central Intelligence Agency (CIA) is an investigative branch of the U.S. government created by the Security Act of 1947. Its director is appointed by the President and approved by the Senate. The Director of the CIA reports to the National Security Council consisting of the President, Vice President, Secretary of State, and Secretary of Defense. The CIA maintains a computer department but little is ever said about it publicly, as is the case with most CIA activities.

During congressional investigations held during 1974 and 1975, it was discovered that a magnetic tape file prepared by the Justice Department on 12,000 political agitators had been turned over to the CIA. The tape contained identifying information, aliases, and any FBI records on the individuals. The group within the Justice Department that prepared this tape for the CIA was deactivated in September 1974. The fact that the CIA uses computers is not disturbing. It is the *misuse* of computerized data that must be prevented.

COMPUTER-RELATED CRIMES

In this section we discuss the new kinds of crime possible with the current widespread use of computers. Especially tempting to criminals is Electronic Funds Transfer. The large amounts of "money" available in EFT may tempt a computer expert to devise a scheme for electronic robbery. Although EFT is not yet widely used, there have already been convictions of people who have discovered methods of accessing computer files and electronically transferring funds from others' accounts to their own. Such electronic thefts usually involve large sums because the opportunity is there to transfer such amounts. Of course, a shrewd criminal will not be so obvious as to transfer, say $10,000 from another account to his/her own. But by writing a computer program to transfer $50 from each of 200 accounts, the same goal is achieved! Furthermore, the possibility of discovering the latter situation is much less than that of finding out about the $10,000 transfer.

Electronic thefts like the one just mentioned do not require that the potential robber be an employee of a bank having access to the bank's computer equipment. Just having access to the kind of terminal EFT makes available to all customers is all that some people need to be able to carry on their criminal activities. The reason for this is that the operating systems (master control programs) for present-day computers are still not foolproof. If a computer expert is persistent, he/she can usually find a way to crack the security scheme of the operating system thus permitting access to information intended to be private. Fortunately, there are not many people in computer-related professions who try such crimes, but if the rewards are great enough the temptation to try is overpowering for a few. Furthermore, as the number of users of EFT increases, the number of potential robbers increases. Consequently, ever tighter security schemes must be devised.

SUMMARY

After reading this chapter, you must be impressed by some of the ways computers have been used for the good of society. Computerized criminal records accessible from any police station should decrease the number of unsolved police cases and make life safer for everyone. On the other hand, massive files of information easily analyzed by computers open up the possibility of reprisals by disgruntled public employees or by politicians in positions of authority. The responsibility for monitoring the use of computers must be assumed by all citizens if computers are to be a force for good. The potential for either good or bad is there. It is up to us to see to it that the positive forces prevail.

EXERCISES

7.1 Answer the following questions about the National Crime Information Center:
   (a) Why was it established?

(b) What agencies participate in it?

(c) How are data entered into and purged from its files?

7.2 What functions of LEAA's Teletype Network are not also functions of the FBI's NCIC?

7.3 How do local police departments use the national computerized systems?

7.4 Discuss methods by which information about a person may get stored on a computer file that may then be accessed by a local police department.

7.5 List some problems associated with the maintenance of computerized criminal records.

7.6 Describe some applications of computers to the judicial process.

7.7 In what ways have computers been beneficial in the handling of police emergency calls.

7.8 Identify some computer applications by the FBI other than the locating of criminals, missing persons, and stolen property.

7.9 Discuss some potentially harmful uses of computer records implemented by the CIA and IRS.

7.10 Debate the following resolution: The use of EFT is beneficial to society.

7.11 Conduct a panel discussion on the use of computerized crime networks. Include a discussion of uses made of such networks by police in your community.

7.12 Prepare a list of congressional bills dealing with individual privacy and write a brief summary of each bill. Of special interest are bills treating computer use of data compiled on individuals.

7.13 Write a report on the automated tax system used by the IRS. Be sure to include some information about the master files kept at Martinsburg, Virginia.

SELECTED REFERENCES

BOOKS AND REPORTS

Allen, B., "Embezzler's Guide to the Computer," *Harvard Business Review,* July 1975.

Anonymous, "Study of Federal Data Systems on Individuals Maintained by Agencies of the U.S. Government", Government Publication 01128, 93rd Congress, 2nd Session, 1974.

Chommie, John C., *The Internal Revenue Service,* Praeger, New York, 1970.

PERIODICALS

Anonymous, "Computers and Drunken Drivers," *Modern Data,* August 1972.

Anonymous, "The FBI's Computer Network," *Datamation,* June 1970.

Federal Bureau of Investigation, *Annual Report of The Federal Bureau of Investigation,* U.S. Gov. Printing Office, Washington, D.C., 1974.

Flato, Linda, "EFT and Crime," *Computer Decisions,* October 1975.

Flato, Linda, "IRS Intelligence Gathering Investigated by Congress," *Computer Decisions,* May 1975.

Flato, Linda, "Justice Admits Feeding CIA Files," *Computer Decisions,* March 1975.

Flato, Linda, "Justice Cuts Data Line to CIA," *Computer Decisions,* May 1975.

Flato, Linda, "Privacy: Commission Staffed, FBI May Get the Shaft," *Computer Decisions,* August 1975.

Internal Revenue Service, *Annual Report of the Commissioner of Internal Revenue,* U.S. Gov. Printing Office, Washington, D.C., 1974.

Whisenand, Paul M. and John D. Hodges, "Automated Police Information Systems: A Survey," *Datamation,* May 1969.

8 COMPUTERS AND YOUR HEALTH

People are concerned about a just legal system; they are also eager to have a good system of health care. There is very little in life as important to a person as his/her health. This is made evident in people's willingness to pay for good health care even though its cost has skyrocketed. Is there anything that can be done to reduce this cost? Many hospitals, federal agencies, and physicians see the application of computers to the health sciences as a means to that end. According to a report prepared by Creative Strategies, Inc., a private consulting firm, sales of computers used in the medical field will go from $156 million in 1974 to an expected $380 million by 1979, an increase of 143 percent over a five-year period. Whereas in 1974 computers in the health care area were most frequently used for accounting purposes (63 percent of total usage), future growth is expected in many other areas.

HOSPITAL USES OF COMPUTERS

Hospital administrators have long recognized the usefulness of computers in financial accounting. Hospitals are, after all, businesses in the same senses as are educational institutions, governmental agencies, and legislative bodies. Records must be kept of hospital receipts and expenditures and reports must be made to various boards and controlling agencies, a situation not unlike that facing any business. Despite these similarities with business and industry, the health care field has, in general, not welcomed the use of computers, but this attitude is changing. In a survey conducted by the American Hospital Association of 5912 hospitals, more than 60 percent of them use some form of computerization. However, the extent of such use ranges from limited access to a special service via a terminal, to completely computerized medical information systems. By far the majority of hospitals fall into

191

TABLE   8.1

CATEGORIES OF HOSPITAL DATA PROCESSING

Administrative	Clinical
Data collection	Medical records
Admission	Pharmacy
Patient census	Nursing
Billing	Radiology
Accounts receivable	Clinical laboratory
Payroll	
Purchases	
Accounts payable	
General ledger	

the limited-use portion of that range. In fact, it has been estimated by reliable sources that not even 1 percent of the 7000 members of the American Hospital Association are currently using medical information systems.

Nevertheless, there is a trend toward implementing such systems. The motivation is economics. The health care field is labor-intensive, and the cost of any kind of labor, unskilled or skilled, has increased dramatically. Health professionals are finally recognizing that routine tasks must be automated if there is to be any hope of keeping health care costs within reasonable limits. There is also a growing realization that the inevitable passage of legislation providing for National Health Insurance will make it necessary to computerize medical records in order to keep track of the massive amounts of data associated with such insurance. How, then, are progressive hospitals responding?

Medical Information Systems

The phrase "medical information systems" again provides the familiar acronym MIS. This MIS is similar to the one encountered in Chapters 4 and 5. Health professionals think of their data processing uses as falling into two categories: administrative data processing and clinical data processing. It reminds us of the two categories of educational computing, doesn't it? A look at Table 8.1 will make it evident that administrative data processing includes the usual accounting operations with slight modifications to meet the specific information needs of hospitals. However, the clinical data processing needs are quite different from anything encountered thus far in this book. Therefore, we will now consider those applications in a little more detail.

Medical Records.   Whenever a person becomes a patient in a hospital, records of previous symptoms, treatments prescribed, and reactions to treatments, follow the person during his/her stay in the hospital. Medical records have, until recently, been paper records. Physicians have written their comments on paper, which become a part of the file. Hospital records are added to the file, and the entire collection becomes a medical history of the patient.

Because it is often difficult to quickly extract the key data in a person's medical record, and because a physician's time must be shared by so many patients, there have been efforts to develop systems for computerizing medical records. Most of the past problems in developing such systems have stemmed from the fact that computers accept input data only if it is in a certain form. Physicians and nurses have not been willing to accept such restrictions as keying code words into terminals, or filling in specified boxes on data-entry forms. In some of the latest systems, physicians' reports are scanned by specially trained people for key phrases which are then used as indexing devices when the report is entered into computerized files. The key phrases can be used by physicians to query computer files in subsequent sessions with the patient and retrieve information that will help them assess how the patient is responding to treatment. The possibility of restricting the terminology that the physician may use in his/her report is also being studied. The objective is to develop a medical record that will help provide the best care and treatment for the patient.

In one hospital, the procedure for adding to a patient's record is as follows:

1. The physician, nurse, or other qualified person dictates the information on telephone-like dictation equipment as shown in Figure 8.1.

2. Any information dictated at step 1 is recorded on a cassette at a central recording station (see Figure 8.2). There each completed cassette is stacked in a special rack. A registered nurse listens to any cassette identified as containing priority orders and handles the orders immediately.

3. All tape cassettes are reviewed by a transcriptionist who keys their contents into a computer video display unit (Figure 8.3) making the new information a part of the computerized medical records system. To be sure all essential information was transcribed from the cassettes to the computer records, a registered nurse listens to each cassette as he/she visually checks the information displayed on the VDU.

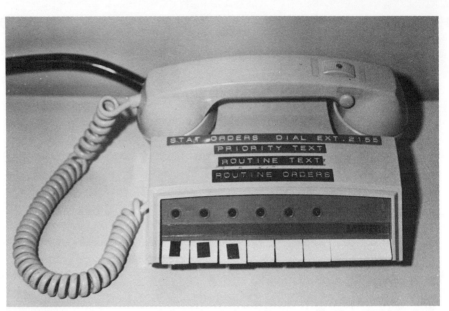

FIGURE 8.1   Medical records dictating equipment (courtesy Canyon General Hospital, Anaheim, California; David G. Knight, photographer).

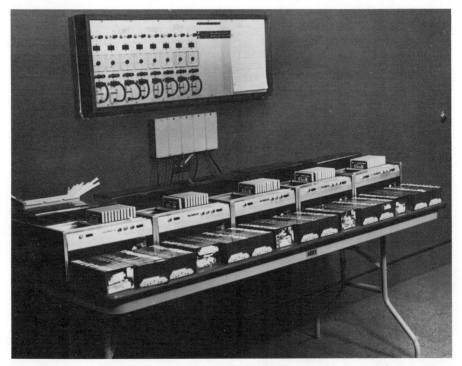

FIGURE 8.2   Medical records tape recording equipment (courtesy Canyon General Hospital, Anaheim, California; David G. Knight, photographer).

FIGURE 8.3   Transcriptionist at computer terminal (courtesy Canyon General Hospital, Anaheim, California; David G. Knight, photographer).

Any future need to review such computerized records can be satisfied by keying special information retrieval instructions at any of the video display terminals. Because of the way these computer files are organized, it is possible to request information in the format most useful to the physician, nurse, or other person requesting the information.

Pharmacy Records.   The pharmacy-records subsystem of a medical information system is the record of all medications used, prescribed, or known to be dangerous to each patient. Rapid processing of prescriptions can almost always result in greater comfort for a patient in a shorter time, and could even affect the recovery time. Quick access to information about drugs to which the patient is allergic could mean the difference between life and death. Accurate, up-to-date historical records of medications used by patients could also have a direct bearing on recovery time.

All of these benefits are being realized in the few systems now in operation. Records indicate that if nurses and pharmacy personnel are trained in the use of terminals (see Figure 8.4), which are usually a part of such systems, there is little

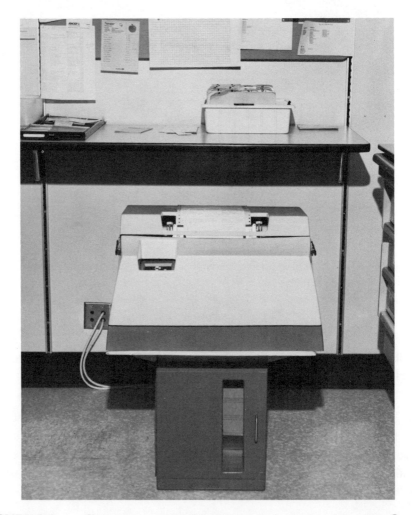

FIGURE 8.4   Computer terminal in hospital pharmacy (courtesy Canyon General Hospital, Anaheim, California; David G. Knight, photographer).

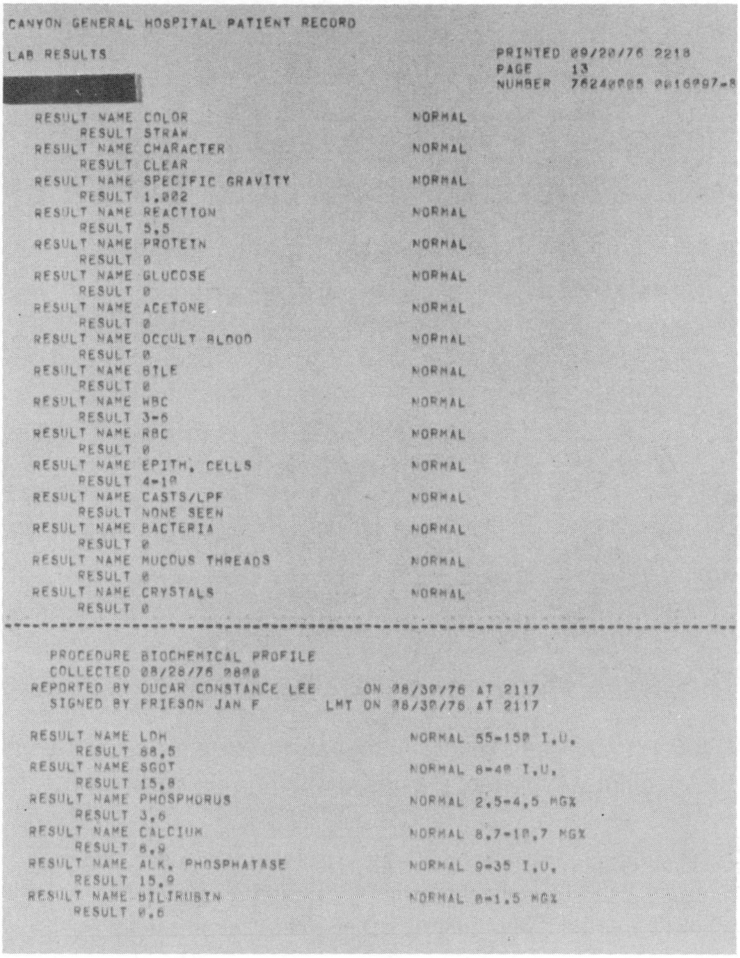

FIGURE 8.5   Typical summary report of a medical information system (courtesy Canyon General Hospital, Anaheim, California; David G. Knight; photographer).

opposition to implementing a computerized medical information system. Another benefit of at least one of the systems in current use is the printing of a "medication profile" at 2:00 a.m. Such profiles help both nurses and physicians to recognize the patients' responses to medications administered. It also provides a complete record of the amounts of each medication and the time administered.

Nursing Station Records.   Once data on patients have been entered into the hospital's computer, it is a relatively simple matter to write a program that

FIGURE 8.6   Computerized radiology terminal (courtesy Canyon General Hospital, Anaheim, California; David G. Knight, photographer).

will generate summary reports to be kept at nursing stations throughout the hospital. Such reports usually provide information about patients that will help the nurses care for them effectively. A report containing medication record, diet record, and temperature and blood pressure records can be very helpful in efficiently utilizing a nurse's time (see Figure 8.5).

Radiology Subsystem.   Radiology is that branch of medicine that uses radioactive materials and X-rays in diagnosis. Computers have been very helpful to radiologists. In fact, in some systems the data from X-rays are transformed into digital signals, transmitted to a computer and analyzed by computer programs designed to detect various abnormalities, and stored for further analysis at a later time. The results of the computer analysis are immediately available to the physician for his/her use in diagnosing the patient's illness. Some computerized radiology subsystems are also used in what is sometimes called nuclear medicine. This refers to the use of a radioactive tracer material introduced into the body (e.g., the blood, the digestive juices, or the air in the lungs). This tracer emits gamma rays that can be detected and used in the analysis of the patient's illness. Sometimes the gamma ray detectors are connected directly to a computer where a special program analyzes the data (see Figure 8.6). Such computer analyses are often more detailed than those any physician could possibly conduct, and their results are always immediately available, a factor that could be critically important in some cases.

     Clinical Laboratory.   In its less sophisticated form, the clinical laboratory portion of the medical information system stores and analyzes the results of laboratory tests. That is, fluid and tissue samples are taken from patients and tested in conventional ways by medical technicians. The results of tests are keyed into terminals by the medical technician or technician assistant, then stored as part of the clinical data, and are subject to analysis by a computer program. The analysis program identifies pathological problems and makes the information available to the physician upon his/her request (see Figure 8.7).

     In more automated forms, devices that actually conduct the necessary tests

FIGURE 8.7   **Computer terminal in clinical laboratory (courtesy Canyon General Hospital, Anaheim, California; David G. Knight, photographer).**

are connected directly to the computer. A nurse may be present to actually take the fluid or tissue sample and then deposit the sample in a special place in the machine. For example, blood samples, urine samples, and solid-tissue samples could be placed in appropriate containers. Then by subjecting the samples to various laboratory tests, all automatically, the chemical natures of the samples are detected by special devices and the results sent on to the computer.

In one or two large cities, automated clinical laboratories were established not as support units for hospitals or medical clinics but as places where people could obtain medical information about themselves. A nurse was there to help the patient draw blood samples and provide other assistance in following the procedures required of the automated laboratory. The usual vital signs (pulse, blood pressure, temperature, and rate of breathing) were measured. After a few minutes, during which time the various data were computer analyzed, the patient would receive a computer-printed statement about the condition of his/her health. If the need for treatment were indicated after the data were analyzed, the patient would be urged to see a physician. As yet, the automated clinical laboratory has not been accepted by society as a substitute for the laboratory associated with a clinic or hospital. If the cost of health care continues to increase as it has, and if automated systems for health care can be shown to be equally effective but less costly than conventional systems, you can be sure people will eventually accept them.

Description of a Functioning Medical Information System.   It might be helpful to describe how a computerized medical information system operates. In one 600 bed hospital, 83 VDU terminals, 48 teletypes, a high-speed printer, and a large amount of disk storage were all components in the computer system installed to support the medical information system. Since the VDU's are all on-line to the central processor, programs are stored in the central processor's memory to provide any one of several formats on the VDU screen for entering information. For example, when a patient is admitted, the data are keyed into a VDU that displays the electronic version of an admittance form. After the admitting procedure is complete, paper copies of the patient's data are automatically printed on teletypes at the patient's nursing station, at the X-ray department, and at the public affairs department.

VDU's and teletypes are located at every nursing station in the hospital as well as in the admitting and business departments (see Figure 8.8). VDU's are also available for physicians to use in entering patient data or for retrieving a patient's record. The pharmacy department also has access to a VDU and Teletype and is thus able to give immediate attention to any pharmacy orders it receives on the system. Once a pharmacy order has been filled, that data also becomes a part of the patient's record, the same record that is updated or reviewed at any of the 83

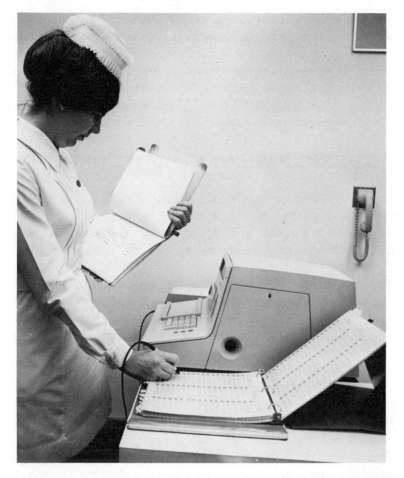

FIGURE 8.8   Computerized hospital nursing station (courtesy NCR).

terminals. That brings up a very important aspect of computerized medical information systems: a patient's record is always kept in exactly one place (computer
storage). That one copy of the record is the only place where additions or changes
are made, so any reference to a patient's record is always made to that currently
accurate copy. Noncomputerized medical records are typically in varying stages of
completeness. The pieces of information from the several departments contributing
to the record do not arrive at the central records library at the same time. Thus
some information in the record is current while other parts of the record have not
been updated for one or more days. For that reason alone one would think that
medical personnel would eagerly accept computerized system.

The fact is that computerized medical information systems have been resisted by most of the people who ought to use them. Physicians have questioned their benefit to the patients. All personnel have been somewhat apprehensive about using new procedures and unfamiliar hardware. But as more and more hospitals are able to reduce expenses by using a medical information system, other hospitals are implementing such systems. This trend has led the American Hospital Association to predict that by 1985 about 50 percent of all short-term hospitals of 200 beds or more would be operating computerized medical information systems.

MONITORING PATIENT HEALTH CONDITIONS

One of the newer and more futuristic applications of computers to the health care field is in monitoring patient health conditions. A prime example is the monitoring of heart patients. In hospitals so equipped, sensors that detect electrical signals associated with heart activity are attached to the patient's heart area. The signals from these sensors are transmitted along wires to a computer programmed to analyze such data. If the incoming data indicate that the patient is doing well, the computer generates no output. If data from the heart indicate the onset of serious conditions, the computer signals an alarm at the nursing station indicating which patient needs human care and the kind of help most apt to be useful. Figure 8.9 shows such a monitoring station.

A similar situation could exist for any of the vital organs in the body. The difference would be that a different kind of sensor would be required to detect the signals associated with other organs, and a computer program for analyzing the new kind of data would have to be present in computer memory.

Going one step further with the monitoring of patient conditions is the implanting of radio-transmitting sensors in human bodies. Such sensors continually transmit signals to receivers at the computer site even when the patient is no longer in the hospital. The signals are then analyzed by computer, and when the signals from the body organ indicate trouble approaching, the computer sets off an alarm at the monitoring station (usually a hospital). If immediate action is needed to save the person's life, people at the monitoring station are dispatched to the location of the sick person.

Perhaps the ultimate in the monitoring of people with malfunctioning body parts is exemplified by the main character in the novel, *The Terminal Man,* by Michael Crichton. This fictional man was plagued with a type of epilepsy. It was discovered that when epileptic seizures were approaching, his brain produced characteristic electrical signals. Furthermore, it was found that stimulation of a certain part of his brain with a mild electrical current from outside his body stopped the onset of the seizure and gave him good mental feelings. These discoveries led to

FIGURE 8.9   Station for computer monitoring of patients' conditions (courtesy St. Luke's Hospitals, Fargo, N.D.).

the implantation of a special transmitting/receiving device in the man's head that communicated to a computer the electrical condition of his brain. When the characteristic signals began coming to the computer, it was programmed to transmit appropriate signals to the device in the man's head to begin emitting a mild electric current to his brain. The effect was to prevent seizures, but because of the good mental feelings that also resulted, the man became dependent on the computer's signals in a manner not unlike drug dependency on the part of addicts. *The Terminal Man* is fiction, but research testing hypotheses similar to the ideas contained in that story has already been conducted, and medical science may soon be ready to try such treatment on more than an experimental basis. Perhaps the time is not far away when every hospital will have a computer dedicated to the monitoring of patients with physical ailments potentially fatal unless constant surveillance somehow alerts them to critical periods in their lives.

DIAGNOSING ILLNESS VIA COMPUTER

In an earlier section in this chapter, the use of a computer in the analysis of data from laboratory tests was discussed. Suppose a computer also had stored in its memory data about the symptoms of any disease or malfunction of the human body. If the physician were to enter into that computer the results of laboratory tests, and symptoms identified by the patient or the physician not apparent from the laboratory tests, the computer could be programmed to compare input data (symptoms and laboratory results) with stored symptoms and quickly isolate the most likely cause of the patient's illness. After all, haven't the best doctors earned their reputations by being able to perform early and accurate diagnoses of patients' problems? What makes some physicians more capable at this than others? Probably the ability to remember information about a large number of diseases and bodily disorders and how to treat them. What could enhance that ability more than a properly programmed computer? Probably nothing. And besides promoting a faster and more accurate diagnosis, the computer could also have stored in its memory the most successful treatments for each physical ailment, including the proper doses of medications to prescribe. Note that the computer in no way replaces the physician, but rather serves as an extension of his/her abilities which make him/her a successful physician.

Here's how it might work. The physician would have a computer terminal in his/her office on which to call up the patient's medical history. The laboratory results, entered by the medical technician, would be a part of that history. During the session with the patient the physician could enter at the terminal data related to other symptoms identified by physician or patient. The computer would send back to the terminal any helpful information related to diagnosis and treatment. The physician would then make the final decision regarding the diagnosis and treatment.

Computer-assisted medical diagnosis is just beginning to be used at a few of the larger clinics in the United States, but its contribution to better health care is almost certain to create an ever-increasing number of advocates.

COMPUTER ANALYSIS OF HEALTH-RELATED DATA

As you know by this time, something a computer does well if it is programmed to do so is to keep track of things. One recent application of that ability to the field of health care is in keeping track of whole blood. Whole blood must be transfused within 21 days after it is drawn or it has no value. Even if it is not to be used as whole blood, if it is to be reduced to plasma, that process must have been started within 30 days. A study by the Department of Health, Education and Welfare indicates that perhaps as much as 25 percent of blood collected for medical use may be lost because of inadequate inventory or distribution procedures.

A computerized blood bank records system was tested in several counties in eastern Pennsylvania and western New Jersey during the spring of 1975. Results of that pilot system indicate that a computerized system can stop almost all of the loss of blood due to faulty inventory and distribution methods. Whenever a pint of blood is needed anywhere in the region, the person requesting the blood keys into a terminal information about the type and amount of blood needed. The system responds by telling where the oldest blood of the specified type is stored. Thus the oldest blood is always used first. Furthermore, whenever the expiration date approaches for any pint of blood stored in the region, the computer system is programmed to transmit a warning message to that effect to the computer terminal located in the office of the manager of the system. The whole blood is then processed for other uses if it is not required for transfusions. If such a blood-bank-records system were put into operation over an even larger geographical area, the results in number of pints of blood saved would be very impressive. Because blood bank agencies often have trouble getting people to donate blood, that type of computer application to health care can only be applauded.

Statistical Analysis of Health Data

Many state and federal agencies collect data related to the health of the nation's population. The amounts of data have been so large, that before the use of computers, it was difficult to draw useful conclusions from the data. In the past few years, however, computers have been used to analyze large amounts of information to reveal some startling facts.

A review of death records, for example, has pinpointed regions where the incidence of cancer is unusually high. When that is known, efforts can be made to determine why this is true. This process led to the discovery that the health of residents around Duluth, Minnesota, and Superior, Wisconsin, was apparently threatened by fibers in the Lake Superior water. These fibers were coming from iron-ore refining operations in which waste materials were being dumped into Lake Superior. Computer-processed statistical evidence pointed the finger at the culprit industry. The legal battle that resulted is still not over but it appears that the problematic pollution of Lake Superior waters will soon stop.

Another situation occurred in the state of Washington. Whether a certain factory producing arsenic (a substance known to be very poisonous to human beings) was complying with federal pollution laws was being questioned, especially by many of the factory employees. The problem seemed to be that employees were dying from cancer. When data from death records and from employment records in the area were scrutinized by computer programs, strong statistical evidence unequivocally pointed to factory conditions as the cause of cancer. The legal struggles to achieve justice are yet not over in that case either.

In still another case, a computer is being used to reduce the potential for infection in hospitals. The cooperating hospitals have installed a system that regularly samples environmental conditions in the hospitals and transmits the results to a computer. The computer has been programmed to recognize the conditions that precede a break-out of infections caused by hospital environmental conditions. When these conditions are detected, the computer sends appropriate warning messages and the problematic situation is cleared up.

These examples are cited to show how computers are being used in undramatic ways to do the thing they do best—process large amounts of information in a short time. The results have been surprising in many situations related to health care. New evidence is regularly made available to assist health authorities in their fight to reduce elements in society that degrade the quality of life.

SOME UNUSUAL USES OF COMPUTERS IN HEALTH CARE

Before we leave the topic of health care, we will consider some unusual applications of computers to the field of health.

In Roanoke, Virginia, a computer is being used to help treat stutterers. The subject sits at a computer terminal wearing a headset microphone into which he/she speaks (Figure 8.10).

The microphone is attached to a device that digitizes the spoken sounds and sends them on to a computer. There a special program analyzes the data and responds to the subject via the terminal. Comments like "very good response," "that was a very good sound," or "that was an awful sound, you idiot" are all part of the computer's vocabulary. Subjects enjoy working with the computer and feel that it is consistent in its judgment of their speech responses. At the present time only single-syllable and single-word utterances are analyzed. The goal is to be able to deal with sounds occurring within sentences. The project director, Dr. Ronald Webster, predicts that soon not only stutterers but people with other speech disorders may go to special terminals (perhaps located in schools or public libraries) and dial up a computer for assistance in their speech problems.

In another project, a computer is being used to assist in brain surgery. Special devices for sensing the electrical activity in the brain are used to help the surgeon detect the exact place where corrective surgery must be made. Signals from these special sensors are transmitted to a computer which, in turn, produces graphical output on the screen of a terminal in the operating room that shows the surgeon where the problem is located.

Computers are being used to help deaf people hear and blind people to

FIGURE 8.10   Computer terminal for treating stutterers (courtesy Ronald L. Webster, Hollins Communications Research Institute, Roanoke, Va.).

see. In the case of the deaf, microphones are used to pick up sounds. The sounds are converted into digital signals that are then sent to a computer for processing. The computer sends electrical signals to the patient via wires attached to areas near the auditory nerve. In a number of cases the patient "hears" sounds via the intermediary, the computer. Similar research has been done with sight for the blind, with the equipment modified to detect light waves rather than sound waves. Computers may soon help such disadvantaged people to function in a much more normal fashion.

CONCLUSION

Undoubtedly there are applications of computers to the area of health care that are not beneficial to society, but such dangerous applications are not readily apparent. Equally certain is that there are many beneficial computer applications to the health sciences not yet discovered. The hope of this author is that as more people find out what things are being done, and gain a better understanding of what kinds of help to expect from a computer, the greater will be the strides toward a good life for all people.

EXERCISES

8.1 What evidence suggests that the health care field is on the verge of dramatically increased use of computers?

8.2 Contrast the kinds of computer applications included in administrative and clinical aspects of medical information systems.

8.3 Identify some aspects of medical records that seem to make them particularly suitable to computerization.

8.4 Identify some problems associated with early attempts to computerize medical records, in particular, why medical people rejected such attempts.

8.5 List advantages and disadvantages of having computerized hospital pharmacy records.

8.6 How might the availability of a nursing station benefit both nurses and patients?

8.7 If you were a patient in need of radiology analysis, why might you be happy if the radiology department were computerized? Are there any reasons for your being unhappy about such a situation?

8.8 List benefits and dangers to the general public if the use of automated clinical laboratories becomes widespread.

8.9 Describe how computers are used to monitor health conditions of patients.

8.10 Describe your attitude toward the use of computers not only to monitor patients' conditions but also to modify patients' behavior by having the computer transmit radio signals to the patients' brains.

8.11 List advantages and disadvantages of computer-assisted diagnosis of patients' illnesses.

8.12 In what ways has the computer been used to benefit people's health through the routine analysis of data?

8.13 Identify some uses of computers in helping people overcome special physical deficiencies.

8.14 Check with your local medical clinics and hospitals to find out ways in which they are using computers. Report on your findings.

8.15 Participate in a panel discussion on the implications to society of using computers to monitor the functioning of vital organs.

8.16 Listen to the audiotape *Mini-conputers and Timesharing in Medical Information Systems* (available as audiotape ACM 10 from Information Cassettes, Inc., 430 North Michigan Avenue, Chicago, Illinois 60611) and prepare a report on the tape.

8.17 Write letters to research hospitals (like those associated with large universities) asking for information on the use of computers in medicine.

8.18 Prepare a report on the book *The Terminal Man* by Michael Crichton.

8.19 View the film *Cybernetics* (a production of Budapest Film Studios, Budapest, Hungary) and participate in a panel discussion on the benefits and dangers to individuals and society associated with the interface of brain and computer.

SELECTED REFERENCES

BOOKS AND REPORTS

U.S. Dept. of Health, Education and Welfare, *The Computer Assisted EKG: From Laboratory to Community,* U.S. Government Printing Office, Washington, 1973.

Creative Strategies, Inc., *The Medical Computer Industry,* San Jose, Calif., 1975.

Bowyer, A.F. et al., "Computer Graphics Simulation of the Human Heart," *Proceedings of the Society of Photo-Optical Instrumental Engineers, pp. 390—395,* August 1968.

Crichton, Michael, *The Terminal Man,* Kopf, New York, 1972.

Sterling, Theodore and Seymour Pollack, *Computers and The Life Sciences,* Columbia University Press, New York, 1965.

Stewart, D.H., H. Erbach, and H. Shubin, "A Computer System for Real-time Monitoring and Management of the Critically Ill," *Proceedings of the Fall Joint Computer Conference,* pp. 797—807, American Federation of Information Systems, 1968.

Stibitz, George R., *Mathematics in Medicine and the Life Sciences,* Year Book Medical Publishers, Chicago, 1966.

Von Neumann, John, *The Computer and the Brain,* Yale University Press, New Haven, 1958.

Wooldridge, Dean E., *The Machinery of the Brain,* McGraw-Hill, New York, 1963.

PERIODICALS

Anonymous, "Computer Assists Stuttering Therapy," *Datamation,* February 1973.

Anonymous, "Computer Center Matches Kidney Transplants," *Computer Decisions,* February 1974.

Anonymous, "Computer Injects Infection Protection Into Hospitals," *Computer Decisions,* August 1974.

Anonymous, "Computerized Eye Doctor," *Science Digest,* June 1975.

Anonymous, "Deaf Hear Computer," *Science Digest,* September 1975.

Anonymous, "Searching for Cancer Drugs by Computer," *Science News,* February 23, 1974.

Avorn, J., "Future of Doctoring," *Atlantic,* November 1974.

Ball, Marion J., "Computers: Prescription for Hospital Ills," *Datamation,* September 1975.

Burkett, Warren, "A Talking Computer Will Help a Blood Bank Save Time and Blood," *Computers and People,* March 1975.

Carren, Donald M., "Multiple Minis for Information Management," *Datamation,* September 1975.

Dorn, Phillip H., "Funding the Operation," *Datamation,* September 1975.

Emmett, Arielle, "The Computer Meets the Doctor," *Science Digest,* September 1975.

Ferderber, Charles J., "A Standardized Solution for Hospital Systems," *Datamation,* September 1975.

Land, Thomas, "On-line Computer Used to 'See' in Brain Surgery," *Computers and People,* April 1975.

Landahl, H.D., "Training Program in Computer Use for Biomedical Students," *Bulletin of Mathematical Biophysics,* December 1963.

Ross, W.S., "Computers: New Dimension in Patient Care," *Readers Digest,* April 1974.

Shapley, D., "Computers in Medicine: Hospitals Cope with Costs," *Science,* February 28, 1975.

Yasaki, Edward, "What Will They Zap at El Camino? The CRT or the Two-Year-Old MIS?," *Datamation,* October 1973.

9 COMPUTERS AND YOUR FUTURE

You have now been introduced to some of the major areas of computer application and have been made aware of some of the implications to society of the widespread use of computers. Although it may seem to you that this book gives the computer a more prominent place than it deserves, the truth of the matter is that we have examined very few of the many uses to which information processing machines have been put. Furthermore, all indications are that the future holds even more spectacular surprises in the way computers will be applied to everyday life. Before we make some educated guesses about the computer and our future, let's look at some of the prevailing attitudes people display when it comes to planning for the future.

ATTITUDES ABOUT THE FUTURE

Many people believe that the problems of the present are too numerous and engrossing to even permit thinking about the future. As Earl Joseph has said,

> For too many, the activity of seeking and shaping better futures seems almost an impertinent triviality relative to the growing chaos and crisis which constantly surround us in each era. Although this estrangement of the future from the present is not new, recently acquired technological and social powers of mankind have jeopardized the continued survival of society in the future.

People who hold such views are too busy getting what they can out of the present to worry much about the future. In fact, the logical conclusion of this philosophy is that there can be no future. "Eat, drink, and be happy, for tomorrow we die!"

211

Other people blame technological development for society's current ills. The complaint of this group is that technology has brought too many changes in too short a time. They conclude, therefore, that technology cannot be good. It has resulted in too many problems for society now and will surely produce more in the future. These people would call for a decrease in technology. Quoting again from Dr. Joseph's paper:

> *Yet, the placing of the blame on technology ends up often misdirected. For example, at the turn of our century horses were a prime mode of transportation in the inner city. On a typical day in 1900, in New York City, 2½ million pounds of manure were deposited on the streets together with 60,000 gallons of urine. Further, the fatality rate due to this mode of transportation was ten times higher than it is now! Thus, the alternative of going back to such a past transportation mode. . .is obviously not desirable for the future. It would be far more nonhumanistic and environmentally degrading.*

As Joseph points out, people who are afraid of technological growth are not always realistic. Still, they see no benefits from technological changes and would like to plan a future without technology. This group would surely predict a small place in the future for computers.

A more realistic approach is to include new technologies when considering alternatives for the future. All of the world's people want to enjoy a higher quality of life, and research on world trends indicates that this goal necessitates the inclusion of *more* uses of technology in any future planning, not less. Thus, the computer looms as a very important device in bringing new benefits to society. Computer-based forecasting is, in fact, one of the most significant tools in planning the future. Numerous other uses of computers just now being conceived will also mold our future.

Within recent years a group of people has emerged who specialize in the study of the future. Some of these pioneers earn their livelihood doing this while others do it as an avocation. They call themselves *futurists,* and they study about and plan for the future. Note that this is *not* a religious cult in any way. Futurists are simply people who believe that the only way to have the kind of future we want is to plan for it today. They believe that through forecasting we can shape the future. Few people would argue that much of the future is controlled by today's decisions. Therefore, why not set policy and goals so that decisions made in the present can help create the future we want? After all, we will live in that future for the rest of our lives. The reader interested in learning more about futurist activities is encouraged to see references at the end of this chapter.

SOME COMPUTER TECHNOLOGY FORECASTS

We consider some predictions about computer technology.

Speed of Computation Increased

By 1980 it is likely that computers will have computation speeds 10 to 50 times faster than today's machines. Recall that computers are now being marketed with speeds of from a few thousand operations per second to 10 million operations per second. The computers of 1980 will be able to execute 100 million to 500 million operations each second. To help you grasp the meaning of that great a computational speed, look at Figure 9.1. If you were the person in the picture and were good in arithmetic, you could expect to add 10 four-digit numbers in 20 seconds. To add as many four-digit numbers as the computer of 1980 could add in one second would take you about 133 years working eight hours a day, 52 weeks a year. If you took normal two- or three-week vacations, it would take an additional five to eight years.

Increased computation speed will cause people to attempt the solution of even greater and more complex problems than have been solved up to now. Whereas computer simulations of world economic systems or of sociological systems have, of necessity, been greatly simplified, by 1980 it may be possible to develop more realistic computer models of such human systems.

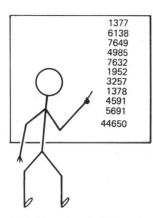

1377
6138
7649
4985
7632
1952
3257
1378
4591
5691

44650

Adds 10 numbers in 20 seconds.
Adds 500 million numbers in
133 YEARS.

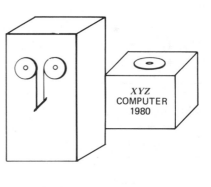

XYZ
COMPUTER
1980

Adds 500 million numbers in
1 SECOND.

FIGURE 9.1 **Comparison of human computation and computer computation, 1980.**

Auxiliary Storage Increased While Cost Decreased

From research currently taking place, it has been projected that within two or three years the maximum auxiliary storage capacity of large-scale computers will double. At the same time, the present cost per character of storage space will be halved. By 1984 it is likely that the cost will have decreased to one-fifth of the present cost.

The combination of faster computation speeds and larger computer storage capacity, all for less cost, will enable people to attempt computer applications hitherto felt impossible. Maybe by 1980 it really will be possible to have completely computerized rapid transit systems that quickly and safely transport large numbers of people.

Computer Networks Will Link Large Files of Data

Today, computer manufacturers are actively researching the development of computer networks. Being investigated are methods of making it possible for computers to communicate with one another and share stored information. Not only is the linking of *two* computers being studied, but methods for connecting *many* computers into a single network of computers are presently being researched. Figure 9.2 is a diagram of this concept. Of particular interest are networks of timesharing computers (see Chapter 3). By 1980 it is quite likely that computer networks like this will be in use. Among other things, such technology will make it possible to have backup computing capability from more than one source. Perhaps more importantly, when such networks become commonplace it will be possible for a user having access to the network in North Dakota to examine information stored on a computer in New York. Imagine that you had a computer terminal in your home and you were doing research that required information from some book in the Library of Congress. Assuming that the electronic equivalent of Library of Congress books have been placed in the auxiliary storage of a computer and that this computer is in the network, you could key certain instructions into the network and, within a few seconds, desired information would appear on your terminal. This scenario might very well take place by 1985.

The EFT system described in Chapter 5 will surely bring pressure for the kind of computer network just presented. It will be economically important for the computers of different banking firms to be able to communicate with each other. This is necessary if a person traveling through Chicago whose bank is in Minneapolis is to be able to conduct transactions in Chicago. Once the technology has been developed for EFT, it will be available for other uses such as education and research.

Another by-product of this technology will likely be inexpensive computer capability for the home. You can already purchase timesharing computer service

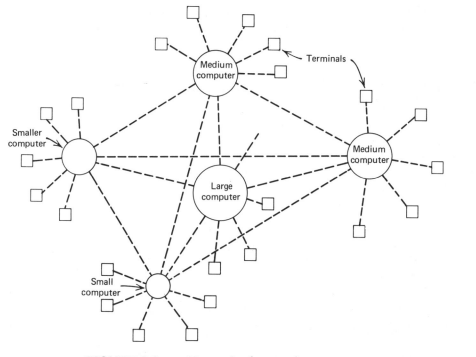

FIGURE 9.2   Network of several computers.

for home use and employ the ordinary telephone line as the connecting link. However, such computer service costs about $10 per minute of computer time, plus the cost of the long-distance phone call if you live in a place outside the local calling area. By 1985 such a computer utility may well be available for one-tenth of that cost, a figure not out of line for any family who could make use of it.

Inexpensive Computer Terminals Will Become Available

A number of computer experts believe that the availability of inexpensive computer terminals will have more impact on society than any other future change in technology. It is quite likely that by 1980 a visual display unit (VDU) will be available for less than $300, and by 1985 a terminal with 16,000 locations of programmable memory will be available for about the same cost. This means that anyone who can now afford color television will be able to buy a terminal. If people can be persuaded that home computer terminals are useful, many will surely acquire them. Perhaps the appeal of being able to shop from the home by viewing items on the VDU then keying in the order for delivery by the store will cause some to buy computer terminals. Perhaps the access to large amounts of educational information will convince others. In any case, when the cost falls below $300 to $500, many people will become convinced that purchasing computer terminals is a good thing.

MICROPROCESSORS AND CONSUMER PRODUCTS

Recall from Chapter 2 that an integrated circuit is a device containing many electronic circuits on a piece of material about the size of the head of a common pin. When integrated circuits were first invented, perhaps 10 electronic circuits could be placed on such a small piece of material. By 1970 manufacturers were talking

FIGURE 9.3   Microprocessor 1000 times actual size (courtesy INTEL Corporation).

about large-scale integrated circuits (LSIs), meaning that as many as 100 circuits could be placed on a 0.004 square inch surface. In 1975, designers of computer circuits began talking about grand-scale integrated circuits (GSIs). They were referring to the possibility of 500 to 1000 electronic circuits on each tiny chip of material. For the first time it became possible to conceive of a computer on a chip. That is, if such a large number of electronic circuits can be placed in such a small space, it is possible to design a collection of circuits that would carry the processing functions of a computer. Such an integrated circuit is called a *microprocessor*. Figure 9.3 shows a microprocessor greatly enlarged.

Microprocessors currently available have the computing and storage capacity of the first electronic computers which occupied hundreds of cubic feet of space. These microprocessors of less than 0.001 cubic inch in size cost approximately $300 including a keyboard and screen for input/output. Such facts are almost impossible to believe when we remember that barely 25 years ago the first commercial computer cost $12 million to develop and required a space of 6000 cubic feet in which to function. As with integrated circuits, the manufacturing process for micropressors is a microphotographic one. The original circuit design is carefully drawn by a skilled human being. Then a high-resolution picture is taken of it and a photographic reduction process produces the pattern used in the mechanized steps culminating in a microprocessor (see Figures 9.4 and 9.5).

Consumer products that utilize microprocessors are already appearing on the market. Automobiles are now available that incorporate microprocessors in the carbureation system. In that system of the automobile it is extremely important to achieve the proper mix of air and gasoline vapor so that the maximum amount of energy can be extracted from the fuel with the least amount of air pollution resulting. Engineers have known about the critical nature of the air/fuel mixture for years but until now have not had the technological means for effectively controlling it in a mobile machine like the automobile. The microprocessor is preprogrammed to monitor the air and fuel intakes via special sensing devices and then adjusts the mix to previously specified ideal proportions. The temperature of the air/fuel mix as well as the electric spark produced by the ignition system are also monitored. Adjustments are made in each of these functions depending on the preprogramming of the microprocessor and the conditions sensed by it. The object of such computer control is to have an automobile that achieves maximum gasoline mileage and produce minimum pollution. The automobile may well be the object of other microprocessor applications. Some functions related to passenger safety could well utilize microprocessors. In fact, in recent studies microprocessors, working in conjunction with special sensing devices, have been used to control an automobile's direction and speed of movement. The on-board microcomputer processes infor-

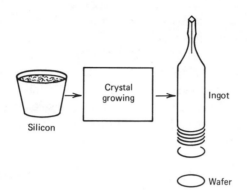

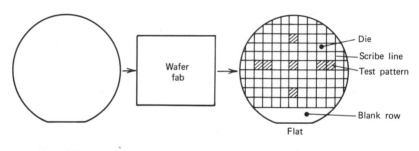

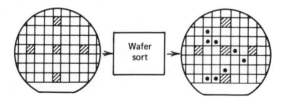

FIGURE 9.4 Diagram of the manufacturing process for an integrated circuit (courtesy INTEL Corporation).

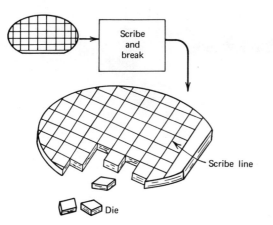

Scribe
and
break

Scribe line

Die

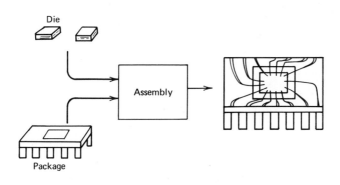

Die

Assembly

Package

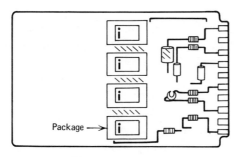

Package

Printed circuit board

219

Figure 9.5 Scene in a microprocessor factory (courtesy INTEL Corporation).

mation transmitted to it by devices that can detect the speed of the automobile, its proximity to other vehicles, its position on the road, and almost any other information essential to accurate control of the vehicle. If such on-board computers are linked to a large, stationary computer to which information about a given road system is being transmitted, freeway traffic could be efficiently and safely controlled. The stationary computer would control traffic lights so that the largest possible number of automobiles and trucks would traverse the road in a minimum amount of time.

Other products that will likely contain microprocessors in the near future are home heating and cooling systems. As in the case of carbureation in the automobile, a microprocessor will be a part of the heating/cooling system and will monitor various functions of such systems. Such monitoring would be designed to the best possible comfort conditions, the most efficient use of energy, and the least harmful effect on the outdoor environment. You will recognize again an underlying philosophy of this book: societal pressures produce technological development. Current concern about the depletion of energy reserves and the preservation of the environment are affecting the development of technology. Microprocessors are being pressed into service in ever more assorted applications in the belief that these marvels of engineering skill can help us maintain a high standard of living without excessively depleting our natural resources.

HUMAN COMMUNICATION AND COMPUTERS

In earlier chapters we described how computers have been used to promote communication among human beings. Recall the example from Chapter 8 in which a computer was used to help people with speech and hearing deficiencies. The crime-information networks of Chapter 7 are examples of computer application to the need for increased communication speed. The management information systems of Chapter 5 and the medical information systems of Chapter 8 are further demonstrations of using computers in special cases of human communication.

Computers and the Switching of Telephone Circuits

We examine some likely ways individuals will be affected by computers. Already computers are being used to determine the routing of long-distance telephone calls so a call is completed in the shortest possible time (see Figure 9.6). Such computer-controlled systems can identify available telephone circuits much more rapidly than human operators did in a previous era. For example, a phone call from New York to Seattle may be most quickly completed by routing the call down the East Coast to Atlanta, Georgia, there westward to Dallas, north to Minneapolis, and finally westward to Seattle. This is obviously not the most direct path, but it might be the least time-consuming if telephone circuits from New York to Chicago to Minneapolis were already in use. In less than a second, computer-controlled systems can examine all options for putting through a long-distance call, then make the appropriate switch settings so as to actually make possible the phone call dialed by the customer. Almost as important as completing the call quickly is the historical record kept by the computer. This enables human decision makers to plan effectively for future equipment installations.

Computers are already a vital component in communication systems that employ earth satellites designed specifically for communication purposes. That role will become even more significant in the near future. Instead of telephone-line circuits, the computer-directed system will select appropriate microwave circuits on which to transmit signals that will complete a call. The principle of selecting microwave circuits is nearly identical to that of selecting telephone-line circuits. Communications satellites would not have the restrictions associated with the need to find an available telephone line. Signals could be sent between any two points on earth having a straight-line access to a satellite (see Figure 9.7). Undoubtedly such a communication system would permit nearly instantaneous information exchange among people.

FIGURE 9.6   Computer controlling telephone routings (courtesy American Telephone & Telegraph).

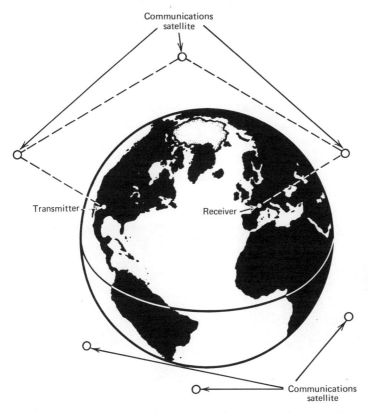

FIGURE 9.7   Diagram of satellite communication system.

Computers and Human Speech

Two areas of research into human communication are just now producing interesting results that may soon be the basis for entirely new applications of computers. One of these areas is human speech. Although most people take for granted their ability to speak, scientists have known precious little about the physical and mental processes that accompany human utterances. Scientific efforts currently taking place at Bell Laboratories in New Jersey and at the Massachusetts Institute of Technology are dramatically increasing our knowledge.

As you can well imagine, the variety of ways in which different people pronounce a given word is so great that the problem of programming a computer to "understand" a spoken word seems almost insurmountable. Most of us have never stopped to analyze the wide range of sound collections which our brains are able to comprehend as the same word. For example, the simple word "dog" is variously pronounced as "dawg," "doughg," "dug," "dog" and many other ways. With almost no difficulty we are able to interpret these pronunciations correctly. How does one program the computer to do the same? Figure 9.8 shows an image appearing on a video display unit during some experimentation being done to help answer that question.

Another source of frustration in researching human speech derives from the fact that speech is continuous. That is, words follow each other without distinct breaks so how does one signal the computer to distinguish one word from another? Really, how do you and I do that?

Considerable progress has been made in overcoming both of these deterrents to producing computers that understand spoken commands. In fact, today

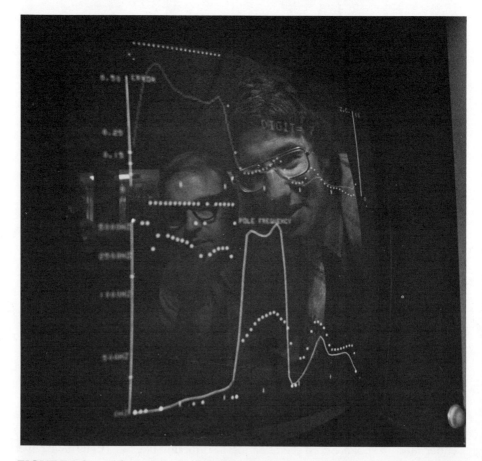

FIGURE 9.8 Computer output during research on human speech (courtesy Bell Laboratories).

computers connected to equipment that converts sounds to electrical pulses can "understand" a very limited vocabulary of spoken words. Not only that, but certain techniques give these experimental computer systems the ability to produce words themselves. That is, not only can these computers "listen" and "understand," but they can also "speak"! It doesn't take much imagination to predict that sometime in the not-too-distant future people will be issuing spoken commands to computers. The machines will carry out the tasks given them, and besides being able to produce printed or graphic reports of the results of their actions will provide oral reports. Does this sound too fantastic to believe? It is being done right now in the research laboratory. Certainly the system must still be perfected before it is marketed but unquestionably that step will eventually be taken. When that time does arrive, the majority of people who want to use a computer will not need to have learned a programming language. A complete, logical description of the task to be done is all that will be needed. The computer can then be programmed by talking to it. Understand that this situation does not eliminate the need for computer programmers. These highly trained people will still be the sources of instruction sets that give computers the "intelligence" to understand speech. However, the average person who needs the computer need not know how to write programs.

How far into the future are we looking when we envision computers that listen and speak? Maybe by 1980, or almost surely by 1985 such electronic marvels will be commercially available. That's barely 30 years from the time when the first computer was made for the marketplace. Unbelievable strides in technology have occurred, and the future holds even more exciting advances.

Computers and Human Memory

As we consider communication among human beings, we should also examine human memory. Most of us have had the task of trying to communicate with someone who has a very poor memory. How frustrating it can be to state and restate a point for such a person only to realize that there is no ability to recall the facts essential to proper understanding. Unquestionably memory is basic to human communication. But just how do we remember things? Is there some way that faltering memories can be shored up? Exactly what happens when we recall information?

Leaders in research into the topic of human memory are Max Mathews, David Meyer, and Saul Sternberg in the Human Information-Processing Research department of Bell Laboratories in Murray Hill, New Jersey (see Figure 9.9). Their research indicates that human brains utilize a short-term memory for mental activities of five minutes or less and a long-term memory for storing facts over longer periods. The short-term memory can typically store from five to ten pieces of

FIGURE 9.9   Test booth for memory experiments (courtesy Bell Laboratories).

information. By contrast, the long-term memory of an average person can retain millions of facts. This situation is not unlike that in a modern electronic computer, which uses memory (short-term) and auxiliary memory (long-term). However, that comparison is incidental to our present consideration. Of prime importance here is (1) the fact that computers are a significant aid to research into human memory and (2) that the potential benefits of such studies to human communication are overwhelming.

Let's explore some possible consequences of a fairly complete understanding of how human memory functions. To begin with, such knowledge will almost certainly enable people to extend their abilities to memorize information. Knowing *how* something happens usually implies possession of the ability to modify the process.

Secondly, and more exciting, if we know the details of the process of human memory, it is conceivable that human memories could be augmented by mechanical memories. Recall from Chapter 8 the reference to implanting special devices in or near the brain that could detect neural activity and transmit appropriate radio messages to a specially designed computer. Why couldn't a similar device augment human memory? A special device implanted in a person's head could detect the mental activity signaling the need for information from the computer's auxiliary memory. The computer could retrieve the pertinent information, transmit signals to the special device (maybe some kind of microprocessor), and provide the person with the needed information. It may even be possible to expand human memory by implanting microprocessors with storage mechanisms containing the desired information. The potential for helping large segments of the world's population is tremendous.

It should be apparent that the situation just described also poses a threat to personal freedom. There is no reason why a powerful government could not use such a technique to control people's memories. Just erase the previously stored information and fill the memories with information supportive to the government. Sure, this sounds a bit Orwellian, but the concerned citizen must be vigilant against any intrusions on personal freedoms.

COMPUTERS AND ENVIRONMENTAL CONTROL

Computers are already being used to control the environmental conditions inside large buildings and huge enclosed spaces such as Houston's astrodome. It is not difficult to conceive of how even larger spaces could be controlled. Plans have been proposed for enclosing entire cities and artificially maintaining suitable environmental conditions. Such plans would almost surely depend on large computer systems intricately programmed to monitor and modify the conditions of such large enclosed spaces.

Humanity's ability to explore space, and, in particular, to walk on the moon, have caused some people to propose human colonies on the moon. Be-

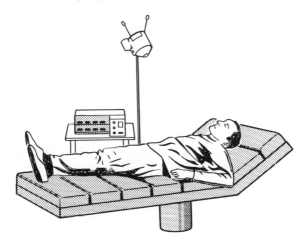

FIGURE 9.10   Computerized home medical center of the future.

cause the environment of the moon is hostile to human life, artificially controlled and enclosed spaces would be necessary if human colonization were to occur. The reader can imagine how properly located sensing devices for heat, moisture, light, and other properties could be used to send appropriate signals to equipment which would probably utilize solar energy to effectively modify conditions, making them situable for human habitation.

Some people have even suggested that computers will in the future be used to control many aspects of life in the ordinary single-family dwelling. Such things as prescribing healthful diets, monitoring bodily functions, providing a variety of entertainment, and making knowledge available about any part of the earth and its atmosphere will likely be routine by 1990. Figure 9.10 shows one version of an imaginary home medical center where physical health is properly checked and analyzed by computer.

COMPUTERIZED SHOPPING

The use of computers in conjunction with home television sets and EFT (see Chapter 6) will very probably make shopping from the home a reality by 1985. With two-way communication via cable television a fact by 1977 (see Chapter 6), the additional features needed to provide for home viewing and selection of merchandise are already being developed. In fact, by 1975 at least one commercial firm had already been organized for the specific purpose of providing member clients with facilities for home shopping. The user of such a system would set the

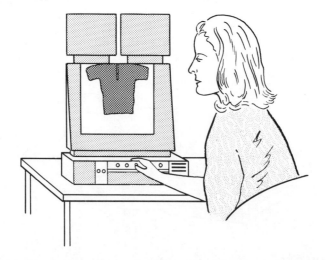

FIGURE 9.11   Computerized home shopping center of the future.

television receiver to an appropriate channel, use an attached keyboard to inform the system which items were of interest and should be displayed on the screen, and finally use the keyboard to select items to be purchased and later delivered to the home. Figure 9.11 shows one conception of such a home shopping system.

CONCLUSION

We have barely started in this chapter to guess some future applications of the electronic computer in the next 25 years. The year 2000 will undoubtedly bring surprises for even the most forward-looking computer fan.

And now as we look back over the subject matter presented in this book, we hope that you, the reader, have learned something about how computers came to be and how they function. Furthermore, you should have acquired some knowledge of how to produce computer programs in the BASIC language. You are now aware of some of the myriad ways in which computers influence your life. Use the knowledge you have gained to help to control the computer's societal impact. Use your influence to bring about computer applications that are *good* for society rather than harmful and dehumanizing. That goal is well worth pursuing and readily attainable if many people become knowledgeable enough and concerned enough to force the issue.

EXERCISES

9.1 State three common attitudes about the future held by many people. Which of the three do you agree with the most? Why?

9.2 What is a futurist? What might be some reasons for a computer manufacturing company to employ a futurist on its staff?

9.3 What computation speed is expected of 1980 computers? Compare this speed with that of Aiken's Mark I and the ENIAC.

9.4 How can increased computation speed affect the society of the 1980s?

9.5 Computers of the 1980s will likely have much larger auxiliary storage at a fraction of today's cost. How will this affect society?

9.6 Name some computer applications that will be affected by the computer networks apt to be commonplace by 1985.

9.7 What is the relationship between computers' effects on society and the cost of computer terminals?

9.8 What is a microprocessor? What impact are they having on our lives at present? What effects are almost certain to be felt from their use in the next 10 years?

9.9 List some ways in which computers affect human communication.

9.10 Why is it so difficult to design and construct a computer that can respond correctly to human speech? Do you think such a computer will ever be built?

9.11 Computers are being used to help us understand the human memory process. What facts have already been discovered and how can increased understanding of human memory benefit society?

9.12 What applications of computers to environmental control are proposed by 1990? Can you think of some potential application in this area not mentioned in the chapter?

9.13 Describe a possible shopping scene of 1985.

9.14 Write a paper of approximately 1000 words in which you compare your attitude toward computers after having completed this course to what it was before you began.

SELECTED REFERENCES

BOOKS

Clarke, Arthur C., *Profiles of the Future,* Harper and Row, New York, 1962.

Fenichel, Robert R. and Joseph Weizenbaum, *Computers and Computation,* W. H. Freeman, San Francisco, 1971.

Forrester, Jay, *World Dynamics,* Wright-Allen Press, Cambridge, 1971.

Greenberger, Martin, *Computers and the World of the Future,* M.I.T. Press, Cambridge, 1962.

Toffler, Alvin, *Future Shock,* Random House, New York, 1970.

Toffler, Alvin, *The Futurists,* Random House, New York, 1972.

PERIODICALS AND REPORTS

Anonymous, "Progress Made in Programming Computers to Listen," *Bell Laboratories Record,* November 1975.

Anonymous, "Where Are We Going with Future Technology?," *Data Management,* January 1975.

Armstrong, Roderick J., Robert Gottdenker, and Robert L. Kornegay, "Servicing Trunks by Computers," *Bell Laboratories Record,* February 1976.

Associated Press, "Computers, TV Would Be a Part of Future Shopping, Study Says," *The Forum,* Fargo, N.D., March 31, 1975.

Joseph, Earl C., "Computers: Trends Toward the Future," in *Proceedings of IFIP Congress 68,* North-Holland, Amsterdam, 1968.

Joseph, Earl C., "Imaging Alternative Future School Organizations: Computer-Based Forecasting," Report to the University of Minnesota Council for Education Administration, Career Development Seminar, December 1972.

Joseph, Earl C., "Towards the Fifth Generation," *Science Journal,* October 1970.

Mathews, Max V., David E. Meyer, and Saul Sternberg, "Exploring the Speed of Mental Processes," *Bell Laboratories Record,* March 1975.

Moster, Clarence R. and Leonard R. Pamm, "The Digital Data System Launches a New Era in Data Communications," *Bell Laboratories Record,* December 1975.

Stephenson, Malcolm G., "Bell Labs: A Pioneer in Computing Technology," *Bell Laboratories Record,* February 1974.

Tenkhoff, P. A. and J. C. Collard, "The Common Carriers' Uncommon Offerings," *Datamation,* April 1975.

Vyssotsky, Victor A., "Computers and Computer-Based Systems," *Bell Laboratories Record,* January 1975.

Withington, Frederick G., "Beyond 1984: A Technology Forecast," *Datamation,* January 1975.

APPENDIX A FLOWCHARTING: A A PROBLEM- SOLVING TECHNIQUE

WHAT IS A FLOWCHART?

A technique that is extremely useful in finding solutions to a variety of problems, especially if the solution involves using a computer, is called flowcharting. Essentially, a flowchart is a diagram of the steps one expects to take in solving a given problem, showing the sequential relationships between those steps.Flowcharts use special symbols with which we must become familiar. Also, there are certain general procedures that make it easier to know how to construct a flowchart. Someone has called a flowchart "a blueprint of an algorithm for solving some problem." That definition is a good one but it includes a word unfamiliar to many people, the word "algorithm."

ALGORITHM

What is an algorithm? Notice that we are not talking about *logarithm*. Logarithms were mentioned in Chapter 1 as a method of doing multiplication and division by means of addition. An algorithm is not this at all. An algorithm is a statement of a procedure one expects to follow to accomplish a given task. Look at this example.

Example 1.

Write an algorithm for cooking two five-minute eggs.

233

Algorithm 1.

1. Place kettle on burner and put 3 inches of water in it.
2. Turn on burner and heat water to boiling.
3. Carefully place two eggs in the boiling water and note the time.
4. Keep water boiling on turned-down burner.
5. Have eggs been in boiling water five minutes?
   If not, go to step 4. If so go to step 6.
6. Run cold water over eggs in the same kettle held under sink faucet.
7. Remove eggs from kettle.
8. Stop.

From this example it may be surmised that a good algorithm consists of (1) a finite number of steps performed a finite number of times, (2) steps that are not ambiguous, and (3) a procedure that actually accomplishes the desired result. It should also be clear from this example that an algorithm can be written for a nontechnical kind of task, one for which a computer would not likely be used. However, since this book is concerned with computers, we will consider a second example.

Example 2.

Write an algorithm for finding the sum of the products of an undesignated number of pairs of numbers such that each pair of numbers is read from a card and the product computed. For each subsequent pair of numbers do the same operations and keep a running accumulated sum of the products. Continue this process until a card with two zeros is encountered, at which time write the accumulated sum on a piece of paper.

Algorithm 2.

1. Write zero in a place reserved for writing the accumulated sum.
2. Read a pair of numbers from a card.
3. Are both numbers zero? If so go to step 7. If not, go to step 4.
4. Compute the product of the two numbers.
5. Add this product to the last number written showing the accumulated sum and replace the last accumulated sum with this new sum.
6. Go to step 2.

7. Write on a piece of paper the last number previously written in the place reserved for the accumulated sum.
8. Stop.

Clearly, Example 2 with its companion algorithm is no more complex than Example 1, but it does seem to be more the kind of task one would assign to a computer. As you study it, see if it has the same three characteristics of a good algorithm identified in connection with Algorithm 1.

Both examples contain loops. A loop is a sequence of steps repeated under certain conditions. In Algorithm 1, steps 4 and 5 constitute a loop. Every loop should include a test that eventually results in an exit from the loop. In the first example, step 5 is such a test. When cooking time reaches five minutes, the loop is no longer repeated, but step 6 is performed. In Algorithm 2, steps 2 through 6 constitute a loop. Step 3 is the test for exitting from the loop. Now we move on to flowcharting and examine the relationship between flowcharts and algorithms.

FLOWCHARTING SYMBOLS

There are quite a number of symbols (25 or more) used by people who construct flowcharts. However, there is no common agreement on the meaning of many of these symbols, so in an introductory book like this one it is appropriate to limit the number of symbols used. We will consider six symbols, the ones on which there is virtually complete agreement as to meaning.

1. *Terminal symbol:*

This symbol, an ellipse, is used to indicate the beginning or end of a solution path. To specify which of the two is being designated, words such as START, FINISH, or STOP are written inside the symbol as follows:

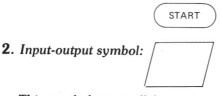

2. *Input-output symbol:*

This symbol, a parallelogram, indicates that information not determined by steps within the plan itself (input) is brought into the solution plan. It is also used to indicate the displaying of results in some form useful to a human being (output). Here are some examples:

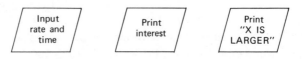

As these examples show, the precise operation being executed (input or output) is apparent from information written inside the parallelogram.

3. *Computation symbol:*

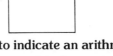

The rectangle is used to indicate an arithmetic process or the manipulation of information or objects previously available in the solution plan. As with the other symbols, specific operations are written inside the rectangle.

Here are some samples:

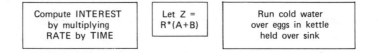

As you can see from the three examples, the size of the symbol has no effect on its meaning. All three rectangles, regardless of their size, refer to the execution of an arithmetic process or of manipulation of objects. For any flowcharting symbol, its size is determined by how much is to be written inside it. The *shape* of the symbol determines the kind of operation being represented.

4. *Decision symbol:*

The diamond is used to show that a test for the existence of a specified condition is to be made and the results of that test determine the next path to take. The test is usually indicated by writing inside the diamond a question that can be answered yes or no, or by writing inside the diamond a statement that is either true or false. Here are some examples:

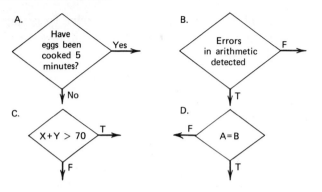

Note the following facts from the preceding examples:

1. the size of the diamond has no effect on its meaning;

2. anything may be written inside the diamond as long as it indicates the testing for some condition;

3. exits from the diamond are at any of the vertices although typically the top vertex is used for entering the diamond.

In example A, if the answer to the question written inside the diamond were "no," the path to follow in the flowchart would be down from the diamond. If the answer had been "yes," the path to follow would be to the right. In example C, if the sum of two quantities referred to as X and Y were greater than 70, the path to follow in the flowchart would be to the right. If not, the path to follow would be downward.

5. *Connector symbol:*

The circle is used to indicate continuation *to* some part of the flowchart not in the immediate vicinity or *from* some part of the flowchart not in the immediate vicinity. For example, if the flowchart were so large that it had to be written on more than one page, then a connector symbol would be used at the end of one page and the beginning of the next. A terminal symbol would *not* be used in this case because such a situation does not constitute the end of the entire flowchart. As with other symbols, size has no effect on the meaning of the symbol. Typically, a number or letter or combinations thereof are written inside the circle. To properly show the continuation *to* and *from*, two circles would have the same information inside them. Consider these examples:

A.   B.

It should be apparent from these examples that there must always be at least two connector symbols with the same information inside. One symbol is the exit point from some path in the flowchart and the second symbol is the continuation of that logical path at some other location in the flowchart. This will be more clearly apparent as we consider entire flowcharts.

6. *Replacement symbol:* ⟵————

This symbol, the left-pointing arrow, is used *inside* the computation symbol to indicate the replacement of information in the location named at the head of the arrow by information in the location named at the tail of the arrow. For example, the symbol means:

$$A \leftarrow X + 3Y$$

replace the contents of a storage location called A by the result of adding the contents of a location named X to three times the contents of a location named Y. Note that only a single memory location is given at the head of the arrow although more than one location with appropriate arithmetic operation symbols may appear at the tail side of the arrow. You will notice in examples of complete flowcharts that arrows are used to connect the various flowcharting symbols. These arrows are *not* replacement symbols. Their function is to indicate the direction of the path along which to proceed in order to arrive at the completion of the task. Only when a left-pointing arrow appears inside a computation symbol is it to be interpreted as a replacement symbol.

DEVELOPING FLOWCHARTS

Now that you have been introduced to the basic symbols of flowcharting, it is time to see how they are used. To do this, refer to Example 1 and Algorithm 1 discussed earlier. A flowchart for the same procedure as that described in Algorithm 1 would appear as follows:

Flowchart 1

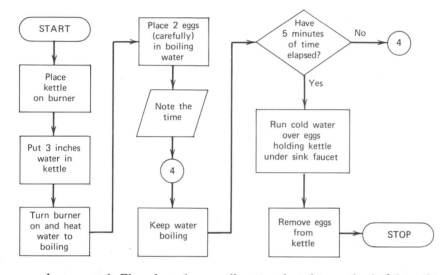

As you study Flowchart 1 you will notice that this method of describing a solution to a problem shows clearly the relationships among the several steps. The different symbol shapes make it obvious *when* specific kinds of tasks must be done in relation to other tasks. You will notice that lines joining the various symbols are drawn either vertically or horizontally, never diagonally. This is a matter of custom but probably does have its foundation in the fact that the resulting diagram is more readable to more people than it otherwise would be. Note also that the symbols are carefully drawn. Of course, you would expect neat illustrations in a printed book, but even hand-drawn flowcharts have this feature. This is possible because a template, a plastic sheet with cutouts of the various shapes, is used. The person constructing the flowchart uses the template to trace out whatever symbol is desired at each point in the diagram.

Now let's consider a flowchart for solving the problem defined in Example 2 and solved by Algorithm 2.

Flowchart 2

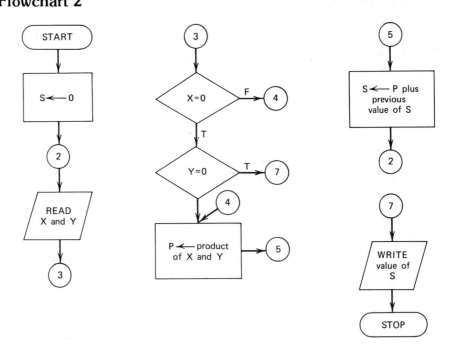

As you refer to Flowchart 2, let us examine some of its characteristics. Notice the use of connector symbols. In order to fit the flowchart neatly in the available space the flowchart was divided into three vertical sections on the page. Connector symbols may be used in any way convenient to the flowchart developer. Their function is to make it possible to provide branching from one place to another and to enable reference to be made to a particular part of the flowchart. For example, right now I ask you to refer to connector ④. You see, a connector symbol makes it easy to pinpoint a specific part of the flowchart. Look at the computation symbol (rectangle) following connector ④. A replacement symbol is used in that computation symbol to indicate that a unit of information called P is computed by multiplying the value of X by the value of Y. As was the case in Algorithm 2, there is one loop in Flowchart 2. Connector ② and the four symbols following it constitute the loop. In this example, transfer out of the loop occurs when both X and Y are zero, that is, at the second diamond following connector ③. Input data used in this way are referred to as *trailer data*. The purpose of trailer data is to cause an exit from a loop which includes an input step. Recall that a loop makes it possible to repeat steps already specified so that tedious rewriting of those steps can be avoided.

Consider the next problem and the flowchart that follows it.

Example 3.

Read a set of data related to a classroom where for each student is given an identification number and three test scores. For each student, determine whether the average of the three test scores is more than 65. If it is, print the student identification number and the word "pass." If the average is 65 or less, print the student identification number and the word "fail." Continue reading student data until the identification number 99999 is read, then stop.

Flowchart 3

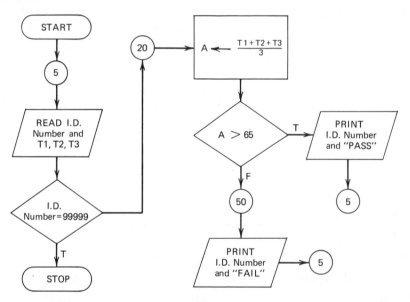

Flowchart 3 demonstrates how an algorithm with a few steps can handle a large amount of data. In fact, this flowchart displays the same logical plan for solution whether there are data for 10 students or 100 students. The key unit of data that will bring the user of Flowchart 3 to the STOP symbol is the encountering of a student identification number of 99999. Remember that input data used specifically to stop any further input are called "trailer" data, or sometimes "dummy" data. The assumption in this case is that no real student will have been assigned an identification number of 99999, so when that number is sensed no attempt is made to process those data and no more data are read.

Let's test Flowchart 3 with some trial data. Trial data are typically small sets of data but contain enough variety to try out all branches in the flowchart. Suppose we use the following:

I.D. Number	T1	T2	T3
10005	75	60	60
10010	58	63	67
10020	80	85	88
10040	65	58	67
99999	0	0	0

Now we refer to Flowchart 3 and when data are read from the preceding table, we assume reading proceeds from left to right beginning with the top row, then row two, and so on. The first symbol to specify an action is the input symbol following connector ⑤ . There we are asked to read four numbers, I.D. Number, T1, T2, and T3. Draw four boxes having those names, like this:

I.D. Number	T1	T2	T3

Taking the data in the order previously described and placing them in appropriate boxes we get

10005	75	60	60
I.D. Number	T1	T2	T3

The next action required in the flowchart is to compare the contents of the box "I.D. Number" with the number 99999. In this case they are not equal so we proceed to connector ⑳ Following that is a computation symbol calling for the establishment of a box named "A" which will contain the average of the numbers in T1, T2, and T3. When this computation is complete, we have five boxes of information, as follows:

10005	75	60	60	65
I.D. Number	T1	T2	T3	A

Continuing in the flowchart, the next step is a comparison of the contents of box "A" with the number 65. In the present situation the contents of "A" is 65, hence not greater than 65, so we proceed to connector ⑤⓪ and on to the output symbol, which asks us to print the contents of box "I.D. Number" and the word "FAIL." The results would be a line of printed information (output) like this:

> 10005   FAIL

Following the output symbol, the flowchart calls for a branching to connector ⑤ . That brings us back to the beginning and we repeat the input operation, using this time as data, the numbers 10010, 58, 63, and 67, respectively. When that operation is complete, the boxes described previously would now have these contents since we assume the former contents were erased.

10010	58	63	67
I.D. Number	T1	T2	T3

Proceeding in the flowchart to the computation of the contents of box A yields the five boxes as follows:

10010	58	63	67	62.67
I.D. Number	T1	T2	T3	A

Note that whenever a box is assigned new contents, we assume previous contents are erased first. This time, again, when the number in box A is compared with 65, the next step is to execute the output operation following connector ⑤⓪ . We have now produced two lines of output:

> 10005   FAIL
> 10010   FAIL

The flowchart next specifies a return to connector ⑤ . As before, we read the next line of information from the table of data, after which the four boxes have the following contents:

10020	80	85	88
I.D. Number	T1	T2	T3

Box I.D. Number does not contain 99999 so box A is computed to give it a value of 84.33. Continuing in the flowchart calls for the comparison of the contents of box A with 65. This time A is greater, so the flowchart specifies the printing of the line:

>   10020   PASS

All of the printed output to this point consists of three lines, as follows:

>   10005   FAIL
>   10010   FAIL
>   10020   PASS

Following the steps in the flowchart returns us to connector ⑤ and to the input symbol where this time we read the fourth line of input data. The four boxes would look like this:

10040	65	58	67
I.D. Number	T1	T2	T3

Again, since box I.D. Number is not equal to 99999, we compute the number 63.33 to be placed in box A. Next, when the number in box A is compared with 65, the flowchart directs us to connector ㊿ and on to the printing of the line

>   10040   FAIL

Returning to connector ⑤ and on to the input symbol results in the four familiar boxes having these contents:

99999	0	0	0
I.D. Number	T1	T2	T3

Comparing the contents of box I.D. Number with 99999 indicates this time that equality exists, so the flowchart sends us to the STOP symbol, telling us the job is completed. All the output generated by this flowchart, given the table of data shown earlier, are these four lines:

10005	FAIL
10010	FAIL
10020	PASS
10040	FAIL

If, in this example, a teacher were providing test results for four students, it is clear that the output would consist of a list of students identified by unique numbers and their grades of pass or fail. It should also be apparent that the same flowchart could have been used to process data for 30 students, or 100 students, or any number of students. The example used data for only four students to keep it reasonably short. It should be pointed out, further, that the simple grading scheme of "pass" or "fail" could rather easily be changed to an A, B, C, D, F arrangement by inserting more decision symbols with appropriate comparisons, each followed by an appropriate output symbol.

SOME HELPS IN CONSTRUCTING FLOWCHARTS

Many people, when first introduced to flowcharts, find their development a frustrating experience. This reaction probably has to do with the fact that the process is new, and seems to have little, if any, relationship to previous experiences. To help you avoid that unpleasantness often experienced by first-time students of flowcharting, the following list of procedures is given:

1. Know the flowcharting symbols and their meanings.

2. Remember that a flowchart is simply a method of describing a plan that accomplishes a task.

3. Before starting the flowchart, make sure you have a precise formulation of the task to be done. You must know what job it is that you are attempting.

4. Before starting the flowchart identify the data available at the start of the task and the information to be produced by completing it.

5. Before starting the flowchart, list any facts, formulas, relation-ships, and so forth that seem to apply to the task. It is better to have too many of these than too few, since you can always discard those concepts that later turn out to have no significant bearing on the task to be done.

6. Begin the construction of the flowchart introducing known data as it is needed to generate further information. Proceed to the compu-tation of new information from that which was previously intro-duced, in turn, using computed information to produce still more information. Throughout this process, refer to your list of facts, formulas, and so on.

7. Use enough steps to keep the transition from step to step smooth, but not so many as to make the final result incomprehensible because of too much detail.

8. Keep in mind the task to be accomplished so that the flowchart terminates when the job is done.

9. Whenever possible, test your flowchart with sample data, selecting the sample so as to try out all paths in the flowchart.

10. When errors in logic appear at the time of testing your flowchart, make appropriate changes and try the sample data again until the flowchart properly handles it.

These procedures should prove helpful as you learn about flowchart-ing. However, there is no substitute for experience. You are, therefore, urged to construct your own flowcharts for all examples given in this chapter without referring to the flowchart in the book. Furthermore, you are encouraged to develop flowcharts for the exercises at the end of this chapter. Please re-member that flowcharts constructed by two different people will probably not look exactly the same. We all use different logical processes in arriving at given conclusions, and this fact will usually demonstrate itself in different flowcharts. There is no reason why any two flowcharts solving a given problem *should* be the same. The important consideration is that both of them provide a plan for accomplishing the given task and communicate that plan to anyone willing to use them.

A FINAL EXAMPLE

Consider now one more example, in which we apply the suggestions listed in the previous section.

Example 4.

For each of some unspecified number of people read the following items of information: sex (1 = female, 2 = male); birthdate (year, month as a four-digit number); state of birth (use two-digit code corresponding to alphabetical listing of states, and use 99 for people born outside U.S.); state of current residence (use same code as for state of birth); marital status (1 = single, 2 = married); and annual income. When a sex code of 9 is encountered, stop reading data. From these data, determine the number of females, the number of males, the average income for females and for males, the average income for people 40 and older, and the average income for people under 40.

The task here is the selection of data based on certain criteria. In particular, average income is to be computed for females, for males, for people 40 years and older, and for people under 40. In addition, we are to find the number of females and the number of males.

The kinds of data provided are clearly listed in the statement of the problem, as are the results desired. This is not always true, however, so you are advised to pay attention to procedure 4 in the previous section as you acquire some experience in flowcharting.

The listing of facts, formulas, and relationships is also not necessary in Example 4, because once it is clear which data are to be provided and what results are desired, no further facts and relationships are needed.

We proceed now to follow procedures 6, 7, and 8 as we construct a flowchart for Example 4.

Flowchart 4

As this flowchart was constructed, it was necessary to keep in mind the concerns stated in procedures 6, 7, and 8. For example, the average income for males and females (computed following connector ⓪ 120) could not be computed before the sums of all income for males and for females (computed at connectors ⑧ 80 and ④ 40 , respectively) were available. A similar situation existed in computing the other two average incomes (see

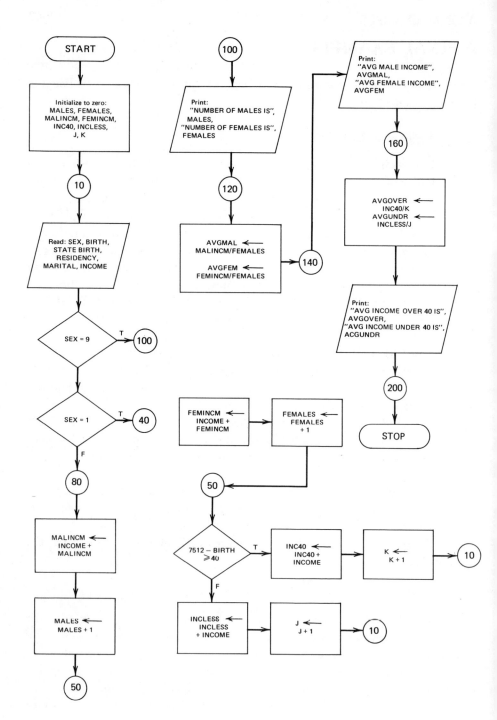

248

symbols following connector ⓢⓞ and connector ⑯⓪). The question of whether a proper amount of detail is shown in a flowchart is a difficult one to answer. Probably a positive answer to the question, "If a person understands the job to be done, can he/she follow the flowchart?" would be a good test to use. Again, experience is the key to knowing best what to do.

The student is urged to apply flowchart 4 to the following set of data to test the flowchart.

Sample Data

SEX	BIRTHDATE	STATE OF BIRTH	STATE OF RESIDENCE	MARITAL STATUS	INCOME
2	2811	23	23	1	15200
1	3201	26	34	1	18500
2	5006	34	23	2	17400
2	5410	23	23	1	12000
2	2404	42	34	2	21400
1	4512	26	34	2	15900
1	4905	34	23	2	13700
9	0	0	0	0	0

As can easily be determined from this table of data, the flowchart, if it is properly designed, should produce the following printed output:

NUMBER OF MALES IS 4 NUMBER OF FEMALES IS 3
AVG MALE INCOME 16750 AVG FEMALE INCOME 16033
AVG INCOME OVER 40 IS 18366 AVG INCOME UNDER 40 IS 14750.

When you work through the flowchart using the sample data, be careful to keep track of the changing contents of various boxes as was done previously during the discussion of Flowchart 3. This time there will be 14 boxes having the following names: MALES, FEMALES, MALINCM, FEMINCM, INC40, IN-CLESS, J, K, SEX, BIRTH, STATE BIRTH, RESIDENCE, MARITAL, and INCOME.

Example. 4 is a case where some of the input data are never used in solving the problem defined. In particular, state of birth and state of residence were never used except as input data. These two items had no bearing on the task to be accomplished. Why, then, were they included with the input data? The answer is probably related to the availability of desirable data. For example, the data shown in the table of sample data may have been collected during a census and recorded on punched cards. Rather than make new punched cards without the state-of-birth and state-of-residence information on them, the original cards are used. It is not hard to realize why this would be done especially if there were data on thousands of people rather than on just seven. This kind of a situation occurs very often in real life.

WHY MAKE FLOWCHARTS?

Maybe some readers see no value in flowcharts, even after these examples. Maybe you are saying to yourself: "Why bother constructing a flowchart? Really all I need is a clear understanding of what information is given and what results I need to produce. All steps between those two I can keep in my head."

You should recognize that the examples given have been simple ones. Whenever a new skill, such as flowcharting, is presented, the task must be clearly understood so there is no confusion in the learning of concepts related to the skill. The real value of flowcharting becomes vividly clear when complex systems with many interrelated subsystems are being developed. For example, if an entire home accounting system were being designed instead of just the portion dealing with reconciling the bank statement, it should be obvious that it would be impossible to keep in mind all the functions required for such a system. Yet by designing flowcharts for each of the subsystems (such as checking account, cash, expenses, and income) separately, then later tying them all together into one system, it is possible to include all aspects of the entire complex of interrelationships. These concepts go beyond the scope of this book. However, once you have mastered flowcharting, the designing of complex systems with interdependent subsystems is not out of your reach.

EXERCISES

A.1. Assume that you have the same kind of data described in Example 3 of this chapter. Now, instead of determining a pass or fail, assign each student a grade of A, B, C, D, or F according to the following information (where AVG is the student's average score):

AVG less than 60 = F
60 ≤ AVG < 70 = D
70 ≤ AVG < 80 = C
80 ≤ AVG < 90 = B
90 or above = A

Modify Flowchart 3 to print a list of student identification numbers with their associated grades.

A.2. Data available are telephone number and blood type (O, A, B, AB) for each of an unspecified number of people. The last data in the set will have a blood type of K to indicate the end of data. Construct a flowchart that handles the reading of these data and produces a list of telephone numbers for those people whose blood type is B.

A.3. Data from an unspecified number of insurance applicants includes applicant number, name, age, and sex (M or F). Construct a flowchart that processes these data (until an applicant number of 00000 is detected) producing a list of applicant numbers, names, and insurance rate codes, where that code is determined as follows: rate 3 if applicant is male and 25 years or younger; rate 2 if applicant is male over 25 years or female 25 years or younger; rate 1 if applicant is female and over 25 years old.

A.4. Moorhead State Company has the following data available on each of its 50 employees: name, social security number, hourly rate of pay, and hours worked this week. Construct a flowchart that reads these data, computes gross wages, and prints name, social security number, and gross wages for each of the 50 employees.

A.5. Suppose the same employee data are provided as in Exercise A.4. Construct a flowchart that computes gross wages where such wages consist of regular pay rate for the first 40 hours per week and time-and-a-half for all hours over 40. Your flowchart should produce the same output as in Exercise A.4.

A.6. An interior decorating firm has just provided you with a detailed list of items to be used in furnishing a new office building. For each item is given a name, an item number, office location number, and cost. Construct a flowchart to read these data, selecting those items that cost more than $150.00, and for each such item, print its name, its item number, its location, and its cost. Your flowchart should stop if an item number of zero is encountered.

A-7. Construct a flowchart to print the parking fee for a lot whose rate schedule is as follows: 50 cents for the first half hour or portion thereof; 25 cents for each additional half hour up to two hours; a total fee of $1.50 is due for parking more than two hours but less than three hours; a total fee of $2.00 is charged for parking more than three hours but less than five hours; for parking more than five hours but less than 24 hours a fee of $3.00 is charged; for each day or portion thereof after the first day, an additional dollar is charged.

A.8. Assume the same data are provided as described in Example 4. Construct a flowchart to find the average salaries for people whose states of residence have codes 23 and 34. Your flowchart should cause the printing of two lines of output as follows:

AVG SALARY FOR STATE 23 is *(COMPUTED AVERAGE)*
AVG SALARY FOR STATE 34 IS *(COMPUTED AVERAGE)*

A.9. Modify the flowchart for Exercise A.8 to read five different residence codes, then find the average salary for each of the five states and print five lines of output similar to those required in Exercise A.8.

A.10. The data to be processed are a set of positive numbers. Construct a flowchart to read these numbers (stopping when the number zero is read) and determine the largest number read. If more than one number has that value, it makes no difference which number is printed since they will all be that same value, and it is simply the largest number that is to be printed.

A.11. Using much of the flowchart developed for Exercise A.10, construct a flowchart to print in descending order *all* of the numbers from a given set of positive numbers. The last number provided will be zero, which you are to use as the signal to stop reading numbers. Hint: Include the steps from Exercise A.10 used in finding the largest number of the set, then, after having printed that number, remove it from further consideration as a "largest number" by changing its value to zero. Now process the set of numbers a second time, then a third time, and so on until all values have been printed.

A.12. The data to be processed are from sales slips and purchase orders; item number and number of items sold or purchased are the data provided. When items are sold, the number of items is given as a negative number, and when items are purchased it is a positive number. Read all such data until a dummy item number of 00000 is encountered. Assume that before processing, the input data have been sorted in ascending order of item number. Construct a flowchart to read these data and produce from them an inventory list, that is, a list of item numbers and the number of items left on hand for each different item number.

SELECTED REFERENCES

BOOKS

Benice, Daniel D., *Introduction to Computers and Data Processing,* Chapter 10, Prentice-Hall, Englewood Cliffs, N.J., 1970.

Bohl, Marilyn, *Flowcharting Techniques,* Science Research Asssociates, Chicago, 1971.

Forsythe, Alexandra I., Thomas A. Keenan, Elliott I. Organick, and Warren Stenberg, *Computer Science: A First Course,* Chapters 2 and 3, John Wiley & Sons, New York, 1975.

Fuori, William M., *Introduction to the Computer, The Tool of Business,* Chapter 8, Prentice-Hall, Englewood Cliffs, N.J., 1973.

Harris, Martin L., *Introduction to Data Processing,* Chapter 6, John Wiley & Sons, New York, 1973.

Rude, Paul A. and John A. Page, *Introduction to Computers,* McGraw-Hill, New York, 1974.

Schriber, Thomas J., *Fundamentals of Flowcharting,* John Wiley & Sons, New York, 1969.

Walker, Terry, *Introduction to Computer Science,* Chapter 6, Allyn and Bacon, Boston, 1972.

Wilde, Daniel U., *An Introduction to Computing,* Chapter 5, Prentice-Hall, Englewood Cliffs, N.J., 1973.

Wu, Margaret, *Introduction to Computer Data Processing,* Chapter 12, Harcourt Brace Jovanovich, New York, 1975.

APPENDIX B
USING A
TERMINAL

B

In this appendix you are introduced to some of the procedures to follow when using one particular computer terminal, the Teletype ASR 33. This is a very widely used terminal, which is why we selected it. You are also given the procedures for making contact with a specific timesharing computer system and what commands are needed to make it perform certain processes. Note that there are many different terminals in use of which the ASR 33 is just one. Consequently, you will probably need some special local instruction if the terminal available to you is not a Teletype. Similarly, the procedures that work correctly for the Univac 1110 computer system (the one used in this discussion) are not exactly the same as for all timesharing systems. Nevertheless, there are enough similarities among terminals and timesharing systems to warrant the inclusion of this appendix.

THE TELETYPE ASR 33

In Chapter 3 you were given some information about the keyboard of a Teletype. In addition to having a keyboard and a printer for computer output the Teletype ASR 33 has a mechanism (called the paper tape punch) for punching coded information into special paper tape and another mechanism (called the paper tape reader) for sensing the information in punched paper tape. These features are helpful in making the most efficient use of computer time. For example, by using the paper-tape-punch feature, one can use the ASR 33 (also commonly called a Teletype) to prepare a program in coded form on paper tape for transmission at some other time to a computer. The advantage of this is that a very slow typist can type information to be produced as a paper tape without wasting valuable on-line time. Then, having produced a coded version

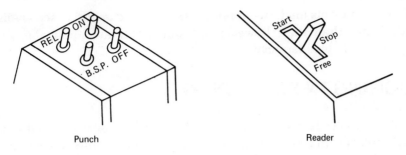

Punch   Reader

FIGURE B.1   Switches for paper tape punch and reader.

of the program using the paper tape punch apart from the central processor, the user can connect the Teletype to the central processor and utilize the tape-reader feature to transmit the program at the full speed allowed by the tape reader, 10 characters per second. This rate is faster than the typing speed of the fastest typist, and thus uses as little time as possible for the central processor to receive the program.

Figure B.1 shows the control switches for the Teletype paper tape punch and paper tape reader. Notice that there are four pushbutton switches on the punch. The two of most concern to a user are the OFF and ON buttons. The other two (B.SP. for backspace and REL for release) are rarely used. Of course, pressing the ON button activates the circuits necessary to cause punching in paper tape whenever a key on the keyboard is depressed. The OFF button deactivates those circuits.

When punched paper tape has been properly placed in the tape reader, the reader switch controls the functions associated with the tape reader. When the switch is in STOP position, the wheel that drives the paper tape through the reader is locked and no action takes place in the tape reader. Placing the switch in FREE position does not cause any action to occur but does allow the drive wheel to move freely. This allows the user to position the punched paper tape anywhere along its length while inserted in the reader. When the switch is in START position, circuits are activated that drive the punched paper tape through the reader, past sensing pins that detect the holes in the tape. The detection of holes causes keys to be depressed automatically and the corresponding information typed by the printer on the paper. If the Teletype also has an acoustic coupler attached to it, the sensing of holes in paper tape produces responses in the acoustic coupler corresponding to the coded information in the punched paper tape.

The keyboard of the Teletype described is virtually the same keyboards of any so-called Teletype-compatible terminals. If you are using a video display unit, any comments made about print lines must be changed to screen-display lines. Other than that, however, all statements are applicable to any Teletype-compatible terminal.

LOGGING-IN PROCEDURE

We now consider how the telephone and acoustic coupler are used to make initial contact with a timesharing computer system. In order to communicate via telephone with a computer, one must know the correct telephone number which results in a telephone-line contact with a line that is connected to a coupler, which in turn is connected to a computer. This number is usually an ordinary seven-digit phone number. To begin using the computer, pick up the telephone receiver and dial the number. If you listen at the earpiece you will hear the familiar rattling sound which indicates ringing of the phone at the other end of the line. After one or two "rings" the communications equipment responds with a high-pitched tone. This indicates contact is being made with the computer. As soon as this tone is heard, place the telephone receiver in the cradle of the acoustic coupler. Be sure the earpiece and mouthpiece are in the proper positions on the coupler.

When the Univac 1110 system is being used, the procedures just described will connect you with the computer. However, the computer expects you to make the first move. Often the user signals the computer by pressing the RETURN key. When this is done the computer responds with

>**PLEASE SIGN ON WITH 'HELLO'**

The "greater-than" symbol produced by the computer is its way of soliciting a response from you. Not all computers produce that symbol but most timesharing systems use some symbol intended to solicit a response from the user. Therefore we'll refer to this symbol as the *solicit* symbol.

If you had been familiar with this timesharing system you may not have pressed RETURN but would probably have typed what is now expected:

>**HELLO MSU0015/PASS** (RET)

where the circle with RET in it means the RETURN key. Every response by the user must end with depressing the RETURN key. In the line just shown, MSU0015 is called the user identification (or user I.D.) and PASS is called the password. Both of these items of information are assigned to each user by the managers of the timesharing system and are examined by the computer to ensure that only legitimate users may connect to the system. If either user I.D. or password are incorrect the computer allows you two more attempts. If you make an error on each of three attempts, the computer signs off and disconnects the phone line. To try again the user must redial the phone number.

If the I.D. and password are acceptable, the Univac 1110 prints a line identifying itself, similar to this:

UNIVAC - SUMITS - 00.00.85 13:54:58 08/15/76

In the preceding line, SUMITS - 00.00.85 identifies the specific timesharing system currently in use. 13.54.58 is the time (as on a 24-hour clock), and 08/15/76 is the date. After the identifying line, the Univac 1110 types the solicit symbol. The logging-in process is now complete and the computer is ready for further commands.

SYSTEM COMMANDS

Associated with every timesharing system are certain words that generate a given response from the computer. Such words are expected by the computer following the solicit symbol. For example, HELLO was such a system command. Other system commands are NEW, OLD, MODE, RUN, LIST, SAVE, UNSAVE, TAPE and others, whose use we will now consider.

The NEW command is used whenever the user intends to enter a new program for processing. Its form is as follows:

>**NEW PROGRAMNAME**(RET)

The characters to the right of NEW constitute the user's name for the program about to be entered and may be any collection of letters and numbers up to a maximum of 12. (This maximum varies from system to system. Find out what it is on the system available to you.)

If the program is to be entered from previously punched tape, the user must enter the TAPE command, as follows:

>**TAPE**(RET)

This causes the computer to activate the circuitry necessary to accept the new program at the full speed of the Teletype. After the TAPE command, the user

must place the prepared tape in the paper tape reader (left front of the Teletype), set the reader switch (see Figure B.1) to START, and wait for the paper
tape to be read. The reading process will automatically stop when the end of
the tape is reached.

Once a program has been entered, the system command that causes it
to be executed is RUN. Its form is

>**RUN** RET

Any output produced by the user's program will appear at the printer. Upon
completion of the program a line will be printed by the system having the
words RUN COMPLETE followed by the amount of time required by the central processor to execute the program.

If the user has a program he/she wishes to store in the computer's
auxiliary memory, the SAVE command is used as follows:

>**SAVE** RET

The SAVE command causes the user's program to be stored under the name
given with the NEW command. To use such a saved program requires the use of
the OLD command. Its form is

>**OLD PROGRAMNAME** RET

Notice that the correct program name must be used; that is, whatever name
was assigned when the NEW command was entered. After the OLD command
the computer responds with the solicit symbol at which time the user gives the
command RUN as previously described.

Whenever a saved program is no longer needed it should be removed
from the computer's auxiliary storage by use of the UNSAVE command. It has
the form

>**UNSAVE PROGRAMNAME** RET

where PROGRAMNAME is the name of the program to be removed.

The LIST command is applied whenever the user wishes to have a copy
printed of the program currently being worked on. The program is printed line
by line sorted in order of line number.

The MODE command makes it possible to use programming languages other than BASIC. Most timesharing systems have more than one language available to the user. The Univac 1110 system assumes BASIC to be the desired language unless the MODE command specifies otherwise. For example, if FORTRAN were to be the programming language used, the command

>**MODE FORTRAN**(**RET**)

must be entered previous to the NEW command as described earlier in this section. Of course, any programs entered following this command must be FORTRAN programs or they would not be acceptable to the computer system.

To terminate a session at a terminal connected to a Univac 1110 system, the command TERM is given as follows:

>**TERM**(**RET**)

The computer then gives an accounting of total time used during the session and disconnects the phone line. The user must, of course, replace the phone in its original position.

CONCLUSION

You have now been introduced to one specific terminal and to one specific timesharing system. Although other terminals function in a way similar to Teletypes there are differences and the wise user will determine what those differences are. Similarly, the commands for computer systems other than the Univac 1110 will vary. But if you clearly understand the commands given here and know the specific words to use for a different computer system, you should have little difficulty using a variety of timesharing systems.

Index